BiG

fat

LiARS

*How Politicians,
Corporations, and the Media Use Science and
Statistics to Manipulate the Public*

Morris E. Chafetz, M.D.

NELSON CURRENT

A Division of Thomas Nelson, Inc.

Published in Nashville, Tennessee, by Nelson Current, a division of a wholly-owned subsidiary (Nelson Communications, Inc.) of Thomas Nelson, Inc.

Nelson Current books may be purchased in bulk for educational, business, fundraising, or sales promotional use. For information, please e-mail SpecialMarkets@ThomasNelson.com.

Library of Congress Cataloging-in-Publication Data

Chafetz, Morris E.
   Big fat liars : how politicians, corporations, and the media use science and statistics to manipulate the public / Morris E. Chafetz.
       p.   cm.
   Includes bibliographical references and index.

   ISBN 1-5955-5008-9

   1. Knowledge, Sociology of.   2. Expertise—Social aspects.   3. self-esteem.   I. Title.
HM651.C46   2005
306.4'2—dc22   2005008696

Printed in the United States of America
05 06 07 08 09 QWK 5 4 3 2 1

To Rose Handell Chafetz, my mother, who gave me life
and to Marion Claire Elizabeth Donovan Chafetz,
my wife, who is my life.

Contents

FOREWORD

I don't agree with all of the conclusions in this book, and I think that the author might be delighted by my caution. Dr. Morris Chafetz reminds us that conventional wisdom changes with the seasons; that there is an expert on every wrong side of a question; and that, in the end, we have to steer through contending versions of the truth and reach our own decisions about how to live.

"Trust and respect yourself," he advises.

We live in a new and improved time when the amount of ways in which we can damage ourselves—and protect ourselves—is vivid, complete, and compelling. Cigarettes are sold with warning labels that can and should chill your soul and stay your hand. By law, automobiles are equipped with seatbelts and airbags (which have been known to cause injury themselves when they spontaneously pop out, unprovoked and unbidden). The largest, most teeming and rambunctious cities in America now have cleaner air than some small hamlets in remote regions of China, India, and Ireland. We can and should be grateful for these changes that have made us safer, healthier, and more alert.

But we also live in times when what Dr. Chafetz calls the false gods of statistics loom over our everyday lives. Studies highlight hazards that are remote but sinister. On any given morning, you can hear expert voices bidding us to cut out sugar, butter, and olive oil, avoid coffee, watch out for the tag under your sofa, be careful not to swallow the nose on your child's teddy bear, make certain you don't get third-degree burns from a distracted server pouring hot coffee onto your lap. (It used to be that the owner of a restaurant would offer to dry-clean your suit. Nowadays, you would be encouraged to refuse the offer, so you can file a class action suit.)

It's enough to make you pull the covers back over your head and hide from life. The statistical gods even urge you on. After all, if you spend all of your life living in a hole, you will never be struck by lightning.

But statistics also misinform. Everyone—and I do mean everyone—who eats mashed potatoes dies. Everyone who has ever eaten a mashed potato in the history of the world will wind up dead. Lincoln, Caesar, George Soros—nobility, power, and wealth cannot save you. *Everyone who eats mashed potatoes dies.* What's stopping the government? Who has the potato lobby bought? Is the butter industry implicated? Why aren't these mashed killers banned? Somebody should do something!

Except, of course, the argument is just a trick of statistics. Everyone who eats mashed potatoes dies. But it does not follow that if you did not eat mashed potatoes you would live forever.

Dr. Chafetz reminds us that everyone who offers a warning, even life-saving advice, has a motive, if not an angle. Can anyone not know by now that it's stupid to smoke cigarettes? (I know more than a few smokers—and they seem to know it better than anyone.) But have the enormous judgments that courts have delivered against the cigarette companies been better for those with scarred lungs, or their personal injury lawyers? Do the high taxes applied on tobacco products practically discourage smoking, or give state governments an interest in the income that smoking provides their treasuries without raising taxes?

In *Big Fat Liars,* Dr. Morris Chafetz encourages us to take back control of our lives from our fears. When he warns about some of the dangers of generalization for the whole, the abuse of scientific knowledge to portray only the worst scenarios, and abolishing personal responsibility by treating all behavior as disease, he invites us to put our own hands on the steering wheel and plot our own route through the perils of modern life.

Readers of this book will be better prepared to examine the pronouncements of experts with their own internal truth detectors and make rational and informed judgments about how to protect and enrich their own lives.

—SCOTT SIMON

PREFACE

A few years ago there was a successful play, and later a motion picture, *Other People's Money*. This book could easily be entitled *Other People's Lives*. It describes the frightening trend by people in power and those seeking it to gain control and power over other people.

Other people.

People like you and me.

Sometimes their motives are pure—or at least they think they are—and sometimes they are not. In all cases, they rely on their ability to convince you and me that we are not bright enough to decide what is best for ourselves.

Democracy is based on freedom. When that freedom is undermined by absolving individuals of responsibility for the consequences of their own behaviors, we face the death of democracy.

In this highly advanced technological age, malignant self-righteousness—the most dangerous cancer for any society—is raging and metastasizing. For example, tobacco, guns, alcoholic beverages, pharmaceutical products, and a host of other products are blamed for human illnesses, frailties, and deaths. In turn, litigation is skyrocketing, and this heightened emphasis on liability cases—often blaming persons, manufacturers, or corporations for things that should have been at least as obvious to the plaintiff as to the defendant—leads to efforts for legislative restrictions on the availability of certain products and activities in the so-called free market.

The assault on personal freedom, disguised as defense of our safety, continues unabated.

The arguments used against supposed instruments of human misbehavior—everything from cigarettes to guns to Frito-Lay potato chips—almost always rely on the corruption and misapplication of science and medicine in general, and the "public health model" in particular. Many individual and group behaviors are distorted to justify legal, political, and economic self-interest to manipulate the public and policy. All this is done under the guise of *goodness,* of *protecting us.* From what? From ourselves and the fruits of our own freedom.

The most destructive aspect of the "blame game," which is growing in intensity in all self-righteous societies, is that the essential aspect of human self-respect—personal responsibility for the consequences of our own thoughts, beliefs, and behaviors—is lost.

Such a loss leads to paternalism in politics and policies. If we desire to maintain individuals and societies by paternalistic behaviors, influences and control by government and other "altruistic" groups over our private lives can only grow. Adults are treated as children. When adults are not responsible for the consequences of their own actions, the most likely outcome is a generalized sense of irresponsibility and lawlessness. This becomes a self-fulfilling prophecy. People who are told that they lack the skills needed to exercise responsibility will find no reason even to attempt to live responsible lives.

The best example of malignant societal harm is the intense tendency to diagnose people who harm themselves and harm others as men-
tally ill or addicted. Persons who seek to harm themselves or others very
probably do have a problem—and that problem very probably isn't the
one that first glance reveals. Treatments that do nothing other than
gloss over problems are temporarily helpful to society, but not in the
long term, and they are of no help to the individual at all. Drugging a
generation of bored school children might relieve society of any sense
that school ought to be more compelling, but the result is bad schools
and a generation that has learned little except that being drugged is the
natural order of things.

A generation ago it was common for families to carry medical insurance to cover the costs of only major medical events. Routine trips to
the doctor were affordable. Then, in the 1960s, government became
involved in paying for medical treatment—and, combined with malpractice lawsuits run amok, the price of doctor visits became unafford-
able to those who have less than comprehensive insurance coverage. As
a consequence, advocacy groups are pushing for treatment coverage
mandated by Congress or state regulations. But it is an obvious fact that
congressional or state regulation of the free market breeds monopoly.
The prices, paid through taxes, would rise, and the quality of treatment
would fall. We've already seen some aspects of this: Despite modern
diagnostic techniques and equipment, the rate of misdiagnosis is no
better than it was not one but *two* generations ago!

An example of undermining self-respect and equal protection
under the law is the tobacco issue. Federal and state governments hold
tobacco companies responsible for the health consequences of smoking, citing tobacco companies as encouraging the purchase and use of
their products. Because we are addicted to simple answers to complex

human and social problems, we forget that the federal government encouraged the use of tobacco products during war time and that federal and most state governments rely on tobacco taxes to make ends meet—yet the government is not holding itself financially or legally accountable for doing so.

We must always keep in mind that liberty and responsibility are inextricably united. The more responsibility people have, the more freedom and self-respect they have. Inversely, the less freedom people have, the less responsibility they are allowed to exercise. This trend serves the interests of those in power, not the interests of the individual. Interestingly, public policy advocates construe individualism as selfishness or egoism. What they do not want to recognize is the fact that self-respect and societal respect for individualism allows for respect for others and altruism. Many of those who want power over people behave as though their morality will always know what is best for others.

From a historical perspective, we need to remember that governments and self-righteous groups (those who know what is best for individuals) have always harmed people more than anyone else has. Public policy and litigation based on the misuse of science and statistics rely on the principle of scapegoating, which is a tendency to blame a minority for the social, economic, and existential problems of the majority. These groups use "experts" in the fields of science, medicine, and academia to influence public opinion.

The misinterpretation and misapplication of so-called science is used to justify, rationalize, and implement disastrous political policy.

The most important purpose of this book is to provide people with the ability to respect themselves—their good and bad features—so that they can respect others. Once that respect has been achieved, it is a small step to regain control over your own life and send packing those who think they know more about you than you do.

1

THE DANGER OF GENERALIZATION

Mark Twain famously wrote that we must take care to learn from a thing not just its lesson but *only* its lesson. A cat that has stepped on a hot stove lid, he noted, will never repeat the mistake. But, he added, it won't step on a *cold* stove lid, either.

Albert Einstein, who many of us would agree was a very bright fellow, said the same thing, though differently: "All our science, measured against reality, is primitive and childlike—and yet it is the most precious thing we have." We can learn from our discoveries, and it is essential that we do so if we are to advance—but we must never lose sight of the fact that even our best discoveries tell us comparatively little of the nature of things.

What neither Twain nor Einstein said is that the world is richly populated with those who would use what little we know, or pretend that we know, to gain power over us.

We live in an era in which we generalize as a matter of convenience, sometimes of laziness. As a result, we seldom get the full lesson of a thing, and almost always we get more of a lesson than circumstances warrant.

We are all different, yet ours has become a nation of lowest common denominators. As a result, the real differences that make us individual human beings often go unnoticed. We have passed laws against the effects of racial and other kinds of prejudice—but prejudice is nothing except drawing a generalization and acting upon it. Indeed, as a result of some civil rights legislation, we have produced a second set of prejudices—the effects of which are as institutionally embedded and as insidious as the evils they were intended to eliminate.

It has always been easier to generalize, and troublesome results have come of it. A friend, now fifty, suffers from chronic back pain. His spine is twisted, though not so you would notice it; but when he stands with his feet lined up as if looking forward, his shoulders are turned slightly to the right.

This is because, as a child, he was in a school where all the desks were built for right-handed students, and he is left-handed. He had to contort his posture, twist to the right, in order to use the desk to which he was assigned. (The reason the desks were all right-handed was that only a few years earlier left-handed students had been forced to pretend that they were right-handed.)

He knew that something was wrong, that each day at school was painful. He was always fidgeting and squirming in an attempt to become comfortable, and as a result he was chided for being disruptive. Before long, he himself actually believed that the problem was behavioral—that something was wrong with him. He learned that erroneous lesson and has a sore back to this day.

His teachers sought to keep control of their classrooms, and when he complained, they decided there was something wrong with him. For his part, he lacked the self-respect to believe himself—that he was in pain each day—and to therefore reject the idea that he was to blame.

His story is a small, simple example of several widespread phenomena in which generalizations have been made, "magically" converted into absolutes, and then used to control everyone, but most especially to control those who fall outside the original generalization.

Today, perhaps, his family would sue the school district. There would be many lawyers involved, at enormous expense. Perhaps the state legislature would become involved, passing laws mandating that school districts place in each classroom a number of left-handed desks equal not to the number of students who are actually left-handed but instead to the percentage of students who are statistically likely to be left-handed—about 10 percent. Of course, by the time it all got resolved, my friend with his twisted spine would be well along in college, perhaps paid for by the settlement from the school district because of the claim—lawyers will be lawyers—that the boy's dignity was compromised by his having had to sit at a right-handed desk.

Or perhaps the legislature would mandate that handedness-neutral desks be provided, which is a fine idea—if a manufacturer could be found who had the proper proportion of minorities and women among its employees and who met the vast range of other generalized requirements imposed by the government in an effort to legislate fairness.

But what constitutes fairness? We live in a society that in large measure rejects notions of right and wrong. It is true that social mores change. The pace of technological development has accelerated at an ever-increasing rate. There have been more significant discoveries and technical developments put to practical use in the last two hundred years than there were in all of history up to that time. Those developments have posed powerful moral and ethical questions, and the questioning of things which were ethically settled—what in the law is called *stare decisis*—has grown as well. In some cases this is a good thing, while in other cases it is not. It is always a mistake to apply the standards of today in judging the actions of persons who lived in the past; consider the absurdity of calling Lincoln a failed war president because he couldn't use the U.S. Air Force to rout the Confederate army in a week's time.

The result is that we live in a society in which a substantial number of people do not believe that there are such things as objective right and wrong. A president who denounces attacks on America (in which thousands of civilian lives were lost) as "evil" wakes up the next day to learn that he is criticized as a religious extremist for proposing that there is such a thing as evil. Even were it possible to pass a statewide or, worse, national law with the object of fairness for everyone, how could that possibly be brought about?

More and more, the denominator is something that has come to be known as "political correctness." From the poetry of the Declaration of Independence that "all men are created equal," political correctness engages in *reductio ad absurdum*—taking those words which define and specify the most fundamental of rights and carrying it to a ridiculous extreme. From "created equal" it derives "just alike, no matter what their abilities are, what they think, or what they do." It carries generalization to the extreme, with the result that ultimately no distinctions at all will be possible. It also carries that sacred document, the Bill of Rights, well past its intention. The first ten amendments to the Constitution of the United States were designed to protect the minority from the tyranny of the majority. Political correctness establishes the tyranny of the minority by seeking to codify the lowest common denominator—to establish a system under which nothing may go forward unless it is approved by the wackiest among us.

This nonsense has infected the very fiber of our country, and has made it possible for scalawags to take control. It has created problems where there were none, and has replaced some problems with other problems.

Political correctness is itself the logical if absurd reduction of a trend that has coincided with the growth of the federal government. The United States is a huge and diverse place. It has regions where it never freezes and regions where it never thaws. It has places where there is nothing but forest as far as the eye can see, and places where the entire vista comprises buildings and pavement. It has cities whose various immigrant communities would themselves make up substantial cities, and towns where "the new family" is the one that moved in twenty years ago. There are regions in near-constant danger of flooding, and regions where the constant is a prayer for rain. In some states, road crews have to deal with the melting and bubbling of the hot tar in the summer heat, while in others the frost heaves of winter make roads difficult. It costs far more to live in some places than in others, yet national taxes are constant, so a person who in one place might be the richest person in town would barely scrape by someplace else. Setting standards for all those places from one central capital is something that a moment's voyage into common sense would tell us is impossible, with any attempt to do so being both expensive and inefficient. There is very little that a national government—a national *anything*, really—can do which will benefit the entire country. The place simply defies generalization.

Nor was this arrangement the one contemplated when the national government was established. But political power tends to consolidate, to do all it can to create more power for itself. This applies to all political power, not just that held by governments. Political science is defined as the study of coercive institutions—institutions which have sufficient power to force obedience. As such, part of this book can be thought of as a critique of those institutions.

But only part. Criticism is cheap and seldom useful unless an alternative is proposed. The alternative is here, too.

We are born alone, usually, and we usually die alone. We have our own individual hopes and aspirations. Yes, we sometimes act in groups, and we hope for the success of the groups of which we are a part. But we individually decide to affiliate ourselves with those groups, whether they be sporting teams, business partnerships, companies for which we work, places of worship—whatever. We decide as individuals to join the group.

There is an exception: the family. The basic unit of humanity is the individual, but individuals are, or—and this is an objective truth— should be born into families. The definition of what constitutes a family would take up a book of its own—and has, several times over. The diminishing importance given to the family, more and more a function of political correctness lest someone whose family is nonexistent feel bad about it, is a terrible thing. Witness the fact that if you have the ability and interest needed to read this book, there is a very good chance that you had a family that served at least some important purposes. If you did not and are reading it anyway, you are probably even more aware of the importance of having one.

Still, while we are most of us born into families and are under the control of our parents during our early years, there comes a time when we are adults and the familial connection is lessened. Then as individuals we decide whether and when to establish families of our own. And even when we are under our parents' roof, we have already begun to grow as individuals, with individual thoughts, plans, and responsibilities. If you fail to take out the trash at age eight, it is you and you alone who are punished; if at sixteen you get a speeding ticket, it is you who stands before a judge appointed not by your family but by society,

6

though you may face additional, perhaps harsher, judgment at home, too.

Judgment from others is difficult to face. When we are born, the judgment of others is the only clue we have. If we are fortunate, we are surrounded at first by people who give us a sense of their unconditional love. As time passes, we learn that the manifestation of this love can be moderated by our behavior. The signals are not always clear: The boy baby with a full bladder who lets loose in daddy's face as daddy changes his soiled diaper, for instance, may well get the sense that daddy doesn't especially love him right now, but mommy is laughing and delighted. Is this a way to please mommy? But it doesn't please daddy. *Hmm.* (If mommy breastfeeds, it's easy to figure out where the decision of who to please will come down, and daddy would be well advised to invest in goggles, though he'll probably just decide that he's "no good at changing diapers" instead.)

As our understanding grows, we learn that some things we do seem to foster greater manifestations of love from those around us than do others; at some point we figure out that we can do things that make that love seem to disappear entirely. In addition to being the source of everything we know, love, and trust, our family is for most of us our first coercive institution, the first place where approval and punishment are administered. We are being taught, and that teaching is based entirely on our desire to receive the approval of others.

At the same time, we are beginning to teach ourselves. We learn that certain things result in pain. But nature is very wise; if we were more perfect thinking machines, we would identify the action that led to the pain and there would never be a second attempt at anything. No one would ever have learned to ride a bicycle.

Thus begins, in our earliest years, a struggle. It is the battle between our own reasoning, as delivered to us at first in things that bring us physical pain or, sometimes, physical pleasure and the desire to please those people upon whom we are wholly dependent. Over time, our dependence on those people—or at least those *particular* people—goes away, but our desire to achieve the approval of others does not.

We go to school, and, for many of us, it is the first time that we have been in a group of people our own age. This brings a whole new perspective on things. The contradictions, the choices, the confusion! We discover that the classmate who misbehaves sometimes gets the approval of others, but not the approval of the teacher. If we emulate that classmate, we get a lesson in nonfamily coercive institutions—the teacher has some clout. We decide whether the approval of our classmates is worth the pain of punishment.

The noted psychologist Dr. Abraham Maslow achieved his fame largely through his observation that there are five fundamental groups of needs, in descending order.

- Physiological needs: We need air, water, and food, and sufficient shelter to keep us from freezing or dying in the heat. We need to be nourished.
- Safety: At a very basic level, we need to be protected from wild animals or from predacious humans, from falling rocks and drowning. We need to feel safe.
- Belonging: We need the love, affection, and association of others.
- Esteem: In Maslow's observations, this takes two forms. The first is the approval of others. The second is self-esteem, our approval of ourselves.

These four he called "deficit needs." By this he meant that if you are lacking in any of them, you will feel it, in gasping for breath, or thirst,

8

or hunger; in fear; in loneliness; in feeling like the outcast; or in shame or a sense of inferiority. All of these things, Maslow said, are essential to our health and well-being.

It is important to point out something here that will be a theme of this book, even as it is the subject of this chapter: It is impossible for Maslow to have known with precision the truth of his observations. If there is a criticism to be made of him, despite his laboratory work with primates, it is that with thinking creatures it is impossible to control all the variables, so psychological experimentation is always in doubt. As with the polls that have converted our electoral process into a sporting event, without listing the margin of error the experiment is highly questionable. In psychological experimentation, it is impossible to know the margin of error. We are all unique. That having been said, Maslow's observations are not without merit.

The fifth need, which Maslow said makes itself less apparent to us than the others, is "self-actualization." It is the desire, having been given life, to make the most of it. To achieve.

A moment's digression: Have you ever pondered the tremendous odds against your even being here? A woman typically emits one egg per month over a fertile lifetime of about thirty-five years. That is 420 months of cycles during which she *could* become pregnant. There are times during this thirty-five years, most notably when she is pregnant, when eggs are not emitted. As most couples seeking a child can attest, even when pregnancy is sought, it is anything but certain. Even for the most prolific couple in the world, 95 percent of those eggs pass unfertilized, and for most families it's more like 99.5 percent. That you are here at all means that your parents engaged in sexual congress at just the right time to give you your one-in-two hundred chance of being born. Now, consider that the odds were about the same—there were factors such as higher infant mortality, but couples had more children to compensate—for your father, and for your mother, and for their parents, and for their parents' parents, and so on, going back to the arrival of humans on the planet. The number of potential people who were never born outweighs, by orders of magnitude, the ones who ever actually drew breath. And the odds against you are higher, actually, if you are relatively young: In the United States there have been on average more than a million abortions each year for the last thirty years; this represents about a fifth of the U.S. birth rate.

Startling numbers, aren't they? They probably make you feel pretty special. And you are in one way, but not at all special in another. Today, there are about 6.5 billion people in the world. Every one of them faced the same odds that you did, give or take a little based on local customs as to family size, health practices, and so on. You are one 6.5-billionth of the world's population. Not so special, huh? But you are, and ought to be, special to yourself. Your life is the only one you've been given. The thought of not existing is abhorrent and frightening to you. You are mortified at the thought of your own death, though perhaps there are things for which you would sacrifice your life—protection of your family, maybe. Before we return to our thoughts of that schoolchild facing the first important decisions, it should be noted that it gets no easier.

If we look at things in Maslow's terms, we instantly discover that our choices in life often pit one need against another. And as we incorporate more and more his fifth need into our lives—the sense that *life has some purpose beyond survival*—the conflicts become even more intense. As the little schoolchild weighs the choices against each other, where is some sense of guidance? What is the *right* choice?

That depends on whether she has learned something that Maslow touches upon but does not fully develop (nor could he; his work was in psychology, not sociology, law, advertising, the media, politics, or any of the other factors that figure so profoundly in our lives). It is something that coercive institutions—social groups, the legal system, the ad agencies, the "news" programs and publications, the politicians, and others—seek to knock down in their pursuit of generalization to achieve power and, sometimes, profit. It is the one thing that doesn't by itself justify your life but without which you cannot set a course for your life that will give it meaning useful to yourself and your family.

It is self-respect.

Self-respect is something you give to yourself, but it is also something whose circle of influence is limited to yourself. It does not come from pretending to be a wounded minority, because each of us is a minority among 6.5 billion other minorities. We cannot and should not expect someone else to grant us our self-respect. Nor can we impose our requirements for self-respect on others. Of course, the exception is in equipping our children with self-respect to the extent that when they go off to school and face the cacophony of choices that entering a broader society brings, they have a sense of what course to take.

Self-respect is confidence in making our own choices and following them through. It is something that is, of course, informed by useful data as they become available, though always with skepticism and examination, always with an eye cast toward the herd mentality that is promoted nearly everywhere today.

It is something that is immune to generalization, even, often, to characterization. Imagine how people around you would characterize you. Be honest. How broad would their brush sweep? Would it differ from the way they would have described you a month ago, a year? Now that you've done the exercise, another question: Who cares? Beyond your family, to whom you are responsible and who deserves some explanation for what might seem to be inconsistency, your responsibility is to yourself.

This isn't some abstract, soul-searching notion. It applies to every decision you make in your life. It applies to whether you smoke, don't smoke, or give up smoking. It applies to how much you eat and what you eat. It applies to your drinking habits. It applies to what you believe, whether or not everyone else believes it.

Self-respect is the recognition that no one else knows you as well as you do.

My left-handed friend arrived at the cusp, between one kind of generalization and another. He has self-respect and has overcome it. All of us have failed in one way or another to separate ourselves from the generalizations that invariably cede power over our lives to some coercive institution when it need not be so. Some of us have fallen victim to this more than others. The entirely worthwhile effort to grant minorities rights equivalent to those of the majority has mutated into a phenomenon whereby it is now a matter of law that minorities are granted special dispensations. This is the announcement and gross generalization that minorities cannot make the grade without special privileges. The only proper reaction by members of minority groups who possess self-respect is *outrage*. How dare the politicians—the coercive institutions—suggest that they are beneath the standards that apply to others?

In fact, minority groups and others are being played by those institutions and by those who would control those institutions. They are, in the name of their advancement, being held back. They are being told that some vague, anti-politically-correct unfairness is keeping them down. They are being told that they should avoid consideration of their own self-respect in favor of some generalized characterization of them as a group.

The examples alone would fill this book, but that is not its purpose. Instead, if this book accomplishes its purpose it will have convinced you that you are, and of right ought to be, the sole master of your decisions—not politicians, corporations, ad agencies, activists, lawyers, or lobbyists.

In my six decades as a psychiatrist and author, I have been involved in politics and national government; I've been broadcast and published, and have seen how those media work; and I have appeared in court as an expert witness and therefore have some knowledge of how the law is administered. As an expert on substance abuse, I have seen the many ways in which things are diagnosed as "substance abuse" that actually have nothing to do with it. In all of this, I have learned much about these coercive institutions. These institutions work together to view people as a generalized group, to deny the value of the only weapon that can let you express your uniqueness as a minority among 6.5 billion, and to achieve the thing that at bottom they think they deserve: power over people.

Including you.

2

IT'S ALL POINT OF VIEW

From time to time a political figure or other leader is criticized for being "divisive," rather than accenting the "things that bring us together." But to do that is merely to recognize facts. We are all different from one another. No two of us, not even identical twins, are alike. To pretend otherwise is to rob us of our individuality and of our self-respect, to treat us as if we are interchangeable parts. We're not.

Human beings have relatively few things in common across the entire species. We are born; we need air, water, and nourishment; and we die. All of us fear death in one way or another. After that, everyone is in the minority or, really, multiple minorities. Red hair? You're in the minority. Red-haired American? A smaller minority still. Red-haired American living in Kansas? Your group is even smaller. We could keep going, keep adding new minorities of which you are a member, until we would arrive at the group that comprises: you. *You alone.*

Beauty, ugliness, what tastes good or bad, what sounds good or bad—these are all perceptions unique to each of us. They, therefore, are not and cannot be matters of fact, except to us as individuals. A word picture painted by the poet does not invoke the same mental image in any two people. The statement that "liver tastes so bad it is inedible" is not true, except insofar as it applies to the person saying it; the statement that "I cannot stand the taste of liver and won't eat it" probably is true.

All of this would be the stuff of greeting cards and vague philosophical ponderings were it to stop there. But it doesn't. Even as we embrace our uniqueness, we also flee from it.

If you had been born in another time and another place, to different parents, it's all but certain that your views, values, and tastes would be different. We noted in the previous chapter that the likelihood of any of us ever being born at all is almost infinitesimal. If we look back on the factors that have shaped the people we are today—individually, not as a group—we would startle ourselves in recognizing how many truly important decisions came to us as the result of seemingly random events. While surely our upbringing plays a huge role in the people we come to be, much of the rest is as leaves in an autumn gust. The choices available to us are vast, and there is no way of inspecting all of them.

A friend, who is not always wise but who occasionally hits upon something worth thinking about, says that his first sense of growing old was the metaphorical sound of doors slamming: The choices available to him "when he grew up" (he was then forty) had become limited. He could no longer head down to the recruiting office and sign up to become a naval aviator. Entering the police academy was not available to him anymore. He now would never be an Olympic skier. Never mind that he had never desired to be any of those things. His anguish, and it was real, was that no longer were all possibilities open to him. It was that idea, the thing we're taught early on about our "being anything we want to be," that had prevented him and many like him from making some important decisions in his life. Committing to one thing, to spending his life in pursuit of a particular career, by its own nature closed some doors. Like others, he had confused "you can do anything" with "you can do everything." It was when age began to make decisions for him that he began to put a life that was not entirely dissolute but was certainly aimless in some kind of order.

We have numerous choices, yet we often exercise little care in making them. There are few tragedies as poignant as that of the man or woman who, upon reaching retirement age, suddenly realizes that the one life available to him or her had been spent without much thought, and now it's too late to live it as he or she would have wished, to do something different.

Much of our life is random. You did not meet your friends through a conscious effort to go out and acquire some friends. You probably did not meet your spouse during an application period in which you reviewed résumés of prospective husbands or wives. While we tend to cling to those with whom we have affinities based on shared interests and views, our having met those people to begin with is largely a matter of chance. And our interests and views are also up to chance to a large extent. You read this book instead of that one. You listened to a speaker who was more skillful in advocating one point of view than the speaker who favored the opposite position. It was a body of water instead of rolling green hills that you passed each day, and therefore you came to have a passion for sailing instead of golf. You watched a televised auto race and from that seed a passion grew for the intricacies of mechanical things, and you became an engineer or a mechanic.

Perhaps you were raised to believe or somehow arrived on your own at the notion that wealth is the end and that the means do not matter. This doesn't mean necessarily that you decided to become a bank robber or swindler, but it may well mean that you embraced a career solely because of its income potential rather than because of any satisfaction you derive from the work itself. Or maybe your motivation is something else. It might be the desire to discover something of use, or to create a work of art that will endure long after you are gone, or to build the better mousetrap—not to get the world to beat a path to your door but because you don't like having mice around. It's your choice, but it is a good idea to remember that other people are entitled to their choices, too.

That said, there is enormous pressure on us to cast off our uniqueness and be like the crowd. Part of this has to do with our nature; while we are not social in the sense of bees or ants, we are not solitary creatures entirely, either. We seek the approval of others, and this sometimes takes the form of wanting to be like them. Such imitation is separate from finding qualities in others that we find admirable and seek to emulate; it is imitation to gain acceptance. The difference is the difference between "style" and "fashion." The former is the inward ability to look and be appropriate in a wide range of situations, while the latter is following the crowd.

Today we live in a world where no matter the direction in which we turn we are encouraged to follow the fashion. This is a matter of some practical reality: There are so many people that it is all but impossible to market to anything except groups. But it is also a function of persons trying to get you to do something for their gain, not yours. In order to make this marketing more effective, it is important for the marketers— and by this I mean anyone seeking to sell a point of view, as opposed to a product—to make it seem more and more important to go along with the crowd.

This phenomenon especially permeates the news media. For instance, consider the coverage leading up to elections. There was a

18

time when that coverage dealt with the positions taken by the particular candidates, which voters were expected to weigh before voting. Today, elections are approached as if they are athletic events. The mechanics of the campaigns—how much money has been raised and where it is being spent, what groups are being courted—are cynically appraised in the way that sporting commentators might discuss training regimens and injuries. Each day the latest "tracking polls" are broadcast, the equivalent of a sports channel giving us the odds for a horse race. But this kind of coverage is of limited use in deciding for whom to vote; instead, it encourages the voter to support whoever is perceived to be ahead.

There is a tremendous accent on polling, with "news" channels, newspapers, and magazines often sponsoring polls on various issues on the Internet. As a measure of anything at all, these polls are useless, but that is not their purpose. They are designed to let the assertive among us get the sensation of having been heard without actually having done so, while allowing those who would follow the crowd to get a sense—also inaccurate—of the direction in which the herd is headed.

Much of what the media do serves to illustrate their lack of respect for their customers. This is especially true of television. We live in a very noisy world, with endless yammering from every direction. In the days since the attacks of September 11, 2001, television news broadcasts have been overloaded with "information." Looking at one of the all-news cable channels just now, I see people talking—well, "talking" is a bit of a stretch; there are two people angrily arguing a political point, casting maximum heat and no light—on a screen also festooned with the time, a changing display of several stock indices, a caption to tell us what the two angry people are fighting about (which is an admission that we would not be able to discern it by listening to them), and a constant stream of headlines traveling in text across the bottom of the screen. It would not be possible for one to follow all of it. It is overload. It dulls our ability to listen, to pay attention, because the screen serves as its own distraction. The only time this cacophony of audio-video noise disappears is during commercial breaks, which seem almost placid by comparison.

I suspect that all of this is deliberate in its effect. Television is certainly the most influential of the media, and it is the locus of a great deal of money. Marketing "scientists" go to a lot of trouble learning what is most likely to have impact upon a viewer. Nothing arrives onscreen without having first been carefully researched. If you watch television news, you might end up with a general impression, but you may have no idea how you arrived at it. You will certainly have the sense of having gotten informed, but have you really?

Ah, but that's the media. Surely we can rely on science, right? Not necessarily. There are many reasons why the science that in the years following World War II we came to view as a more reliable replacement for the God of earlier generations falls short. One is that scientists themselves are corruptible. It is possible to find a scientist who will say, for money, just about anything you wish to have said, as the transcripts of trials show. Another is that scientific findings are limited by the assumptions that go into the design of experiments. Yet another, which applies most especially to experiments involving human beings, is that it is impossible to control all the variables—to do that, you would have to produce a "lab rat" population of humans whose every detail would have to be monitored from conception, and even then you would fall short because of genetic differences among us and the effects of having lived in a certain environment. Still another is the fact that science is not the omniscient thing that in the optimistic 1950s and '60s we believed it was. Many of the modern scientific discoveries from the research and development labs came about by accident, when the problem that was solved was not the one for which a solution was sought.

We tend to overestimate ourselves as a species. We believe that we can ultimately know everything. Perhaps this is so, but perhaps we are to the universe as the ant is to the human: incapable due to our own limitations of fully grasping its nature, its significance. Worrying about this is an issue of faith, not demonstrable fact. But it is important to be aware that even seemingly simple problems we think could be easily solved sometimes aren't.

For example, I play tennis. The physics of tennis ought to be something simply explained. Yet on August 30, 2004, the *New York Times* reported that it isn't: "Andrew Ashcroft, a doctoral student in engineering at the University of Cambridge in England, had an arsenal of data in his study of how the ball strikes the racket. His conclusion? 'We don't understand how the ball interacts with racket strings,' he said. 'We can't correlate through mechanical tests what players perceive.'"

Science cannot prove what I, as a player of some experience, have come to learn works for me.

Yet surely I know that unless I slather my arms and legs with sun-blocking cream, I run an increased risk of contracting skin cancer, most worrisome of which is deadly melanoma. No, actually, I do not. Nor do you—not with any real certainly. Dr. A. Bernard Ackerman, a New York dermatologist, describes much of the research that leads to such a conclusion as "nonsense." He may be right. He may be wrong. His credentials are at least as good as those of researchers in the field. He is sixty-seven years old, and he has decided not to use suntan lotions. He has concluded that epidemiological research on cancer is unconvincing.

Yet conventional wisdom says that defending ourselves from the sun is settled scientific sense.

In a time when there are more choices in our lives than ever before, it is more difficult to arrive at intelligent decisions and easier to go with the flow. The flow always leads downstream.

The result is that it is ever more difficult to maintain your own sense of things, to make your own personal decisions about your own life and the lives of the children in your care. Reports that we are overweight and out of shape (and therefore cannot ever attract the sexual partner of our dreams) are interspersed with advertisements for pills that tell us that we can lose weight effortlessly, or with advertisements for machines that—it is claimed—will enable us to achieve the physique of a body-builder (and therefore obtain that sexual partner that somehow we always thought would never give us a second glance) while never breaking a sweat. And for those times when breaking a sweat is desirable—after we have lassoed the sexual partner we have been promised if only we purchase these products—there are advertisements for pills for achieving arousal. We are told that we are victims, and soon thereafter we are treated to advertisements which urge us to sue our oppressors. The government issues a new report on smoking that lists so many diseases attributable to that practice that if the report were true there would be no smoker left standing, and the news account of it is followed by advertisements for pharmaceutical or herbal smoking cessation aids.

Society, as manifested in the media, by the government, by lawyers, by advertisers, and by plain old busybodies, has decided that your point of view is not valid and must not be countenanced. But it has done more than that, and it is the one thing that is designed to inflict maximum damage on your self-respect. You do not make the choices that you make (as opposed to letting others make those choices for you) because you are stupid, or of evil intent, or simply contrarian. Oh, no: It is because you are a victim. You did not make your choices because they were your choices; you made them because you were unduly influenced—the claim made by those who want to unduly influence you instead.

Making your own choices is more difficult now than ever before, and finding information that lets you inform those choices with facts is a roll of the dice. In a world that wants you to be part of the herd, strays are punished severely.

3

I'M OKAY, AND IF YOU WERE LIKE ME, YOU'D BE OKAY, TOO

God created man, the Bible tells us, in His own image. But, it points out, that doesn't mean we are like gods. Indeed, the book of Genesis says that the fall from grace came when the serpent said that eating the forbidden fruit would allow Adam and Eve to become gods themselves—and we know how that turned out. Nevertheless, we try to recreate the people around us in our own image. We constantly play God. Sometimes this is with altruistic intentions; sometimes it is for selfish reasons. But it seldom works out well.

There are distinctions to be made, certainly, and some of them are subtle. We offer assistance when asked, and sometimes we offer assistance—"You don't want to take that route; the bridge is out"—without being asked. It is when one urges people to become better by being more like oneself that the trouble begins.

Why do we want others to be as much like us as possible? The reasons are varied. At a very basic level, we long to be part of a group. We have clung to groups from our earliest days as a species because they provide safety or the illusion of it. This clannishness has stayed with us

25

over the millennia. So has our sense that we are ourselves special, but everybody else isn't—because, of course, they are special only to themselves. Thus, it has become second nature to us to favor others by holding out the hope that they can be just like us.

The flip side is that others have a different idea: They want to favor us by holding out the hope that *we* can be just like *them*. It isn't just that the two are mutually exclusive, it's that both are impossible. But still we try. Sometimes this is out of fairly straightforward selfishness. An old *Peanuts* cartoon comes to mind, in which the character Lucy describes herself as "idealistic." She continues: "I want to make the world a better place for me to live in."

A friend moved to the country to obtain some peace and quiet. He was troubled upon learning that near his home was what is called an "airway intersection," meaning that commercial airliners were often assigned a point nearly directly over his home as a waypoint. Airliners would be directed to that point, then given a new heading to another waypoint or to their final destination. The effect is that though he was out in the woods, there was the constant dull roar of jet airliners high above. He was annoyed. Were there a way he could have brought it to an end, he would have. To his credit, he did not hire a lawyer to file suit. His case is not unlike the one found near many airports. Airports are often built some distance from population centers, precisely because airports are noisy places and airport authorities would rather inconvenience fliers by making them drive farther to catch their flights than spend time in court battling angry homeowners. But after the airports are built, people start to build homes nearby, and soon everyone is in court anyway. There was a time, ending in the 1960s, when the loud booms characteristic of jet airplanes exceeding the speed of sound were common across the land. Now, though, supersonic flight is illegal over the U.S. except in times of emergency. People had complained; some had sued and had prevailed, resulting in an end to hopes of supersonic coast-to-coast passenger service. My friend in the country endures jets passing far overhead, but his fillings are not shaken out by constant sonic booms.

Alas, the airplanes proved to be the least of his concerns. Several months after he moved into his new home, construction began on a house down the hill from him, in sight of his back porch, which had until then been a relatively quiet and very private place. He thought that the construction noise would only last a few months, and he was right about that. But soon thereafter the home's owners moved in. They were from the city where lights are bright and the noise of commerce and civilization is constant. They seemed frightened by the peace and general quiet of the place. In the city, in darkness often lies danger. The new neighbors cleared all the trees from a broad area around the house. They planted grass. They installed outdoor lighting—lots of it. Where once my friend could step out on the back porch and enjoy the moonlight shimmering on the tops of the leaves, the vista now is of a place down the hill that is lit up like a nuclear power plant.

Because the neighbors want their lawn to be perfectly manicured, they run very loud mowers much of the year, and leaf blowers during other parts of the year, and snow blowers other times. Much of my friend's reason for moving to the country had been taken away, and with it some of the value of his homestead, to say nothing of the quality of his life. This was all the more galling because he had gone to some lengths to be a good neighbor: When he mowed the lawn, he did so late enough in the day that it was not likely to interrupt anyone's sleep or breakfast, and he made a point of being done before the noise would impinge on neighbors' evening meals. He cut his own firewood, which is a noisy process involving a chainsaw, splitting maul, and sledge hammer, but he restricted the hours during which he did this so as to minimally annoy others.

In an ironic twist that should come as no surprise in this day and age, it was the neighbors with the bright lights and noisy implements who complained, and they complained about my friend. They had a child, they said, who was allergic to the odor of wood smoke, which drifted down the hill, highly diluted.

My friend's home was soon on the market, and he looked for a new place, deeper in the woods (and in a hilly area unsuitable for airports).

There are worse things that happen, of course, every day. Yet my friend's experience illustrates two things. The first is a matter of "rights." Is there a right not to be annoyed? Did my friend have a right to insist that the light and noise from his neighbors stop at his property line? Did the neighbors have a right to insist that the smoke from the fireplace be directed elsewhere? Beyond that, to what extent are we obligated to get along with those around us? My friend did not complain to or about the neighbors, beyond some general grumbling. But the neighbors went to the authorities and, of course, threatened to sue. (Whether they would have prevailed in court is another matter, but it costs a lot of money to defend even a ridiculous lawsuit—something we will cover in depth in later chapters.)

Our rights end at the other guy's nose, or so the saying goes; that saying was coined in a time when the only thing you could do to the other guy's nose about which he might have a legitimate complaint was punch him there. Today, people complain, with a straight face, that their rights are violated by foul odors (and, if it comes to court, often trot out hired "experts" who present some "scientific" evidence that the odor is unhealthy). There have been lawsuits (and even legislation in many places) over light and noise "pollution." We have become uncompromisingly selfish. We want it all, but we do not want anyone else to have his or her version of "it all," if it does not fit in with our plans.

Sometimes we wish to rule other people's lives not out of direct selfishness but because we think we know what is best for others and imagine that they would be healthier, happier, and generally better persons if only they did as we said.

Today, rights that were enumerated in a straightforward fashion in the amendments to the U.S. Constitution have gotten blurred. It will be no surprise that lawyers often come to be involved. It should be no surprise that "science" is often invoked as part of the campaign to get people to do not what they care to do but what someone else cares for them to do.

The classic case is smoking. It may well be that for at least some people, smoking is a harmful thing. The science on this is not as absolute as you might suppose, but there is cause to believe that for some people under some circumstances at some times in their lives smoking is inadvisable. That it is not for everyone is neither questionable nor questioned. No one is forcing anyone else to smoke.

Yet it was decided that people should be discouraged from smoking. (It should surprise no one that this came about coincident to the federal government becoming involved in healthcare through its Medicare and Medicaid programs, which in turn set the prices for medical care in the U.S. at a level such that medical insurance became an expensive necessity.) The government, without sufficient or scientifically convincing evidence, announced that smoking is invariably bad, and the announcement was accepted uncritically.

Some people stopped smoking because of the announcement, but many more did not. We will get into what happened at a government level in the next chapter, but on a personal level people undertook to make others quit smoking.

For example, "No Smoking—Driver Allergic" stickers began appearing in New York City taxicabs. Now, it may well be that cab drivers object to tobacco smoke. It may be that a few of them actually suffer from some medical condition that makes it inadvisable that they spend a lot of time in smoky environments. But the stickers are in most and maybe all cases simply a lie. That is because despite extensive research on the subject, no one has ever found an antigen to tobacco smoke, which is to say that as far as it is known no one is genuinely allergic to it. The standard reference on the subject is a paper which appeared in 1989 in the publication of the American Lung Association, the *American Review of Respiratory Disease*. The stickers are a perfect example of people hiding behind science to force others to do something (or, in this case, *not* do something).

The problem cuts both ways. Taxi drivers hide behind science rather than simply say that they would prefer it if passengers refrained from smoking, as surely is the driver's right. This may well be justified to some extent by passengers who believe that it is their right to smoke no matter what; perhaps there is a belief that the sticker imposes some kind of legal bar to smoking in taxicabs.

But the stickers do something else. They elevate what is always or almost so a matter of personal preference to a scientific certainty, an inviolable fact. The driver achieves a superior, almost holier, position in the matter. That the stickers are always or—let's give the drivers the benefit of the doubt, scientific evidence notwithstanding—*almost always* a lie never enters into it. Who is going to engage in a scientific debate with the cab driver?

The issue of allergies in general has come to be abused, such that "I am allergic to [something]" is often nothing more than a synonym for "I don't like [something]." This can be a murky area, because allergies vary in intensity, and it could be that in some cases our aesthetic distaste for some food item, plant, or something else has come from a mild physical reaction to it. But that is a far cry from the announcement that you are allergic to anything that in fact you simply don't like.

The psychologist Nathaniel Branden has concentrated on and written several popular books having to do with the issue of "self-esteem." As with many subjects that have a basis in scientific fact, self-esteem is a part of our personalities that is sometimes worthy of attention. And as with many such subjects, it can be taken to a ridiculous extreme—that a bank robber suffers from low self-esteem must, at bottom, be *his* problem, not the bank's; never mind whether low self-esteem is the "cause" of bank robbery, which in all likelihood it is not. In his books and workshops, Branden offers the view that the first and most important step one can take in enhancing one's self-esteem *is to tell the truth.*

When we lie about an allergy in order to bring about a desired action by someone else, we are saying that we do not think enough of ourselves to believe that a mere statement of our wishes will have any effect. We are also saying that we think so little of others that we do not believe they have the decency to take our wishes into account.

Tragically, this has been built into society to the extent that it is now exceptional when people negotiate calmly (let alone cordially) to find a way where both parties can be happy or where such discomfort as is inevitable can be evenly or justly assigned. The story is told—and I am assured that it is true, though today it sounds apocryphal—of two neighbors who shared a long common driveway. Asked how they maintained it without dispute, one of the neighbors said, "It's easy. We each do more than our share." That is, really, the recipe for success in any relationship, be it commercial or personal. But it is also something that we no longer feel compelled to do.

I know of a nice, energetic, retired couple who enjoys after-dinner walks around their neighborhood. These relax them, or used to. Now their walks make them nervous wrecks, because several of their neighbors have purchased large, apparently vicious dogs, and do not keep them under control. Consideration on the part of all involved, plus respect for others, would make this a nonissue. The people have the dogs for protection because other means of assuring one's security at home—such as a firearm—have been socially stigmatized (and in some cases prohibited by law). But they take this a step too far, by allowing the dogs to run free. Their "right" to have a dog, as with one's "right" to smoke or not smoke, carries responsibility.

If self-esteem requires you to tell the truth, then self-respect requires you to bear the responsibility of your decisions, and there are few decisions that do not bring with them some kind of responsibility. Your handling of the responsibilities that you assume through your decisions is the most visible announcement of your own self-respect and the respect you have for others. Many of life's decisions involve the lesser of evils; in fact, most of them do. You decide the speed at which you drive your car, and you have a choice: Drive very fast and increase the likelihood of being in an accident and the likelihood that that accident will be serious, or drive slowly and make it less likely that your life will be shortened by an accident—at the price of giving up some of your life in the extra time spent reaching your destination.

I once saw a calculation of the price in human hours of a one-hour traffic delay on the Beltway around Washington D.C. at rush hour. While each person lost only an hour, so many people were involved that the total time lost, when everyone's hour was added in, amounted to several lifetimes. In a sense, this is worth considering when we look at our approach to topics such as speed limits. Higher speed limits cost more lives in terms of number of people killed, but do they save more lives in terms of the total number of hours that humans are doing things other than traveling from place to place? Are we agreed that it is good that each of us gives up a little bit of his or her life—and more than a little bit over a lifetime of driving—in order to keep someone else from losing life entirely? Remember, the life that is saved might be yours. Things like this are worth thinking about, even though there is no real "right" answer, because they help illustrate how just about everything is a trade-off, even things that do not at first seem so.

A related issue is what we have come to call "road rage" and its far more common predecessor, impoliteness among drivers. It is easy to take one's frustrations out on another driver. It is a kind of communication that is both direct and relatively anonymous, with little likelihood of any immediate, painful effect. But what does it gain you, other than the knowledge that you have assaulted an anonymous stranger? Compare it to the satisfaction you get when at a stop sign you wave the other driver through ahead of you. Yet the latter course of behavior is on the decline, while the newspapers tell us, as does observation, that the former is more and more commonplace.

I think much of the reason for this is that we have imparted a certain nobility to victimhood. We believe, and are encouraged to believe, that we are victims (which we'll discuss more in the next chapter). It used to be considered a virtue to suffer in silence, but now all the attention goes to those who suffer, or pretend to suffer, as noisily as possible.

It is a fact that life is a series of trials and decisions at the end of which you die. This is inescapable. No way around it. Those decisions may to a large or small extent determine when you die, but not whether you will. Relatively few of those decisions are absolute. If you eat a spoonful of powerful poison, you will die. If your parachute doesn't open, the odds are overwhelming—though it is not certain, there having been survivors—that you will die. If you drive fast, you might die, and if you drive slowly, you might die also, though there is statistical evidence that suggests your likelihood of dying is somewhat reduced.

We can control some things, and some things we cannot control. Life is not fair, and it cannot be made fair. People have died at home in bed when airplanes crashed into their houses. They have also died at home in bed, despite lifetimes of care for their own health and safety, when some blood vessel ruptured.

But when we seek to be victims, we must do something to elevate ourselves beyond being victims of life's vicissitudes. We cannot be just victims—we must be victims of something. Or someone. Preferably someone.

When we are victims, we gain a degree of sympathy that can be leveraged into power over other people. And when we are victims—this is the part no one mentions—we can be more easily controlled.

4

PLAYING GOD AS AN INSTITUTIONAL RIGHT

The Oxford don and author C. S. Lewis once made an observation about those who would help us: "Of all tyrannies, a tyranny exercised for the good of its victims may be the most oppressive. It may be better to live under robber barons than under omnipotent moral busybodies. The robber baron's cruelty may sometimes sleep, his cupidity may at some point be satiated; but those who torment us for our own good will torment us without end, for they do so with the approval of their own conscience."

Society has made a point in recent years of doing all it can to remove the responsibility from some actions while canonizing others, all with little objective reason, but often with an ulterior motive.

Our tendency to encourage others to be like us takes on new power and great danger when it is indulged in by our governments and other institutions. Yet those institutions flow naturally toward telling others how to live, for several reasons. The first and most obvious is institutional convenience—it is far easier for any institution that affects many people if there is no exception, if everyone is identical, as with the teacher and the left-handed student. There is also the assumption that the group is surely more knowledgeable and wiser than the individual.

The U.S. Constitution has appended to it the Bill of Rights, the purpose of which is to protect the minority—the individual—from the tyranny of the majority in certain areas. But the majority's tyranny writ small is evident throughout our institutions. Candidates may be elected after having appealed to our basest prejudices and fears. News media survive on their ability to appeal to the largest possible group. Research grants are awarded, often, more on the ability of the researcher to gather a following than on the nature of the work proposed. Infomercial hucksters offer quick, easy solutions to problems or imagined problems, and their success depends on their ability to persuade viewers to send them money.

All of it feeds, and feeds upon, the idea that there is one right way and one alone, that people should be alike, that there are ideals of thought, belief, appearance, and behavior that should be attained even by coercion if necessary. But this assumption of ideals is erroneous when applied to individuals. It benefits not us but the institutions that employ it. Their underlying goal—influence—is different from their stated goal—helping us have better lives.

The reason we do not see this is our desire to be part of a group, to achieve what Abraham Maslow described as "belongingness." We are willing to override our own knowledge of what's good for us in order to succumb to the lure of the group. In so doing, we cede power over ourselves to the group, be it political party, trendy fashion in clothing, scientific "truism," or a dime-store psychologist who claims to have the one true recipe to make us happy.

This uncritical willingness to abandon our very right to think for ourselves is bad enough. What makes it worse is that our institutions are so often wrong, either deliberately or by accident. Worse still is that over time the purpose of the institutions becomes solely to maintain their power over us, by whatever means.

The issue was illustrated nicely by British health secretary John Reid, as reported in the June 9, 2004, edition of the Manchester *Guardian:*

> Mr Reid said that the middle classes were obsessed with giving instruction to people from lower socio-economic backgrounds and that smoking was not one of the worst problems facing poorer people.
>
> "I just do not think the worst problem on our sink estates by any means is smoking, but it is an obsession of the learned middle class," he said. "What enjoyment does a 21-year-old single mother of three living in a council sink estate get? The only enjoyment sometimes they have is to have a cigarette."

Nor does it stop with smoking—and the problem is one that affects many cultures, though the "enlightened" West is especially vulnerable to institutional meddling. The current craze—which suspiciously coincides with a vast marketing effort for a diet regimen that is itself highly questionable—has led to the assumption that something called the "obesity epidemic" is a fact, and that it is our obligation to rush forward and—what?

Again from England, and again from June 2004, comes the story of a three-year-old girl who was, supposedly, England's youngest victim of morbid obesity. The story is all the worse for its having appeared in an official report, commissioned by the House of Commons, where the anecdote was in the second paragraph, where it was sure to gain attention. There was a media frenzy, with the British press searching records to learn more about the girl, even offering her family thousands of dollars for exclusive rights to her story. London's *Independent* takes it from there:

> Then it emerged that the girl was not, after all, a victim of the "obe-sogenic" environment—one which encourages over-eating and sedentary behaviour. Instead, she had a rare genetic defect which affected the appetite control mechanism located in the hypothala-mus in her brain. The result was she had a ravenous appetite immune to the efforts of her parents to control it and unaffected by junk food advertising, school sports policy or government behaviour.

You may rest assured that the error was not reported with anything like the fervor that characterized the reportage of the original, incorrect story, and no doubt there were some who were perfectly willing to let the truth in this case fall victim to what in their minds was the greater good: increasing public awareness of the obesity epidemic.

Beware the phrase "increase public awareness." Almost without exception is it a euphemism for "drum up a mob." But it also means that the person or organization using the phrase supports the cause over which the mob is to gather its pitchforks and torches. It means that you are supposed to become outraged without stopping to think about it.

There are many groups, organizations, and institutions vying for their respective pieces of our outrage; if we were to follow them all, we would sleep fitfully and awaken to blind anger that would last until we again dozed into fitful slumber. (There are those who do believe them all, and that is the kind of life they lead.) Animal rights groups want you to be angry that a shampoo maker would check ahead of time, by use of lab animals, to see if its product produces blindness—they would rather it be tested on your child in your home. (And if it does blind your child, you can always sue the company!)

Environmental organizations, the result of perfectly reasonable conservation movements taken to ridiculous extreme, want nothing short of the shutdown of Western civilization, which allows them to become angry over nearly everything.

Political candidates seek to gain power by pitting one group of citizens against another in class warfare, and often do not feel obligated to employ the truth (and seldom do they feel obligated to employ the entire truth) in making their pitches.

Scientific research organizations and academicians, scrambling for the grant money that comes from public popularity, do not accent the limited or tentative nature of their study findings, and even if they did, the news media would gloss over those caveats in covering the stories and the legal profession would, too, also for financial gain.

Honesty has become a prerequisite to nothing, and perception has replaced objective, demonstrable truth in the areas where truth is available.

Institutions champion what they want, which is fine and to be expected, through campaigns in which they present it as being good for you, whether it is or not—and that is *not* fine. Institutions that are supposed to advise us, to raise the red flag, are increasingly complicit in this endeavor. Once-trusted newspapers, many recently embroiled in scandal, have given up any appearance of or attempt at objectivity and are openly partisan, allying themselves with causes that they immunize from criticism. Broadcasting networks do much the same; some admit their bias up front, while others do not, and while still others appear to be at least willing dupes eager to parrot any claim so long as it is sufficiently outrageous.

The real story is practically always more complicated than you are led to believe. You are given one piece by groups, in their effort to exert godlike control over what you think, and another piece by different groups, often for the same reason. You can take the time to assemble the pieces and—if those pieces are all true, which in this day and age is itself a leap of faith—try to estimate what the real story is.

A word about the media: Their task is more to sell a product than it is to present an accurate and complete account of events. Yet we believe them.

Consider: Have you ever seen a news story about a subject with which you are personally familiar? It might be a "hard news" event, such as a terrible car or airplane crash, or it might be something softer, a feature story. Is it not true that when you read or viewed or heard the news account, you noticed that it contained inaccuracies? And yet did you not then go on to assume that everything else in the newspaper or newscast was absolutely true?

We are led to discount the evidence provided by our own eyes, ears, experiences, and reasoning. We are taught to be sheep and to follow the shepherd, in a world of competing shepherds.

All of it is to gain power over you. And you alone have the power to stop it. It begins by keeping your own council and making your own judgments rather than accepting the prepackaged ones served up to you. It includes recognizing that your judgment may not be the same as that of your neighbor or someone across town or across the country— and that both judgments might be perfectly valid.

It means having respect for yourself and having respect for others as well. And recognizing that "one size fits all" often means "one size fits all equally poorly."

5

THE NEW GODS DON'T KNOW EITHER

Over the last several decades, the convergence of powerful institutions—government, academic, scientific—and broad and pervasive news media have created new gods: the god of statistics, the god of correlation equaling causation, the god of science. We are encouraged to worship at their altars and are shunned if we do not.

As a result, numerous theories have unjustifiably taken on the mantle of fact and have become the assumptions upon which policies have been formulated. Our lives have been changed, at our economic and psychological expense, at the cost of the quality of our individual lives—and it has often been based on scientific "proofs" that are anything but proof and often demonstrably wrong.

An examination of history demonstrates that this is not new—what's new is the speed and certitude with which errors now come to be taken as fact.

The incidence of this phenomenon is now so widespread that it would be impossible to list every time it occurs. Some of the most glaring examples will be examined in the following chapters; sometimes the argument over how to solve a particular problem obscures whether the problem itself is properly defined—as it often isn't. But one example familiar in some respects to everyone should serve as an illustration of how well-meaning authorities can go terribly wrong, all the while pointing to science and wholesomeness as their motivation, while debating solutions to a problem that may be nothing like its generally accepted definition—and ruining anyone who dares to disagree.

It is the story of Acquired Immune Deficiency Syndrome, also known by the acronym AIDS. It began in 1981, when there were published accounts saying that there had the previous year been more cases of a rare cancer, called Karposi's sarcoma, in New York City alone than were normally found in a year in the entire country. Each victim, the accounts detailed, was a homosexual man.

Soon there were more reports of this disease among homosexual men, not just in New York but in other cities in the U.S. and then abroad. This was followed by statistics listing an abnormally high death rate among homosexual men from other diseases. It was all lumped together and called AIDS.

Everyone who had an opinion weighed in, with views in both extremes. Some claimed that this was divine retribution for the sin of homosexuality. Others, equally extreme (but they prevailed in the end), offered the view that linking homosexual behavior to AIDS was politically incorrect and bigoted. Groups formed, first to look at and deal with the puzzling statistics and to see if there was something that needed to be done, later to become politically active in a variety of polite and outrageous actions to increase the strength of homosexuals as a group.

More and more diseases were added to the list of ailments of which it was decided AIDS was composed. This necessitated a search for a common element. As long as the definition of AIDS coincided with the sudden upsurge of cases of Karposi's sarcoma, the search was manageable, if not easy. But in an effort to make the problem seem other than an outbreak of a rare cancer within a particular group, which itself existed in a statistically interesting but small group of people, incidents of apparently disparate diseases involving not just gay men but other groups were added. Students of the phenomenon, irrespective of political point of view, suggested that the Reagan administration wanted to reach out to groups in New York and, later, other big cities where what was now diagnosed as AIDS was becoming increasingly common. Unstated, perhaps because those who care about such things take it as a given, was the fact that research dollars are typically awarded based not on how interesting a problem is—and a sudden burst of Karposi's sarcoma in a small population was certainly that—but on how many people are affected. It therefore made sense to exaggerate the nature and scope of the outbreak.

Nevertheless, the homosexual community, which was able to say that which political correctness prevented others from saying, believed that a disease was killing them. It is a human tendency, especially in our society, to blame someone for everything bad that happens, and the gay community blamed Ronald Reagan, who had recently become president. Reagan was not, they said, doing enough to combat this strange new disease, and his lack of action proved, they said, that he did not care about homosexuals. (It should be noted as a matter of historical record that Reagan had been an actor and came from a world where homosexuality was not unknown, yet no one from that world offered the slightest evidence that he had ever expressed any discrimination with respect to homosexuals. It should also be noted that presidents have not traditionally been called upon to come up with cures for diseases.)

A year passed, then two, then three, and there was no "cure" for the "disease" of AIDS. (Adding to the problem was that no one died, or dies, of AIDS. Deaths come from other diseases; AIDS is said to make its sufferers more vulnerable to those diseases.) The media, in part frightened that sexual promiscuity could result in the dreaded and, it was thought, invariably fatal syndrome, and in no way enamored of Reagan, turned up the heat. As the 1984 election approached, the pressure was great for the government to come up with some advance in connection with AIDS.

It came to pass that on April 23, 1984, Dr. Robert Gallo of the National Institutes of Health appeared along with Health and Human Services Secretary Margaret Heckler at a news conference at which it was announced that a retrovirus, called Human T-cell Leukemia virus Type-III or HTLV-III, was responsible for AIDS. Gallo said that the virus had been isolated from AIDS patients. He further said that a test for its presence had been developed.

While the media and many, many people accepted the claim uncritically, Gallo's assertion was immediately on shaky footing; it would have collapsed underneath him thereafter if the one goal of AIDS research had been getting at the truth, which some believe still has not been revealed. Two years earlier, Gallo had blamed AIDS at least in part on HTLV-I, but that hypothesis was immediately shot down, primarily for three reasons: HTLV-I was associated with leukemia, but AIDS patients did not suffer from that disease with any greater frequency than the general population; tests of antibodies determined that the population with greatest exposure to HTLV-I was in Japan, yet no one in Japan had come down with AIDS; and French researchers had come up with a more likely candidate, which was called Lymphadenopathy Associated Virus (LAV).

Before his announcement, several investigations by private and government organizations concluded that Gallo had not discovered HTLV-III but instead had merely renamed the French virus, of which he had been provided samples and then claimed it as his own discovery. The investigations cast doubt on the whole proceedings, but by then Gallo's hypothesis had been taken as fact, a status which it continues to enjoy. (The French had claimed in 1985 that Gallo had stolen their virus. The matter was resolved not by scientific research but by a negotiated treaty signed in 1987 by Gallo, by the discoverer of LAV, Luc Montagnier of the Pasteur Institute, and by Reagan and French President Jacques Chirac, in which Gallo and Montagnier were named codiscoverers.)

Another investigation, chaired by Yale biochemist Frederic Richards, concluded that papers published by Gallo and colleagues in the prestigious journal *Science* in conjunction with the announcement of HTLV-III (later called "HIV" for "Human Immunodeficiency Virus") as the cause of AIDS did not accurately describe the lab work that had been done. The NIH's Office of Scientific Integrity conducted an inquiry and decided that Gallo had "created and fostered conditions that give rise to falsified/fabricated data and falsified reports" in his AIDS research.

The NIH's Office of Research Integrity reviewed the OSI report and itself found Gallo guilty of scientific misconduct.

Despite what was at the very least some extremely questionable behavior on the part of the NIH's AIDS researchers, nobody in any of the investigations dared to suggest that perhaps the conclusions reached by that research might be tainted. There was a reason for that. The OSI report had been completed in 1992, and by then it was common knowledge that the careers of those who dissented from Gallo's findings were being systematically destroyed. It was death to one's career to suggest that Gallo might be wrong. By then it was a "fact" that HIV caused AIDS. That was that. It simply was not to be discussed further.

A textbook example is that of Dr. Peter Duesberg, a professor of molecular and cell biology at the University of California–Berkeley, and, until he dared open his mouth about Gallo's findings, on many people's short list of researchers likely one day to win a Nobel Prize. Duesberg thought Gallo was wrong and said so.

Duesberg is not, or at least at the time was certainly thought not to be, some mad scientist from the fever swamps. He had been elected in 1986 to the National Academy of Sciences and awarded an Outstanding Investigator Grant by the NIH itself. But credentials be damned. For suggesting that HIV might not be the cause of AIDS and that AIDS might be nothing more than a collection of diseases diagnosed as AIDS when HIV was present, Duesberg was transformed into a scientific leper, his arguments never receiving serious consideration.

At first his arguments got published, some of them in very prestigious journals. But they were quickly and loudly attacked in overwhelming numbers; it has been suggested (and there is cause to suspect) that this had to with NIH having accepted Gallo's research as its official position. The National Institutes of Health control an enormous amount of research money, and it would not hurt to stay in NIH's favor if one were seeking a grant.

Duesberg's assertions are stark: Not only does HIV not cause anything one might call AIDS, it does not and cannot cause anything at all and is in fact harmless though communicable, he says. The initial diseases that led to the rubric of AIDS, he asserts, can be attributed to the use of various drugs and chemicals popular in the homosexual community, with Karposi's sarcoma being induced by "poppers," butyl nitrate inhalants that provide a rush of pleasurable energy for a brief period. Many people who die of AIDS, he says, are killed by the long-term use of the powerful drugs and chemicals used as prophylactic treatment when one has tested positive for the presence of AIDS.

He notes that babies born infected with HIV have in some cases become free of the virus without intervention. He argues that the rush to establish something called AIDS and the even more fevered rush to find cause and cure were politically and socially—not scientifically—based.

Duesberg soon saw grant money dry up; he was shunned by colleagues and in some ways even by his own school.

Yet he may be right.

To this day, no proof has been offered of any connection between HIV and AIDS, or indeed that there even is such a thing as AIDS beyond a list of diseases which, when there is also HIV present, are called by that name. As Dr. Roger Cunningham, director of the Center for Immunology at the State University of New York at Buffalo, noted in 1994, "Unfortunately, an AIDS 'establishment' seems to have formed that intends to discourage challenges to the dogma on one side and often insists on following discredited ideas on the other." Dr. Harvey Bialy, author of an excellent book about Duesberg and his punishment for having failed to sing along with the chorus (and himself the former editor of *Bio/Technology* and *Nature Biotechnology*), says that "HIV only contains a very small piece of genetic information. There's no way it can do all these elaborate things they say it does."

Today, the term "AIDS" is applied to twenty-six diseases, many of which are relatively common. If one gets pneumonia, one is said to have pneumonia and the case is so labeled for statistical purposes. If, however, one contracts pneumonia and is HIV-positive (which is to say, in a test one is shown not necessarily to have HIV but instead to have developed anti-bodies that suggest exposure to it) that person is diagnosed as having AIDS and the case is reported as such to the statisticians.

For a decade we have been hearing truly heartrending stories of the "AIDS epidemic" in Africa. The federal government has pledged billions of dollars to fight that "epidemic." But in many affected regions of Africa, one does not need to be HIV-positive to be diagnosed as having AIDS—any of the twenty-six diseases alone will do. African nations lack the laboratory facilities, trained technicians, and financial resources to conduct the tests, so it is simply assumed that those diseases are AIDS caused by HIV. Bialy goes so far as to say that much of the American aid to African nations to combat AIDS is simply bulk purchase by the U.S. government of drugs from U.S. companies, which are then shipped to Africa where, if Duesberg is right, they will merely make sick people even sicker.

Tragically, if the dissenters' view is accurate, then money that might be applied to immunization and treatment of sick people—of whom no one disputes Africa has many—is being used instead for worse-than-useless, actually harmful drugs.

This long saga is not widely reported. It is inconvenient and messy. It does not fit in a one-minute story for television. It rocks the boat. If you look hard enough, you can find it, but for every mention of it you find you will find, too, ten thousand mentions of HIV as "the AIDS virus," no questions asked.

I do not know who is right, but it is clear that factors other than scientific probity led the way in determining how the "scientific" story would unfold. And it was done with your dollars by people pledged to serve you.

Feel served?

Look at it from different directions. The statistics proved the existence of AIDS—except that those statistics may be no more valid than would be statistics in which red-headed people were singled out and twenty-six diseases, when they occurred among those people, were attributed to "red-headed disease." Noted scientists have staked their professional careers on there being such a disease, and that disease being caused by HIV—yet some of them have been shown to have engaged in questionable practices in arriving at that claim, some others have something to gain by agreeing or remaining quiet, and still others have paid a heavy price for disagreeing. Ah, but there is correlation: Every person who dies of AIDS is HIV-positive (if we forget a few million untested Africans)—but the very definition of AIDS is to be HIV-positive, so such a person who dies of nearly anything can be said to have died of AIDS and, officially, has.

Statistics, science, correlation-as-cause: All are tools, and, like all tools, they can be misused—accidentally sometimes, or deliberately by those who have something to gain from doing so.

At the beginning of this chapter you probably "knew" to a moral certainty that HIV causes the fatal disease known as AIDS. You're probably less certain now.

And that is just one example.

Another involves a raging dispute in the psychotherapy field, with a substantial number of psychotherapists arguing that psychological treatment is more art than science, while another group argues that therapists should employ standardized therapies based on statistical appraisals of what is believed to have worked for the greatest number of people. Much of the concern arises from a financial consideration: Insurers look at a chart that describes psychological complaints and lists the amount of therapy that studies show typically resolves the problem—

and after that amount of therapy the insurer will no longer pay. Some therapists are outraged, while others find little problem with the arrangement.

A debate about the relative value of much in psychotherapy is probably a good thing; testing and retesting assumptions usually are. What is troubling, though, is the idea that the full range of conditions incorporated in the human psyche can be reduced to a series of categories. For such categorization to be of real use, there would need to be a category for very nearly every human on the planet.

Consider. It would be easy to divide patients seeking treatment for psychological disorders into two categories: those whose troubles do not prohibit their functioning and living self-sustaining lives, and those whose problems are so severe that they are, in effect, nonfunctional. The chart at this point might say that the second group ought to be hospitalized, and the first group, unhappy though it may be, sent home with no treatment at all. If the interests of the megaorganism we call society are the ones being considered, such a chart might even make sense.

Perhaps the next division of the chart, were it to be made more complicated, would be to divide the first group based on whether the person is likely to become a danger to himself or others, and the second group based on whether hospitalization provides any service that the patient needs—whether treatment might be as effective if the person stayed home (or its inverse, that hospitalization makes the person no better).

The division could continue, but it would not be accurate until a category existed for every single person. The reason is simple: Human beings are unique, complicated creatures. We are the sum of our experiences plus our innate makeup—our intelligence, our genetic predispositions, our aptitudes (which may or may not be functions of the other things). No two humans are alike.

I often ask friends if, had they been born to different parents in a different time and place, their view of the world would be the same as it is with the parents, time, and place that fate assigned to them. The answer is, of course, no. While that is a very broad question, it survives when made far narrower. No two of us perceive a thing in exactly the same way, because no two of us have the same point of view, either experiential or physical. I love playing tennis. Someone else might not, for any of a multitude of reasons or combinations thereof. Maybe he or she was once forced to play the game as part of a physical education class or summer camp and did not do well and was laughed at. Such an experience goes far in precluding a second attempt unless the person is sufficiently motivated to overcome it. One person, upon seeing a horse in a field, might think serene thoughts, while another may remember a broken arm from being thrown from a pony in childhood.

Our perceptions are in as great a profusion as are we ourselves. If there is anyone of entirely pristine mental health, living an utterly untroubled life and responding "appropriately" to every circumstance, I have never heard of that person. Yet in another sense, we all respond "appropriately" to everything, all the time. Something leads us to do what we do, and it is the combination of our experiences, intelligence, and mental health that determines our response to literally everything. When responses consistently make things worse, or when we consistently misread the stimuli, we have a problem. But that is entirely different from "appropriate" response being defined by others.

Still, defining appropriateness and seeking to sway our perceptions are two ways in which those out of power seek power, and those in power seek to become ever more powerful.

6

THE ENVIRONMENTAL MESS

It used to be called *conservation,* and it used to be a good thing. But what we have come to know as *environmentalism* is nothing more or less than a new flavor of the same old Statist religion, in which a once-worthy movement has been coopted, sanctified, and used to promote failed socialist goals, which by definition gain control over individuals.

Conservation, before it took on its current fragrance and before it became a political movement, advocated the avoidance of waste, as the word suggests. It meant not destroying things on a grand scale thoughtlessly. It meant not eating the seed corn.

Fine things came from the idea of conservation, and some even came from government. The Soil Conservation Service, part of the Department of Agriculture, taught farmers how to avoid losing their topsoil to erosion due to wind and water. From that agency and other groups, from university extension services and from private organizations, we were taught to get maximum yield from our land while keeping it rich in the nutrients that would let it remain fertile so we could get maximum yield next year, too.

Hand in hand with this was the notion of conservation of wildlife, which is of value beyond the aesthetic. Tragedies such as the extinction of the passenger pigeon and the elimination of the herds of American bison, both of which were deliberate, and the loss of the heavy, gawky dodo, which was accidental, show that human beings can drive other important species out of existence. Hunting is a recreational activity enjoyed by many, and there are a lot of families who eat better, and for less cost, due to having a hunter within them. The spring morning is alive with the sound of birds, and our lives would be lesser were they silenced, as has happened when house cats have been allowed to return to their feral state.

Over the years, ignorance led us to do things that we should not have done, with the introduction of foreign plants and animals. The locale where this is most readily apparent is southern Florida, where little is native anymore, and where the sky, ground, and waters are filled with foreign creatures, from fish to birds to giant snakes, that have been released there and have driven out other, native species. The waterways are choked with foreign vegetation, and the landscape is littered with huge, often toxic, melaleuca trees, which, once planted (as they were, primarily by government agencies), are nearly impossible to kill. Even the English sparrow, now one of the most common of birds in many areas of the country, was introduced.

So conservation, as with the political philosophy with which it shares a linguistic root, means to be circumspect in acting, taking into account the likely effects of actions and weighing them against the perceived benefits before acting. It does not mean calling a halt to everything; indeed, in some cases doing nothing allows bad situations to which we have contributed to worsen. Many parts of the country face a terrible overpopulation of deer, for instance; in the Northeast it is not uncommon to see deer grazing in front yards like goats. This is not so much due to our destruction of habitat—a huge majority of the country remains largely untouched by developers—as our destruction of the predators that kept the deer population in check.

So while there are worthwhile environmental concerns, they need to be approached calmly, rationally, and with the recognition that human beings live here, too.

But that is not how it has worked out.

A case in point is what we have done in connection with the pesticide DDT, in many ways the first action of the modern environmental movement.

First used during World War II to control lice that carried typhus, DDT was sprayed *on* U.S. troops, refugees, and concentration-camp survivors. Entire cities in Italy were dusted. It proved tremendously effective, with no discernable side effects, even at extremely high doses. In 1948, Swiss chemist Paul Müller, who first reported DDT's insecticide properties, was awarded the Nobel Prize.

In the postwar period, DDT was used to control mosquitoes carrying malaria. In 1935 the United States had approximately 130,000 cases of malaria and about 4,000 deaths from it annually. By the 1950s, DDT spraying had virtually eradicated malaria in the United States and southern Europe. Greece saw its malaria rate drop from 1 to 2 million cases a year to close to zero. In Italy, the number dropped from 411,602 in 1945 to 37 in 1968. Between 1946 and 1951, Sardinia saw the number of cases drop from 75,000 per year to nine.

Similar results were seen in developing countries. In 1943, Venezuela had more than 8 million cases of malaria; by 1958, the number was down to 800. India, which had over 100 million cases (and 2.5 million deaths) in the 1940s, had 285,962 cases in 1969. Pakistan's rate plummeted from 7 million cases in 1961 to 9,000 in 1967. Malaria rates in Sri Lanka dropped from 2.8 million cases and 7,300 deaths in 1946, to 17 cases and no deaths by 1964. In Zanzibar the prevalence of malaria dropped from 70 percent in 1958 to 5 percent in 1964. DDT used in northern Zambia reduced malaria cases in the area by about 50 percent in one year. Taiwan, which had over a million cases before DDT was used, saw the number drop to less than 600 within five years of spraying.

By 1969, of 146 countries originally classified by United Nations World Health Organization as malaria-ridden, 36 had accomplished eradication, according to J. Gordon Edwards, professor emeritus of entomology at San Jose State University. In addition, 53 more were engaged in eradication programs, and 27 were carrying out significant malaria-control programs. In the course of this global campaign, DDT saved 50 to 100 million lives, estimated the WHO.

In the midst of this, what was perhaps the greatest public health triumph in history, fell a bombshell.

In her 1962 book *Silent Spring,* Rachel Carson wrote that a 1956 article in the *Journal of Agriculture and Food Chemistry* had reported that DDT "may seriously affect reproduction" of birds. (In fact, the article she cited found that 80 percent of the eggs of quail fed high levels of DDT hatched, compared to 83.9 percent of the eggs of quail fed no DDT, while pheasants fed high levels of DDT hatched more than 80 percent of their eggs, compared to 57 percent of the eggs of pheasants fed no DDT—so if the study was accurate, DDT harmed quail slightly and actually *helped* pheasants.)

Ms. Carson, an editor for the Fish and Wildlife Service with an M.A. in zoology, instantly became the media's number one expert on epidemiology, toxicology, and environmental cancer. In 1963, CBS produced a television special, *The Silent Spring of Rachel Carson,* which trumpeted her allegations against DDT to millions.

After her death the following year, the National Audubon Society began making a nice return on its newly established Rachel Carson

Memorial Fund. The fund, in turn, provided financing to a group of New York regulatory lawyers to lobby and litigate for a ban on DDT. They founded an organization for that purpose called the Environmental Defense Fund (now called simply Environmental Defense).

By 1970, environmental agitation had reached a watershed: the first Earth Day; the passage of the Clean Air Act, Clean Water Act, and Endangered Species Act; and the establishment of the Environmental Protection Agency. Environmental groups had the ear of the media, which had discovered the mesmerizing power environmental terror could exert over an audience. The *CBS Evening News* summed up the messianic mood of the times in the title of its series, "Can the World Be Saved?" As the avuncular Walter Cronkite—the most trusted and authoritative voice of the day—reported in February 1970:

> Again and again we see a frightening pattern—a science so far behind technology that it can't even predict which of two opposite catastrophes will occur. Yet our society, obsessed with short-term gains and gross national products, continues on its course. The scientists I spoke with disagree about the schedule of disaster, but we found not one scientist who disagreed that some disaster portends.

Let us pause to parse the substance of Mr. Cronkite's sonorous dispatch: The experts say—with scientific certainty—that something terrible is going to happen, but they are not sure what, or when. "And that's the way it is."

This prediction—that something bad is going to happen, sometime—is worthy of Nostradamus. No wonder it elicited that rare bird, the unanimous scientific consensus: Who could disagree with such a vague prognostication? After all, there will probably be another war sometime, an assassination, a riot. If not, there is always the next earthquake, ice age, or asteroid collision. Eventually the sun will go nova, then there is the heat death of the universe to look forward to (unless the universe continues to expand forever, turning into frozen, isolated rocks meandering their lonely way through space—the scientists cannot agree on that one, either).

What this report conveyed was precisely zero information, but a great deal of terror—employing the terms "frightening," "catastrophe," and "disaster" (twice!).

The experts don't know when we will get our comeuppance or what form it will take, but it is apparently due to our obsession with "short-term gains and gross national products." And here the media find their groove: Our wealth, our prosperity, and our unprecedented GNP are unforgivable, and we will be punished. No matter what our retribution is to be, or when, the expert voice says, to avoid it we must reduce our standard of living.

Not that you should expect experts like Mr. Cronkite or Ms. Carson to take a pay cut. The experts require certain accoutrements to power. It is the public—you—who needs to reduce your standard of living, to return to the quality of life of the "good old days" of family farms, homespun cloth—and malaria.

Under a relentless media barrage, President Richard M. Nixon in 1971 took authority over pesticide regulation away from the Department of Agriculture and handed it to the new EPA. It was a momentous decision.

After seven months of hearings involving 9,000 pages of testimony, the EPA hearing examiner, Administrative Law Judge Edmund Sweeney, concluded, "The use of DDT under the regulations involved here do not have a deleterious effect on freshwater fish, estuarine organisms, wild birds or other wildlife."

Two months later, EPA Administrator William Ruckleshaus overruled Sweeney, banning DDT in the United States. Ruckelshaus admitted that he had not attended any of the hearings, and his aides reported that he had not even read the transcript. USDA scientists used the Freedom of Information Act to request the materials upon which Ruckelshaus had based his decision, but he stonewalled, saying the documents were "internal memos."

Ruckelshaus's decision served "to enhance the activist image he sought to create for the agency, and without prohibitive political cost," explains the EPA's official history. His decision also "demonstrated the effect public pressure could have on EPA policy decisions," states the agency.

Ruckelshaus himself admitted that "decisions by the government involving the use of toxic substances are political . . . [and] the ultimate judgment remains political. . . . [In] the case of pesticides, the power to make this judgment has been delegated to the Administrator of EPA." Thus, both Ruckelshaus and the EPA admitted that his decision was political, not scientific.

A scientific study had found a questionable risk, minor if it existed at all; a talented and emotive writer exaggerated the study's findings; the media further amplified her distortion; activists used this misrepresentation to raise money and pressure the government; and the politicians, well, acted like politicians.

This ugly interaction of science, media, and politics has since been replayed many times with many issues, often with harmful results. But never has it issued a more deadly result than the war on DDT.

The United States could afford to do without DDT—after all, we had already eradicated malaria in the U.S. (using DDT) by 1972 and could afford more expensive (and harmful) substitutes.

But when the EPA prohibited the manufacture of DDT by U.S. companies, it cut off the world's major supply. The international repercussions were devastating, especially in the developing world. In countries where DDT was still desperately needed, governments began producing it to make up for the loss of the U.S. supply. China, India, and Mexico began producing DDT in substantial quantities.

U.S. international aid agencies, both public and private, responded by withholding aid from countries that used DDT. By 1986, the U.S. Agency for International Development had prohibited funding for any program using DDT. As a result of this pressure, Belize and Bolivia stopped using DDT.

Other sources of international aid have since followed suit. In 1997, the World Bank gave India $165 million in credit, on the condition that the funds could not be used for DDT. Similar pressure forced the government of Madagascar to stop a successful program of house spraying.

In Eritrea, where 50 percent of mortality and 60 to 80 percent of morbidity is attributed to malaria, the World Bank, UNICEF, and USAID provided aid for mosquito nets and "environmental assessment," but not for DDT. As a condition of its aid, the World Bank actually required Eritrea to phase out DDT use within two years.

The WHO told Mozambique that countries using DDT must phase it out, says Avertino Barreto, Mozambique's deputy national director of health, epidemiology, and environmental health. DDT use in Mozambique "was stopped several decades ago, because 80 percent of the country's health budget came from donor funds, and donors refused to allow the use of DDT," according to a 2000 report in the *British Medical Journal*.

In 2001, Mozambique reported 3 million cases of malaria, out of a population of 17 million. In some areas, 90 percent of children under five years old are infected, and malaria is the leading cause of death in children.

Governments are not the only parties pressuring malarial countries to abandon DDT. In the early 1990s, for example, a U.S. tobacco company told farmers in Zimbabwe that the U.S. might stop buying tobacco from them unless the country ceased using DDT for malaria control. (Since then, Zimbabwe's dictator, Robert Mugabe, has so thoroughly trashed his country's economy, in part by allowing his unskilled supporters to seize productive farms and turn them into unproductive farms, that the issue is now moot.)

Both the governments and industries that are pressuring others to stop using DDT are responding to the fear of public opinion, fomented by the media and "experts" from environmental groups. But sometimes such groups apply pressure directly themselves. For example, Greenpeace protested to shut down the last major DDT production facility in the world, at Cochin, India. In response to this pressure, the Indian government promised Greenpeace that that it would shut down the facility in 2005. Likewise, another group, the International Pesticide Action Network, says it is "working to stop the production, sale, and use" of DDT worldwide. Such groups lobbied to attach to NAFTA a requirement that Mexico stop using DDT.

"Countries are banning or reducing the use of DDT because of continuous international and national pressures against DDT," said a 1997 study published by the CDC.

As a result, malaria is making a devastating comeback. "The period from 1959 to 1978 can be characterized as a period of insecticide-controlled malaria," said the study. "The period from 1979 to 1995 can be characterized as a period of decreased use of residual spraying and geometric growth in malaria incidence."

In Zanzibar—where the prevalence of malaria had dropped from 70 percent in 1958 to 5 percent in 1964—it was back up to between 50 and 60 percent by 1984.

"When I was working [in India] in 1966 [during the period of DDT spraying], I saw almost no malaria," recalled National Institutes of Health director Harold Varmus. "But when I returned in 1988 [after spraying was curtailed], there was a raging epidemic."

In Latin America, the decline in house spraying resulted in an average annual increase of 4.8 malaria cases per 1,000 population from the mid-1980s to the mid-1990s, according to Donald Roberts, professor of medical entomology at the Uniformed Services Hospital of the Health Sciences. For Latin America as a whole, at least 1.8 million additional cases of malaria were occurring each year up to 1996. Case rates have continued to grow since 1996, and "we can reasonably expect that the number of excess cases is now much greater than in 1996," says Roberts. Only Ecuador, which has increased house spraying, has seen a reduction in the number of malaria cases—61 percent overall.

Today, some two million people die from malaria every year, mostly pregnant women and children under the age of five, reports WHO. That amounts to a death every thirty seconds—equivalent to crashing seven jumbo jets filled with children every day. In some parts of Sub-Saharan Africa, one in ten infant deaths and one in four deaths of children under four years old are attributed to malaria, according to the United Nations Environment Program.

Describing the problem in the *Washington Post* of July 12, 2004, Enriqueta Bond (president of the Burroughs Wellcome Fund) noted that the proscription of DDT is now more than anything else a matter of faith, unsupported by facts: "Upgrading preventive techniques by, for example, scrapping misplaced taboos to allow internal spraying of African homes with DDT is essential."

Other mosquito-borne diseases are also on the rise. For example, DDT was used until the 1970s to eradicate the *Aedes aegypti* mosquito from South and Central America. The resurgence of this mosquito since then has brought horrific outbreaks of dengue fever, dengue hemorrhagic fever (from which a victim literally bleeds to death, often from bodily orifices—not a pretty sight and not a painless death), and yellow fever. During the DDT campaign, there was a decline in many other insect-borne diseases, such as kala azar, sleeping sickness, typhus, and West Nile virus, all of which are making strong comebacks today.

Terrible is the toll the experts have imposed on people in malarial regions. That our media, activists, and politicians are willing to kill literally millions of innocent men, women, and children—whether for money, power, or whatever motive—should raise a sober caution in us. If they are able to impose such horror on their fellow man, what would the experts not do to us if they could?

Yet there are a few rays of hope amid this vast horror. In 1996, the new government of South Africa succumbed to international pressure and, after fifty years, stopped DDT use. As a result, South Africa's annual malaria rate saw a more than five-fold increase in just four years, from 11,000 in 1996 to 62,000 in 2000—overtaking the number of new cases of "HIV/AIDS infection," which is to say twenty-six other diseases, some very common, combined.

Neil Cameron, chief director of communicable diseases for the South Africa Health Department, reacted, despite condemnations from environmentalists, by reinstating DDT spraying in 2000 in KwaZulu Natal province. As a result, the number of malaria cases there fell by 80 percent that year.

Anyone with a shred of humanity must applaud this decision and give support and encouragement to those willing to do the right thing and save lives, even at the risk of a questionable 3 percent reduction in the quail population.

As its reward, the South African government faced opprobrium from UNEP, which was meeting in December 2000 in Johannesburg for a conference to draft a treaty on Persistent Organic Pollutants (POPs), intended to ban DDT globally.

"We are now facing the unprecedented event of eliminating, without meaningful debate, the most cost-effective chemical we have for the prevention of malaria," concluded the 1997 CDC study cited above. "The health of hundreds of millions of persons in malaria-endemic countries should be given greater consideration before proceeding further with the present course of action."

In protest against the proposed ban, more than four hundred concerned scientists, Nobel laureates, and doctors from fifty-seven countries signed an "open letter" pleading that DDT be permitted for malaria control. The letter demonstrated how at least one environmental group at the conference, the World Wildlife Fund, "inaccurately conveyed the conclusions of some studies to discredit DDT." "In essence, WWF has cited a study that says 'there is no association between DDT and breast cancer,' as support for its position that DDT creates a risk for breast cancer." (Note how the WWF here carried Rachel Carson's technique to its logical conclusion.)

At the urging of these specialists, the United Nations exempted DDT use for malaria control, eliciting predictable denunciations from the environmentalists. The fact that the government of South Africa stood up to these true believers, that four hundred specialists were willing to speak the truth about them, that even the UN can finally be shamed into doing the right thing, all of these are rays of hope for the future.

"Rachel Carson's legacy is not entirely positive," says Robert Gwadz, a malaria researcher at the NIH.

Of course, it may well be that the environmental movement welcomes a disease that has the potential to kill millions; sometimes it is difficult not to believe that the one species whose extinction the environmental movement would favor is *Homo sapiens*. Certainly it believes, and has believed for decades, that overpopulation threatens to wipe out the planet. The political philosopher Thomas Malthus, in his *An Essay on the Principle of Population,* raised this very issue in 1798, though without the shrillness achieved by Paul Ehrlich in his book *The Population Bomb* 170 years later.

Ehrlich, for the record, has been predicting the imminent demise of the planet for four decades, but if he has turned out to be right about anything, anything at all, it was so minor as to escape notice. Yet he continues to come up with a new theory of our impending doom every so often, and he is still listened to; perhaps it is thought that by the sheer law of averages (and the observation that even a stopped clock is right twice a day) he will one day make a prediction that comes true—his earliest certainly did not. "The battle to feed humanity is over. In the 1970s, the world will undergo famines. Hundreds of millions of people are going to starve to death in spite of any crash programs embarked upon now. Population control is the only answer," Ehrlich memorably and erroneously said.

Ehrlich's 1968 wolf cry led to movements such as "Zero Population Growth," a Vietnam-War-era agitation organization that would show up to demonstrate whenever and wherever anyone else was demonstrating against anything. It achieved a patina of respectability for a time, but faded away when it became clear that the group was little more than howling at the moon. Still, its artifacts remain, not the least of them the abortion movement (as opposed to the "pro-choice" movement, which is itself largely pro-abortion but doesn't say so in so many words), which argues that the one of the most important uses of foreign aid is to pro-vide abortions to Third-World women.

Interestingly, in Europe, where the environmental movement has cast off any pretense of being anything more than a militant socialist (and sometimes Marxist and even Maoist) organization to form the Green Party and seek political office, the population bomb has implod-ed. Were it not for immigration there, chiefly from the Islamic nations, the populations of many European nations would be plummeting. Call it the Population Dud.

Unsurprisingly, environmentalists rejoice at the notion of fewer humans on the planet. This from the *New York Times* of August 29, 2004:

> For decades, the rise in human numbers has been seen as the chief force threatening rain forests, depleting fisheries, choking the air and polluting the waters. So would an end to humanity's growth spurt make possible a not-too-diminished world with enough room for some wild things, with reasonably breathable air and drinkable water, with a livable climate?
>
> Many demographers, economists and ecologists are guardedly, often very guardedly, optimistic.

At that first Earth Day in 1970, when the environmental movement was still listening for the ticking of Ehrlich's population bomb and when some involved in it were truly concerned with the environment, many posters and placards demanded that we turn to "Nuclear Power Now!" That being one of the few sensible positions ever taken by the environmental movement, it was quickly abandoned. The idea of nuclear power suffered a fatal blow, for no good reason, when in March 1979 there was an accident at the Three Mile Island nuclear power plant in Pennsylvania.

Before we go any further, we should note that no one was killed or even injured as a result of the Three Mile Island "disaster" (for that is how the media played it, as a disaster, letting sensationalism obscure facts). For the record, more people will die from rabies in the United States this year than have died due to radiation in the entire U.S. nuclear energy industry from the beginning of time until now. The old joke is that more people have died in Sen. Edward M. Kennedy's automobile than died at Three Mile Island; the old joke is true.

It is unquestionably true that nuclear power is something that must be undertaken very carefully, the stakes of a catastrophic failure being, well, catastrophic. It is also unquestionably true that it is within the realm of human ability to succeed at that endeavor. But as a result of Three Mile Island, the environmental movement has succeeded in getting some nuclear power plants shut down and approval of others denied. It is as if Ralph Nader, in his diatribe against the Chevrolet Corvair, had leaped to the claim that it proved that all automobiles should be banned. He didn't. That proposition would await Al Gore's *Earth in the Balance: Ecology and the Human Spirit,* published in 1992 and again in 2000.

What is most telling is how in abandoning its support of nuclear power the environmental movement revealed its true motives. Absent nuclear power, we must chiefly rely on the combustion of fossil fuels to generate electricity. (There are "alternative" energy sources that have been touted from time to time: wind power, solar power, even hydroelectric generation by harnessing the tides. Each has its drawbacks; for instance, windmills tend to chop up migratory birds—not all that environmentally friendly, is it?—while using the tides has a small, almost imperceptible, but real effect on the relationship between the Earth and the moon that over eons could bring the two crashing into each other. This would certainly spawn a doomsday book, probably by Paul

Ehrlich—though in this case the threat, though slight, is real, so maybe not.)

There are problems in the use of fossil fuels. They are largely of foreign origin, for one thing, which renders us vulnerable to foreign blackmail, as in the Arab oil embargoes and resulting fuel shortages of the 1970s. But the problem that belies the stated goals of the environmental movement is their purported concern over air pollution. The burning of fossil fuels creates substantial pollutants, while nuclear power generation does not.

Evidence supports the idea, though, that the real goal of the environmentalists is to keep you from using energy at all. Their real complaint has to do with your standard of living. The lowliest among us has, or has readily available, a standard of living higher than that in most of the world, which does not bode well for a movement that is at its heart so far to the left that were its actual motives known it would be a loud, annoying, but powerless fringe. Consider ANWR. The Arctic National Wildlife Refuge is a huge expanse of land—more than 19 million acres—in northern Alaska, owned by the federal government. It contains an estimated 10.3 billion barrels of easily recovered oil—more than twice that in Texas. The oil could be drilled for and pumped away with little or no effect on the wildlife there, nor on the primitive beauty of the place, for the oil is located in an area of 1.5 million acres, or less than 10 percent of the place.

Drilling for oil there seems an obvious choice, particularly given our reliance on oil from unstable and often unfriendly parts of the world. But the environmental movement has been monolithic in its opposition to drilling in ANWR. And because that movement has been so successful in assuming a mantle of inviolability, we do not drill there. Ponder that the next time you look at the prices on the gas pump, or look at your electric bill and note the extra charges due to the price of oil.

Indeed, the environmental movement, already at the fringes were its true motives known, has its own fringes which have taken up terrorism. There are organizations with names such as "The Eco Anarchist Club" (which lists its philosophy as "libertarian socialist ecology," a contradiction in terms if ever there was one) and most especially the "Earth Liberation Front," which is alleged to have firebombed multiple businesses that do not fit its view of how the world should be. These include enemies of the planet such as car dealerships.

From the straightforward and noble goals of conservation, it has come to this corrupted political movement that wants nothing less than to destroy your way of life. From the "victory garden" idea, that by growing some of your own vegetables you could save the materials needed to package and the fuel needed to transport commercial ones, we have come to militant "environmentalists" whose real target is American business in all its forms—including, perhaps, the one from whence you derive a paycheck. That movement has achieved tremendous power through the complicity of media who do not investigate before they report, and through a population that still sees only the facade, not the underlying truth.

It is up to you to decide whether "conservation" means what the environmental movement has turned it into—whether you would accept demonstrable lies over demonstrable facts.

7

GLOBAL WARMING: MORE HEAT THAN LIGHT

What do you think of global warming? Pretty frightening, isn't it? After all, turn on the television or pick up a magazine or newspaper and you'll see that global warming is a fact; that it will be the death of the planet or, at least, life as we know it. Our industrialized society and our labor-saving products and devices have changed the planet forever. Because of this, the Earth will one day be uninhabitable. So we are told, incessantly, despite the fact there is no proof and precious little evidence to support the global warming theory as it's popularly presented, and of the evidence that exists for warming, practically none of it supports the notion that human activity has had or even can have much of an effect on the climate.

Not long ago, scientists and the media (and therefore the public) became terribly concerned, almost panic-stricken, over the Earth's climate. Change was coming, and it was all our fault. We needed to do things differently, drastically differently, and at once.

If we did not, global cooling would greatly alter life on Earth.

Global *cooling?*

That's right. Through the 1970s and much of the '80s, the concern was that the planet was becoming colder, that the polar ice caps would grow, that much fertile land would cease to produce crops, and that life would be dismal for those who managed to survive.

Today, the same evidence is being employed in the same way by many of the same people to convince us that the mercury is rising menacingly and it's all our fault, and the only hope of stemming it is to do things drastically differently. If we do not, they say, global warming will greatly alter life on Earth.

The fact is that a single volcanic eruption, spewing tons of toxic gas and ash into the atmosphere in one destructive belch, can have more effect on the climate than has the total of everything done by the human race since the beginning of time. There is no evidence at all that we are significantly affecting the climate.

What, then, motivates the climatic Chicken Littles? Why is so little attention paid to research that disputes their claims? And why have government, the media, and many of us chosen to follow them?

Many influential people today warn that catastrophic global warming threatens the planet. Skeptics on the right have discounted such warnings, charging that similarly dire warnings about "global cooling" were popular in the 1970s. For example, in 1991, Anna J. Bray, then a lowly intern at the Heritage Foundation, wrote in a journal published by that conservative think tank:

> While scientists, politicians, and the media alike present global warming as an imminent catastrophe, we might do well to remember what was, 15 to 20 years ago, regarded as an inevitable environmental catastrophe. It was widely believed that an ice age threatened to destroy civilization.

The following year, three eminent scientists—including the late Roger Revelle (the man Al Gore credited with his own views on global warming)—reiterated Bray's assertion in the pages of the prestigious journal *Cosmos*. The trio chided global warming enthusiasts about "a quarter-century decrease [in global temperature] between 1940 and 1965 when concern arose about an approaching ice age." The same year, MIT climatologist Richard Lindzen, writing in a journal of the libertarian Cato Institute, repeated the charge:

> [T]he global cooling trend of the 1950s and 1960s led to a minor global cooling hysteria in the 1970s . . . the cooling hysteria had certain striking analogues to the present warming hysteria.

The list of one-time global-cooling alarmists who now are sounding the tocsin about global warming is long and distinguished. Merely citing them all would run into many thousands of words. One might begin to think that it doesn't matter to them what they're upset about, as long as they can be upset about something—and one could find more evidence to support that conclusion than one can find to support, say, allegations that global warming is real.

Here is, in its entirety, what we know: The Earth's climate changes over time. Thoughtful climatologists are interested in the nature of that change and the scope and duration of swings in terrestrial temperature.

Then there are those who have another axe to grind, and they're happy to hone it on whatever is available. When the world's temperature trend seemed to indicate that cooling was underway, they screamed and wept about the coming ice age—and announced that it was the result of industrialized society. When the ice age failed to materialize and there was short-term data that could be beaten into a claim that the world is getting hotter, they screamed (and are still screaming) about that. And they are saying that it is the fault of industrialized society. It appears that the crime doesn't matter, as long as industrialized society and its driving force, capitalism, are found guilty in the end.

It is no surprise that those who carry the pitchforks and torches of the global warming army are nearly universally of a liberal political bent, which tends to oppose capitalism for other reasons as well. Nor is it surprising that political and philosophical conservatives pooh-pooh global warming as they a generation ago refused to believe the horror stories of global cooling.

Before we go any farther, let's agree to a brief but adequate pair of definitions. Conservatism has been described—by one of the nation's most prominent conservatives—as "standing athwart history and shouting 'Stop!'" While that is probably a little extreme, the conservative philosophy serves as the brakes to the liberal philosophy's accelerator. Liberalism favors change where possible, while conservatism opposes change that isn't for a good, demonstrable reason. In the matter of global warming, the conservative idea is that it's a bad idea to act until we are sure we know what we're doing, while the liberal claim is that by then it might be too late.

When conservatives and scientific skeptics draw parallels between the fear of global warming and earlier fears of global cooling, their rhetorical purpose is clear: If environmentalists reversed their prediction so dramatically and so quickly in the past, they implicitly ask, how are we to know they won't do so again?

Yet the fact that someone was wrong in the past does not mean he is wrong today. The earlier prediction may have been based on incomplete data or a flawed theory that has now been corrected. However, a raging desire to enact sweeping changes based on incomplete data or a flawed theory indicates a less-than-exacting approach that is worthy of suspicion.

To assess the competing claims, it is necessary to review whether the skeptics' charges hold water, and, if they do, to see whether environmentalists today are avoiding the pitfalls that led them into error in the 1970s.

The atmosphere warmed steadily from about 1890 to about 1940, but in the 1940s, a pronounced cooling trend set in.

It is hard to remember these days, when any warming is considered catastrophic and when even intelligent and educated people point to a normally hot summer day as evidence of the apocalypse, that during the cooling of the 1970s, people looked on the prior warming with fond nostalgia. As *Fortune* magazine reported:

> [F]or nearly half of the current century mankind was apparently blessed with the most benign climate of any period in at least a thousand years. During this kindly era the human population more than doubled. . . . [It] began with a pronounced warming trend after about 1890. Mean temperatures peaked in 1945 and have been dropping sharply ever since.

Let's pause a moment and examine this, for it is instructive. The best weather in the last thousand years took place in a period that topped out in 1945. This alone suggests that the Earth's temperature swings take place over far longer periods than can allow any of them to be attributed to human activity, because the human activities that are often blamed for climate change are relative newcomers. Global cooling and global warming have both been blamed on the use of fossil fuels, particularly in automobiles. Those were not in common use a hundred years ago.

"The central fact is that after three-quarters of a century of extraordinarily mild conditions [which is to say, global warming]," agreed *Newsweek,* "the earth's climate seems to be cooling down."

"[S]tudies of both short-term climate patterns (the past three hundred years or so) and of long-term cycles (thousands of years) point to the same tentative but harsh conclusion," concurred *Popular Science.* "We've been living in warmer than normal times—and we may have to face an increasingly cold future."

These two excerpts, too, are useful, though the first one is not of help in the way its author probably intended. What it tells us—and the *Popular Science* item underlines—is that climatological data assembled over seventy-five years or even three hundred years are not of much use, except in predicting short-term trends. To use those data to diagnose a cataclysmic problem and, moreover, to lay blame is simply laughable.

Yet some of the most prominent media outlets (*New York Times, Science, Newsweek,* etc.) and scientists (Stephen Schneider, Chrispin Tickell, Paul Ehrlich, etc.) now pushing global warming were active in the global cooling hysteria.

As with global warming, some in the media had a tendency toward sensationalism about global cooling, downplaying scientific uncertainties and focusing on worst-case scenarios. Some blamed human activities for the cooling and called for regulatory approaches to combat the threat.

The evidence brought forward for cooling involved theories such as air pollution reflecting solar energy away from the earth. It involved extrapolation from trends such as the ice age/interglacial cycle and the 1940–75 cooling. It involved anecdotal evidence from regional weather events, animal migrations, famines, etc.

The theory was wrong. The extrapolation was wrong. And the anecdotal evidence, it appears, was misinterpreted. Just as *Newsweek* once reported equatorial warming as evidence of global cooling, we now see stories reporting that record cold and record snowfalls are evidence of global warming.

On the basis of bad theory, proponents of global cooling demanded international action to mitigate global cooling, including halting aerosol emissions, diverting rivers, covering the polar caps with black soot, and intentionally increasing greenhouse gas emissions.

If we had heeded their advice, we would have saddled the world's people with an economic burden of inconceivable proportions. What is more, if current theories are correct, when the temperature trend reversed in the mid-1970s, such approaches would have dramatically intensified the warming about which these same people are so exercised today.

The global cooling hysteria could have been avoided by paying attention to the uncertainties of theory, to the arbitrary nature of future extrapolation from past trends, and to the inherent weakness of anecdotal evidence.

Following these guidelines can help to extricate us from global warming hysteria today. No, let me modify that: Following these guidelines, applying common sense to what we hear, may help us as thinking individuals who respect our own thought processes from being swept up in the new flip side of the climate hysteria. When we read in the popular press of the "certainty" or "scientific consensus" behind global warming theory, it might help to recall that the same experts once agreed that the same causes were leading us to just the opposite result, yet nevertheless to our doom.

The common narrative of both scares is instructive: Modern civilization is destroying the world, and only global governance can save us. Free people are inherently self-destructive; to save themselves, they must turn over their power over their own lives to the experts. At bottom, what this means is that you don't know what is good for you, but experts do.

Only, as we have now seen, experts don't, and repeating the same lie a thousand times makes it no more true. A better question than the one posed by the claim of global warming is this: What is the *real* motive of those who once peddled the terror of global cooling and, their predictions having proved false, now seek to tell you that the world is heating up?

I propose that the answer is simple. Following the technological advances of the 1940s, 1950s, and 1960s, scientists took upon themselves a role almost like that of Plato's "philosopher kings." They knew what was best. They were infallible. Their vision for the world rapidly outgrew their knowledge, indeed the entire body of scientific expertise. Any fairly literate individual looking at what is known about the Earth's climate could tell almost instantly that nothing useful can be determined about the climate based on even hundreds of years of data. The world's climate swings are to human lives as the seasons of the year are to bacteria whose life span is measured in hours. For humans to claim responsibility for climate change based on our use of technologies that have been in existence for less than two hundred years is the crowing cock claiming credit for the sunrise. To then recognize that far greater climatic shifts have regularly taken place, going back far before people were doing anything at all, puts the lie to that crowing.

Our species is extremely egotistical, both overall and individually. The center of the universe is wherever we happen to be standing, or so we tell ourselves. Our knowledge knows no bounds. We know what is best, especially for others.

8

BEHAVIOR AS DISEASE

Let us suppose something: Nobody does anything without a reason.

Now, it is true that the reason might be arrived at without much thought, or that the reason, even if it is arrived at with considerable thought, might not be a good one. We are all the sum of our experiences as interpreted by our intelligence and emotional state, which all together give us our ability to reason and the solutions we find to real or perceived problems—for every action is our attempt to solve a problem.

Our reasoning is therefore, by definition, with an eye toward consequences.

The political philosopher James Burnham offered the view that it is impossible to do just one thing, meaning that our actions have consequences that extend beyond what we had in mind. The night's passion may not have anticipated the disease, or the infant nine months hence (or, more likely today, the abortion); the bank robbery is not committed in anticipation of free room and board (and some new, very close friends) at state expense; the lottery ticket is not bought with the idea that the dollar may just as well have been burned. We do things for reasons, and the things we do produce results, and those results are not always happy ones. Sometimes the unhappy results are the *anticipated* consequence, too.

Sometimes the results are very unhappy, if not for us then for others. If what we do is sufficiently harmful to other people, we can, or should be able to, anticipate that we will be called to account for our having made the decision we did, taken the action we took, and produced the results that it did. In some cases, especially involving businesses—for which the vision that hindsight now offers is expected to have been available as foresight (described in Chapter 16)—there is no forgiveness, and many businesses have been destroyed as a result.

But for individuals, especially those who fit in politically correct classifications, there is a growing movement that suggests that nothing they can do is wrong, because anything that they might have done has occurred due to "disease." It is, therefore, excusable.

Nor must the "disease" be organic, or even a particular attribute of that individual. The movement, in a strange offshoot, has posited a kind of group disease which frees all members of that group from culpability.

For instance, within the group that opposes the death penalty there is a substantial number of people who believe that capital sentences should never be carried out because the defendant, by virtue of committing the crime for which the death penalty was awarded, is *prima facie* insane and therefore not responsible. While such reasoning has failed to win the day as an argument against capital punishment, it has moved into mainstream mental health policy and practice in a number of areas where what was once an offense is now labeled a disease.

As a result, crime is now considered as much a public health issue as a law enforcement one. In some cities, the response to domestic violence is a mandatory visit to the emergency room. A variety of behavioral issues are now medicated, even in young children. Lack of self-discipline is no longer recognized at all.

As with noted apocalyptic and politico-apocalyptic novels, it is now supposed that all discomforts can be cured or at least reduced pharmaceutically. Conversely, the punishments and "reeducation" that were once reserved for bad behavior now are used to combat a lack of political correctness.

It begins, now, at an early age. Children who are bored in school or who would rather be doing something else and say so are not misbehaving, as was once the diagnosis (and one that appeared to work quite well). No, they are victims of attention deficit disorder or attention deficit hyperactivity disorder. Often as not, they are drugged into a stupor, making them docile. There is debate in scientific circles whether these diseases even exist. Yet there have been incidents of parents being hauled into family court for removing their children from the pharmaceuticals when school officials had decided that drugging the children was in order.

It cannot pass without mention that one reason students might be bored and angry is that teachers, who appear to owe their allegiance to teachers unions rather than the children they are supposed to be teaching, are on average doing a pretty poor job, if the controversies surrounding standardized tests are any indication. But it's easier to force pills down a kid's throat than it is to force competency from the throat of a teacher.

An increasingly common phenomenon today in dealing with problems—or, more accurately, in avoiding dealing with them—is to describe them as a disease. Thus, we end up with stories such as this one, published in the *Oregonian* in the late spring of 2004:

A Portland lawyer says suffering by African Americans at the hands of slave owners is to blame in the death of a 2-year-old Beaverton boy.

Randall Vogt is offering the untested theory, called post-traumatic slave syndrome, in his defense of Isaac Cortez Bynum, who is charged with murder by abuse in the June 30 death of his son, Ryshawn Lamar Bynum. Vogt says he will argue—"in a general way"—that masters beat slaves, so Bynum was justified in beating his son.

The slave theory is the work of Joy DeGruy-Leary, an assistant professor in the Portland State University Graduate School of Social Work. It is not listed by psychiatrists or the courts as an accepted disorder, and some experts said they had never heard of it.

DeGruy-Leary testified this month in Washington County Circuit Court that African Americans today are affected by past centuries of U.S. slavery because the original slaves were never treated for the trauma of losing their homes; seeing relatives whipped, raped and killed; and being subjugated by whites.

It should probably be noted that the fellow accused of killing his little son had never been a slave nor had he been within one hundred years of slavery in the United States. This kind of detail is often left out, and it is not politically correct to bring it up. Nor is the idea that in offering his defense the lawyer is tacitly making the claim that all black people are somehow diseased.

Over time, though, even ridiculous theories such as that of the Oregon lawyer come to take on a kind of currency, to be accepted as if they are true, and even though they do not usually succeed, they end up being treated as if they were facts. A textbook example involves the 1977 case of fifteen-year-old Ronnie Zamora of Miami.

Zamora burglarized the home of a neighbor, the elderly Elinor Haggart, and he murdered her. His counsel, Ellis Rubin, was not a "celebrity lawyer" at the time, but the case made him so. Rubin pursued an insanity defense, claiming that Zamora was the victim of "television intoxication." Zamora, Rubin argued, had been made violent by watching violent television programs. The jury apparently wanted nothing to do with it and found Zamora guilty; Zamora's appeals included the claim that he had had "ineffective counsel" at trial (which any convicted criminal could claim, in that the desired effect was the avoidance of conviction), but higher courts turned him down.

Nevertheless, the television-causes-violence notion crept into national discourse, and it came to be treated as if it were a fact. As "proof," experts point to children who engage in "violent" schoolyard play, in which they engage in what in a less politically correct time was the near-universal game of cowboys and Indians. Those games did not lead to generations of murderous sociopaths, yet today students guilty even of pointing a finger and saying "bang" are treated as if they already are threats to society. It might be noted, too, that in an era in which children were allowed to play their "violent" games, they did not later plot to kill everyone in their schools. There is cause to suspect that by denying children their play, the experts plant the seeds for the real thing later on, rather than make events such as the Columbine High School murders in Colorado less likely. Again, it is not always easy to gauge the effects of actions, and it is impossible to do just one thing.

One wonders if perhaps today Zamora would get off the hook for his brutal actions.

To hear the lawyers, sociologists, psychologists, and their media lapdogs tell it, the typical American today is a weak and timid person, nothing more than the sum of his or her "traumas." What is a trauma? Anything, apparently, that makes anyone unhappy for any period of time. It is also an excuse for nearly anything. There was a time when unhappy events troubled people, maybe caused them to have bad dreams from time to time. Today, they are "traumatized." (Actually, "trauma" is a prescription excuse; the over-the-counter version is "stress.")

"Trauma" makes it a wonder that we can function at all. Fortunately, it is a relatively new arrival on the scene. Imagine the wagons heading west 150 years ago. The hardship was great. Wagon trains often arrived with fewer people in tow than had been present at the beginning. Disease, accident, and foul play of several sorts resulted in deaths and burials, after which the wagons would proceed. Had those travelers paused for the arrival of "grief counselors" or melted into puddles of traumatized humanity awaiting a government bailout, we probably wouldn't have made it much past the Mississippi River. Success is about overcoming adversity, not succumbing to it and using it as an excuse.

Many illnesses and behaviors were for hundreds of years ascribed to such things as the presence of demons. Those who are clearly insane have for many years been excused, at least to some degree, from being held accountable for crimes they have committed, the usual standard being whether the person who committed an act knew right from wrong at the time and was capable of assisting in his own defense. But now, with the movement away from objective notions of right and wrong, distinctions blur. What of the criminal who commits a crime but at the time believes (or later says he believed) that it was the right thing to do? In 1981, John W. Hinckley Jr. shot President Ronald Reagan and several others outside a Washington D.C. hotel. It emerged at his trial that he believed that the actress Jodie Foster might fall in love with him if he shot the president. (Such a notion was a sign of insanity then; today it might be viewed as an accurate if somewhat cynical appraisal of political bitterness.) Hinckley was adjudged insane, but he was locked up for decades.

While he might have thought he was doing the right thing, and perhaps should be pitied for that, it was deemed nevertheless unacceptable for him to walk the streets in that condition.

We have now cast out our demons and replaced them with illnesses. Not the demonstrable illness of John W. Hinckley Jr. and not only in court. People rush to sign up for the latest and trendiest theoretical syndromes that might relieve them from responsibility over their own lives.

This is perhaps best illustrated by the boom in twelve step programs.

The twelve step idea came from a fellow named Bill Wilson, who drank too much. Employing philosophies and techniques that had been previously used by religious groups, he put together a course of action that he believed would help himself and others like him to stop drinking. This came at a time when physicians and psychologists first were thinking of excessive drinking as a disease. Wilson's idea grew to become Alcoholics Anonymous, which many heavy drinkers say has helped them stop drinking. The problem—and there is one, a very big one—is in the first of the twelve steps: "We admitted we were powerless over alcohol—that our lives had become unmanageable." If we are powerless over alcohol, then our having succumbed to it is scarcely our fault, is it?

Imagine if the sentence were recast: "We decided we possess power over alcohol, which we had allowed to make our lives unmanageable." The difference is potent: In the original, responsibility is denied, while in the second it is embraced. The original one allows the "victim" to wallow in self-pity and deny responsibility for having made a mess of his or her life, while the edited version offers hope of rising above it all by truly claiming responsibility.

In an article in the *Washington Post* in November 2003, the writer Mark Gauvreau Judge described how the twelve step idea is perverted, exchanging reliance on alcohol for reliance on wallowing in the horrors of having drunk too much for too long. He described one of the last meetings he had attended:

> It was a beautiful day, I had just published a book, and I was feeling fine. I shared with the group how great things were going and joked that I was ready to win my Pulitzer Prize. The words were barely out of my mouth when a hand shot up behind me. "We are not here to win prizes," the man hissed. "We are here to get sober one day at a time." I felt humiliated, and at the next meeting I dutifully stuck to the topic—the drinking that isn't part of my life anymore.

While Judge sees great value in Alcoholics Anonymous, he disagrees with the idea—an article of faith in AA—that one is forever "in recovery." Even Bill Wilson recognized that his twelve steps were not the end but the means. On his deathbed, in pain, he asked his nurses for three shots of whiskey. His request was denied.

"I don't know why Bill Wilson was denied those three shots of whiskey," wrote Radley Balko in a May 2004 article in the *Wall Street Journal*. "Perhaps alcohol would have reacted poorly with the medication he was on. Perhaps it was against the policy of the hospital or medical center where he was staying. Whatever the case, I'm not at all shocked or horrified that Bill Wilson asked for whiskey as he was dying. But I am saddened that a dying man was denied one of the few things that may have given him some comfort."

Perhaps it was thought that "recovery" was the inescapable morass that so many involved in it have caused it to become.

"In recovery." The phrase has come to be worn as a badge of honor by many. It has become the catch-all excuse for inappropriate behaviors of many sorts, involving substances and not involving substances; the behavior is usually referred to as "my disease." The twelve steps now have been applied to just about everything. And because the very first step is to admit one is powerless over (fill in the blank), a handy excuse is presented. They cannot be blamed, after all, for that over which they have no power. By rushing under the "recovery" umbrella, one is provided not only with an excuse but with what in modern society is seen as a very high honor indeed: the mantle of victimhood. Alas, poor me, I am a victim of promiscuity, or of a love of pornography, or of bad relationships, or of a desire to consume various substances. Pity me, for it is a wonder that I have survived at all.

We have returned to the old notion of demons that must be cast out, appeased, or kept at bay. But you cannot have self-respect, nor can you respect others, if you claim that you are powerless over some demon.

9

ALCOHOL AND ALCOHOLISM

My life's work has been largely concerned with problems people have related to alcohol consumption. I have worked at the Alcohol Clinic at Massachusetts General Hospital, founded the National Institute on Alcohol Abuse and Alcoholism, and served on the White House Conference for a Drug-Free America. I have been inducted into the Health and Safety Hall of Fame.

It was over twenty years ago that I served as chairman of the Education and Prevention Committee on Ronald Reagan's Presidential Commission on Drunk Driving. To this day I regret my failure to act on a major societal concern: underage drinking.

The recovering alcoholics on the commission were pushing hard to raise the drinking age in all states, since there were variable drinking ages between the states. The representatives of the wine and spirits industries went along, convinced that young people did not use their products; the beer industry representative had to acquiesce, because he did not want his industry to look as though it were pushing kids to drink beer.

I alone fought it. I fought it because, while it was a long time ago, I was once a kid. I remembered "a don't was a do" for a young person. Who struggles for what they can have? A kid who is denied something wants it all the more, a phenomenon not unknown among adults. The pressure for me to make the position unanimous was strong, and, to my regret, I went along to support unanimity within the commission.

Underage drinking is perceived as a continuing major problem. What strikes me, as I approach the end of my fiftieth year dealing with alcohol issues, is that we cannot learn from others.

Portugal, for example, doesn't even have a drinking age and yet has the lowest incidence of alcohol problems in the developed world. There, alcohol is a part of life, of meals, and not subject to any special treatment, either stigma or special approbation. Children grow up around alcohol and come to think of it not as forbidden fruit but as a part of life which one's own taste rules, as with any other food or beverage. Yet in at least sixteen states, it is against the law even for parents to offer their own children alcohol in the privacy of their own homes. The logical question is: Why do we not teach children how to drink? We teach them how to drive a car—and the misuse of cars is a substantial killer in all societies that have them. We teach them all kinds of other social responsibilities. Why not teach them how to use alcohol responsibly?

Perhaps the reason we do not is that there is nothing more noble than saving children. Therefore, for us to feel noble, we are making certain that underage drinking is a major problem. Can we ever learn?

Can you imagine: A person is old enough to marry, sign contracts, join the military, vote, and take a host of other social actions, but cannot legally purchase or consume an alcohol beverage.

Most other nations have legal drinking ages ranging from sixteen to eighteen. But not the United States, where twenty-one was forced on states by threatening them with a loss of 10 percent of their highway funds if they refused to adopt the higher drinking age—an especially malignant form of financial coercion of one unit of government over another and a slippery way around a little something called the Tenth Amendment.

Unfortunately, during an era of remarkable technological advances, we religiously fail to learn from history.

During the mid-1820s, when the per capita consumption of alcohol was extremely high (largely because water supplies were contaminated, and alcohol did not carry the pathogens that drinking water did), a movement began to lower and limit the amount of alcohol consumed. During the same period, smoking was attacked and eating the "right" foods (graham crackers, for example) was promoted along with exercising for health. The movements against alcohol and smoking and for proper diet were derailed by the greatest tragedy the United States ever suffered—the Civil War.

But in the 1890s, the self-righteous started stirring again, moving to impose their images and values upon the rest of society. A campaign against alcohol and smoking and for eating the right foods led to the only amendment to the U.S. Constitution ever to be rescinded: prohibition of the manufacture and sale of alcohol beverages.

Though somewhat changed, that movement is still in effect. Let us hope an event as terrible as the Civil War is not needed to derail it. Perhaps instead we could simply exercise common sense and teach our young people how to drink responsibly. We could lower the drinking age to the age of majority, no more than age eighteen in public settings. At the same time, we might create programs to teach children how to drink.

Teaching young people to drink could start at an early age, which could remove the magic and mystique of alcohol consumption, which causes inexperienced drinkers to overdose or behave irresponsibly. Lessons could be provided for families to teach responsible drinking at home, or, if the parents chose not to, schools and other academic institutions could provide the teaching. Teaching alcohol responsibility to young people would also teach them how to be responsible in many other aspects of their lives.

As it is, young people are taught that they must not consume alcohol, which often causes them to seek it all the more. But having crossed the line with their first sip, any notion of responsible drinking no longer has an opportunity to enter their minds. Thus we hear that a large portion of underage drinking is "binge drinking," which is to say drinking to the point of drunkenness and, sometimes, beyond.

We live in a society in which young people are issued condoms rather than chastity belts at school. The idea of teaching them responsible drinking is a very modest notion by comparison, and one for which the need is even more apparent.

I first voiced that view more than two decades ago. It was not seriously considered. The drinking age was raised via the threat of monetary penalty to the states. Problem solved, right?

Don't bet your lunch money.

On October 25, 2004, the *New York Times* ran an opinion article written by Jim Gogek of the Pacific Institute for Research and Evaluation, described as "one of the nation's preeminent independent, nonprofit organizations merging scientific knowledge and proven practice to create solutions that improve the health, safety and well-being of individuals, communities, nations, and the world." (Keep that statement in mind and recall the aforequoted observation of C. S. Lewis: "Of all tyrannies, a tyranny exercised for the good of its victims may be the most oppressive. It may be better to live under robber barons than under omnipotent moral busybodies.")

Said Gogek, "A year ago, at the request of Congress, the National

Academy of Sciences issued a nationwide strategy to reduce underage drinking. It hasn't been adopted, and since then more than 3,000 Americans have been killed and nearly one million injured in traffic crashes, shootings, stabbings, beatings, drownings, burns, suicide attempts and alcohol poisonings—all linked to underage drinking."

The critical reader ought to have hackles raised anytime the phrase "linked to" is employed, because it is junior-writer sloppiness at best and a desire to stretch the truth at worst. It gets worse: "And there have been more than 1.1 million property crimes and nearly 400,000 incidents of high-risk sex among youths, according to research conducted over the years by our institute."

Having failed to establish a correlation he is proud of enough to specify and instead glossing it over with "linked to," the fellow now provides an important scientific research term, "over the years." Pretty shoddy work. Predictably, Gogek called for "a lot more help from Washington," "[federal] legislation," "a national media campaign and the establishment of an independent prevention foundation," "curbs on alcohol advertising," "increased enforcement to stop sales to minors"—from whom? the FBI?—and "real political commitment." He bemoaned "a paltry $19 million to combat a problem" (which, presumably based on data "linked . . . over the years") that "costs the nation about $62 billion a year."

In short—it's not working, so let's do more of it.

The societal view toward alcohol contributes to its abuse by more than the young, in my view. As this book was in its early stages, a close friend of a good friend of mine died a terrible death, the result of many years of excessive drinking of alcohol. By all accounts among the most wonderful and compassionate of men, this fellow had been a television newsman, had studied to be an actor, and had been hired for some small parts on the New York stage but instead took a job in a supporting role for a famous author and publisher. It came to pass that he drank more and more; over the years he began the day with what in America is sometimes called an "eye-opener," that first-thing-in-the-morning shot of liquor that the British more colorfully call "a hot start."

His close friends knew of his problem. They also knew—and this will surprise you—that his problem was *not* alcohol. His dreams of an important network newscasting job or of acting stardom had not panned out. Viewing what he had seen as his own failure—had he not worked hard enough? had he given up too easily?—led him to lose all respect for himself. He didn't like himself, and he didn't like the life he was living. He found that a few drinks would, at first, let him think a little better of himself. He allowed this to grow until he was living his life drunk. He became skilled at appearing to be sober, though of course he wasn't, and his work, relationships, and other aspects of his life suffered—leading to even less self-respect, more drinking, and so on.

He died the day before he was to enter an alcohol abuse treatment center for the third time. There he would have been taught, again, how he should deal with the problem of alcoholism.

Over the years, I have seen major changes in society's views toward alcohol. What had been called "being a drunk" came to be called "alcoholism," and drunks, "alcoholics." Alcoholism became defined as an "addiction," and addiction became a "disease." I must admit that I played some role in these changes. The idea was that by removing this behavior from the realm of personal responsibility to that of illness, we could reduce social stigma, and thus encourage more people to seek treatment.

The preferred treatment has involved programs such as Alcoholics

Anonymous, which stress acknowledging one's helplessness and turning to a "higher power" in pursuit of abstinence. The results have not been encouraging. Some people who are apparently "alcoholics" become controlled drinkers or abstainers without such programs, and AA does not appear to improve the success rate of people dealing with alcohol problems. Indeed, there is evidence that counseling people to drink moderately is more effective than urging them to pursue abstinence. Stressing personal responsibility and power appears to be more beneficial than instilling powerlessness.

That's why the fellow mentioned above did not have success at his first two sessions at the alcoholism clinic—he was told that he was powerless over his disease. But as may well often be the case, alcohol wasn't the disease at all. His affliction was a collapse of his own self-respect. Alcohol was his way of treating *that* problem. He had no desire at all to stop drinking. Certainly, he knew that if he didn't it would kill him—but if he did quit, it would return him to a life that in his view wasn't worth living. There was a problem that deserved attention, but drinking too much was not the problem and instead a symptom of the problem, which was his own lack of any sense of value, replaced by a sense that he was powerless over his own life, which anguish alcohol assuaged.

Yet the alcohol experts continue to push the disease model of alcohol addiction, emphasizing the helplessness of the drinker over the drink. They have acquired a vested interest in persuading others of their powerlessness, in order to obtain power over others for themselves.

The experts say they are advancing a value-neutral, clinical approach to a disease that is no more related to one's choices than epilepsy—rather than "blaming the victim" by moralizing about failures of willpower, vices, or sins. But are they really? AA and similar twelve step programs are overtly religious. The demand that one acknowledge one's powerlessness before temptation and turn one's life over to a "higher power" echoes St. Augustine and Martin Luther. Their insistence on total abstinence—and hostility to moderation and controlled drinking—is essentially moralistic, following the prescriptions of the Temperance and Prohibition movements, which originated in the Methodist and Quaker religions. (When citing St. Augustine as an expert it does not hurt to note that the fourth century philosopher was possessed of an immense sexual appetite, which he hoped—someday—to overcome. This led to his most famous prayer, "Make me chaste and continent, but not yet!")

Such demands are often called puritanical, but this is a slur upon the Puritans. The pilgrims carried more beer than water on the *Mayflower*, and landed at Plymouth Rock only because their beer barrels had run empty. The first Thanksgiving featured beer, brandy, gin, and wine. The early colonialists made alcoholic beverages from carrots, tomatoes, onions, beets, celery, squash, corn silk, dandelions, goldenrod, and just about anything else they could find. Harvard College, a Puritan institution, made construction of a brewery one of its first priorities. Colonial New England's largest and most prosperous industry was rum. Indeed, during the debates that led to the Declaration of Independence, there was talk of the "triangle trade," in which New England, which cast a disapproving gaze on slavery, provided ships to the Caribbean and the southern colonies that would, depending on the leg of the journey, carry rum, slaves, or molasses.

Methodists and Quakers, in contrast, saw drinking alcohol as a sin. They had some difficulty with the fact that Jesus drank wine and was castigated by the Pharisees as a "wine-bibber." Yet wine was and is an important part of many religious rituals and celebrations. The turning of water into wine at the wedding at Cana was regarded as a miracle not just because of the transformation but also because the transformation was seen as for the better. In the Eucharist, it is wine that is transubstantiated into the blood of Jesus. And it is not hard to see why turning water into wine would be regarded as purification. Water supplies in biblical times often were contaminated by human or animal wastes, containing pathogens causing scourges such as dysentery, hepatitis, typhoid fever, and cholera. These were major killers until the nineteenth century, rivaling plague in mass destruction. Alcohol is an antiseptic, killing such pathogens in water. By mixing alcoholic beverages with water, it was possible to purify the water for drinking.

Only in the past century, as a result of chlorination, have most people had access to safe water supplies. The realization that microorganisms caused disease and the institution of sanitation finally made water a safe beverage in the West. It was these scientific and technological breakthroughs that allowed the Temperance movement to break out of the churches into the political arena.

Enjoying alcohol in moderation seems to be a natural part of being human, just as alcohol is a naturally occurring substance. Whenever honey or fruit "spoils," it ferments: Yeast produces alcohol as a natural by-product of metabolizing sugar. The fact that humans have a gene for an enzyme to metabolize alcohol suggests that our progenitors must have encountered alcohol relatively frequently, over a very long period.

Certainly excessive consumption of alcohol leads to a host of health problems, and social problems, too. Recognition of these facts led to Prohibition. But while Prohibition may have reduced alcohol consumption, it produced social costs widely perceived to be even worse than those engendered by alcohol consumption itself.

No doubt, the traditional social stigma attached to drunkenness deterred many who needed treatment from seeking it. Compassion and solicitude toward such people is understandable. If telling them that they are victims of a power outside themselves or greater than their will encourages them to seek treatment, why not?

Perhaps the pendulum has swung too far. In our desire to encourage problem drinkers to seek help, we have told them that they are powerless victims of their genes or of chemicals. In weakening the stigma of antisocial drunkenness, for example, have we encouraged the trend of binge drinking and drugs among young people? In promulgating a "noble lie," have we engendered social costs even worse than those of Prohibition?

Many people "diagnosed" as alcoholics seem to "cure" themselves without AA or any other treatment. When that happens, the experts can only say that they must not have been "true alcoholics" in the first place. But if that is so, there is no way to diagnose this "disease," short of the patient coming down with some objectively diagnosable disease such as cirrhosis, or else drinking himself to death. And if we tell him that he is powerless in the face of his addiction, do we not make that more likely? What drunk would fail to welcome the news that he is not responsible for his drinking? A diagnostic system that leads us to this impasse is not useful; it is harmful.

Before the disease of alcoholism spawned the industry that it has, it was not uncommon to hear of people who had been through "a bad patch," who for a period of time had consumed enough alcohol to be a source of embarrassment to himself, his family, his friends. Sometimes this was tied to other events—a business reversal, loss of job, the end of a marriage—though it is not possible to generalize as to which led to the other. But in those days, too, it was not seen as a one-way street. People emerged from their bad patches and continued with their lives. They were said to have gotten control of their lives, and there was no particular social stigma attached to it unless they had killed someone while driving drunk or had gone on an intoxicated shooting spree, or suchlike. More often than not, those persons would thereafter drink socially with no ill effect.

But now drinking to excess is deemed a disease; more than that, it is an incurable condition.

The central problem is that we are defining behavior as disease, or diagnosing a disease on the basis of "symptoms" that are merely behaviors, or subjective symptoms such as "craving." This technique does not yield trustworthy diagnoses, but it does give tremendous power to the diagnostician—power not over disease, but over human beings. You cannot help yourself, we say; you must do as I say, or you are doomed.

Moreover, when we tell a patient that he is helpless, powerless, do we really help him, or do we create a self-fulfilling prophesy? The placebo effect works both ways. If I tell you with authority that you cannot have even one drink without drinking to intoxication, do I make it easier for you to deal with your problem or harder?

Many people who have alcohol-related problems do bring their drinking under control and are able to drink in moderation. Understanding that this is possible makes it easier to do so. By telling people otherwise, the experts are depriving people of hope, and so bear a heavy burden of guilt for the inevitable tragedies that result. Medical practitioners must surrender some control to the patient in order to empower him to recover. The conflict between our personal power and the interests of the patient must be resolved in favor of the patient.

It is said that when all you have is a hammer, everything looks like a nail, and so it is with the medical and paramedical approach to alcohol consumption. The noted writer William F. Buckley Jr. mentions in one of his books an acquaintance who is an "alcohol counselor," by which he does not mean helpful bartender. This woman, he writes, diagnoses as an alcoholic "anyone who has ever finished an entire beer." While this is an extreme example, it illustrates the approach that the alcoholism industry takes toward those who drink.

Alcohol has an effect on people, on that we may all agree. That effect is physiological as well as psychological. A person who has a drink to soothe himself upon hearing of the death of a friend is, certainly, using alcohol as "a crutch." Is this any different from the person who has a headache using two aspirin as "a crutch"? For that matter, is it any different from a person who has a sprained ankle using a crutch as a crutch?

The issue is further clouded by research that suggests that some people benefit physiologically from alcohol consumption. For decades, physicians have told some patients, particularly those suffering from heart and circulatory ailments, that a beer or a glass of wine each day might be therapeutic. In recent years there have been statistical studies which have seemed to confirm this, though the reason it might be so has been a mystery. (Much speculation has resulted, as researchers ascribed beneficial effects to this liquor but not that one, wine over "hard" liquor, drinks that are red or brown in color instead of clear, and so on; but no one offered much evidence beyond a reshuffling of statistics, and most of the reports suggested that it was something other than the alcohol itself which provided the beneficial effect.) In September 2004, Ron Korthuis, chairman of the Medical Pharmacology and Physiology Department at the University of Missouri School of Medicine, announced the results of research that suggest alcohol prevents blood vessel damage during heart attacks. His observational study found that alcohol is involved in the production of a protein that protects blood vessels from the damage caused by white blood cells released during a heart attack.

Even from a therapeutic point of view, the finding, if accurate, poses a question: Is the problem drinker who has heart disease to eschew alcohol and face increased risk of sudden death from a heart attack, or is that person to learn to drink moderately—something the alcohol treatment community says is impossible—and live, perhaps, a longer life?

I have focused on alcohol treatment in this chapter because it is the area in which I have had the most personal experience. But the problems I have outlined in the dominant approach to addiction are much broader than alcohol. Today there is scarcely anything, from shopping to eating to sex, that is not governed by this paradigm. The result is a wholesale transfer of power across the board from the individuals involved, who make up the public, to the so-called experts.

Nor is the problem of defining behavior as disease limited to addiction. As we shall see, it permeates much of psychiatry today and is beginning to corrupt medicine, science, politics, and law. By outlining this process in the following chapters, I hope to empower you to take back from the experts what they have stolen from you.

But there is something more that deserves to be said, as unpopular and potentially controversial as it might be. It's this: You and only you have the right to decide how much, if any, to drink. You do not have the right to get drunk and go driving or speedboating, because the effects of alcohol combined with those activities endanger others. Nor do you have a right, if your choice is to drink an enormous amount, to expect society to look after you if that drinking leads to illness. And you do not have a right to leave a family uncared for if you get sick or die from overindulgence. You have a right to drink, but you do not have a right to be irresponsible. Your rights end somewhere before the point at which you're throwing up on someone else's shoes.

With those caveats as prologue, it is possible to justify, at least in some cases, the choice of drinking a great deal. Consider the great poet, Dylan Thomas, who died at age thirty-nine after a lifetime of truly epic alcohol consumption. A man dead from drink at thirty-nine is surely by most standards a tragedy. But there are questions worth pondering. If Thomas had lived a life of abstemiousness, would he have been able to write as he did? Or, conversely, might he have achieved even greater literary heights had he, free of the bottle, lived another fifty years? We cannot know the answers, and the fact is, it's none of our business. The only ones to whom the answers rightfully would have mattered are Thomas himself and those whose caring about him was personal rather than societal or literary.

He had been warned that excessive drink was taking its physical toll. He chose to continue to drink. It was his choice to make, and we are not entitled to second guesses.

The arts are filled with similar stories. They are often accompanied by lives that in every aspect but the arts were disasters, tragedies. We poetically say that the brightest lights burn most briefly. It has happened frequently enough that we cannot discount the possibility that there is something to it. From this we can establish no useful correlation—the dimmest lights also burn briefly, in all probability, but we never hear of them.

We cannot say that drunkenness contributes to artistic triumph. We can, however, say that some who have achieved artistic triumph believed that in their cases it did.

This is by no means an argument for drunkenness, far from it. It is instead an argument for people being allowed their own choices. Every year some people die in the hobby of skydiving. It is an exciting sport that always carries the very real possibility of sudden death, and for some that possibility is transformed into reality. They know the dangers, and they choose to jump out of the airplane anyway. Ought we pronounce them diseased?

Of course not. Nor should we so judge those who ride motorcycles, live in cities whose crime rates are high, or even drive to and from work (because many thousands of people are killed each year in automobile accidents). They have weighed the risks and made their choices. (Perhaps they have fooled themselves with erroneous notions of immortality, the sense that it won't happen to them. But who among us is exempt from *that* self deception?) This is their right—as is true of those who drink, and sometimes even those who drink to excess. And for those who suffer from some dysfunction that leads them to an unhealthy reliance on alcohol, the last thing that makes sense is to convince them that they are powerless and to treat them as if alcohol is the problem, when in all probability the real culprit is deeper and defies such easy generalization.

10

MUSHROOMS AND THE MISUSE OF THE PUBLIC HEALTH MODEL

Consider for a moment the poisonous mushroom.

Poisonous mushrooms are common. Practically everyone has encountered them. While mankind had known of their existence for thousands of years, there is still no antidote to their toxin, amanitin, which produces prolonged, agonizing death.

But the symptoms of poisoning to do not appear at once. They may not present themselves until hours or even a day or more after the offending fungus has been consumed.

At the beginning of this book, Mark Twain's admonition on the importance of learning the right lesson from every experience was remembered. Think now of the process that must have taken place as our species correctly identified poisonous mushrooms—and, more, recognized that some other mushrooms are not only safe to eat but tasty and good.

Surely some people ate poisonous mushrooms and died. It probably took a long time to make the connection between the mushrooms and death, in that time passes before the onset of symptoms. So it could be that many people died. Even now we hear from time to time of whole families who have perished as the result of a meal of toadstools or Destroying Angels or some other toxic fungus.

Moreover, poisonous mushrooms often resemble harmless varieties. To make things still worse, some creatures are unaffected by amanitin. The common woodland box turtle—probably most often seen as a crushed creature on the road—not only eats poisonous mushrooms but gains some protection from them: The toxin is stored in its fat, making it a meal fatal to predators. This is an observational issue worth noting.

Imagine the first person to eat an oyster. He or she must have been awfully hungry, no? This ravenous individual saw fit to smash open what probably looked like misshapen rocks attached to seaside boulders and then to consume the mucous-like contents. An oyster does not appear at first glance a likely candidate to become part of a wholesome meal. It is entirely possible, though we cannot know, that the first oyster eaters watched birds devour the bivalves. Similarly, our use of clams for food very possibly began when we saw birds drop them onto rocks to break open their shells, then swoop down for a meal.

That kind of observation isn't helpful to the fellow who sees the box turtle eat the toadstool. And the first person who thought a stinging jellyfish looked good to eat no doubt soon regretted it. Meanwhile, the people who consumed fiery hot chili peppers and who may have regretted it at first for some reason stuck with it, and we are better for their having done so.

If we examine, for instance, Old Testament dietary laws, we discover that they make a great deal of sense, especially in an age in which the reasons for illness were not understood. The proscription of the eating of pork, for example, was significant because pork can be host to trichinosis, a debilitating disease. Today we're told the danger can be eliminated by thoroughly cooking it, but to nomadic peoples it would have been obvious that pork dries out when completely cooked, making it unappetizing—and in any case it's unlikely anyone knew that even infected pork could be rendered safe by thorough cooking. Likewise, the ban on consumption of shellfish. In a hot locale and a time before refrigeration, marine invertebrates would spoil very quickly. Those potential morsels are not as easily preserved as are fish and meats.

It is probably safe to say that if a thing can be placed in the mouth and swallowed, someone has done it. We have known which things are edible and which things are harmful to eat for a long, long time. A lot of people got sick and a lot of people died as we assembled that body of knowledge. What is most surprising, though, is the precision with which over the millennia we have learned about plants and animals not just as foodstuffs but as medicines and for other purposes. We almost always learned the lesson but just the lesson—we didn't exaggerate. It could not have been easy. As with our friend the harmless box turtle, there were misleading things thrown in our path: For instance, some people are deathly allergic to items that for everyone else are healthful and nutritious. How was this reconciled among peoples who had no knowledge of allergies? Or is it possible that we used to be sturdier, less subject to things such as allergies, because those who were of puny constitution often died before extending their bloodlines? There is much room for speculation here, and the reader is encouraged to undertake it. It is a good practice to spend an afternoon in silence and solitude, just thinking an abstract problem through. In the course of it, one might even learn that it is not necessary to have the flashing television or blaring radio to be entertained—

one's own mind can provide good and useful entertainment, and, as with our other faculties, it benefits from exercise.

As our thinking over the millennia grew more complex, more abstract, we sought to bring order to the random observations that had until that time been our only way of advancing the collective knowledge of humankind. Plato codified the notion that it was useful to think not just of particular things but of the idea that those things represented—*the* wheel as opposed to *that* wheel. This enabled us to generalize in a useful way: What is it about a wheel that makes it a wheel? From here the next step was the effort to learn how to use observations in order to arrive at *useful* generalizations. It wasn't easy: Some apples have worms in them and some don't, so the mere knowledge that a thing is an apple provides no clue as to whether or not it is infested.

So we added something new, a way of converting observations into generalizations *along with a way of determining the extent to which those generalizations are true*. It is called the scientific method.

The scientific method involves more than simply going about things in a fastidious manner, essential though that is. It is a very specific set of steps that carries us from an observation to a generalization in which we can take some confidence. It begins with an observation: That apple has a worm in it. It is followed by a hypothesis: Apples have worms in them. The hypothesis leads to a prediction: That apple over there has a worm in it.

Here we hit a bump. That apple over there, when cut open, might not contain a worm. If it doesn't, the hypothesis has been disproved. Does this mean that if the second apple does contain a worm, the hypothesis—that apples are infested with worms—is proved? No, and the "scientist" who published his new generalization about apples at this point would have difficulty in convincing anyone of anything ever again (to say nothing of the wrath of apple growers). But our imaginary scientist is more careful. He cuts open another apple. Let's say that it contains no worm. His tally so far is two apples with worms, one without. If he were lazy or unimaginative, he might at this point say that based upon his research two out of three apples contain worms. This is certainly convenient, protecting him as it does from being confronted with a worm-free apple had he published his initial finding that all apples contain worms. He might even get away with it, if getting away with something were his goal.

But if his goal were instead to advance knowledge, he would continue, cutting open more and more apples. At the end of the day he would have a number of apples that contained worms and a number of apples that didn't. From this he might begin to derive a ratio of infested versus uninfested apples. The more apples he dissected, the greater his statistical precision—with some caveats.

There is a joke told in the scientific community of the four scientist-philosophers who took a train ride across Scotland, in a region where sheep herding was the principal agricultural activity. "Look," said one, pointing out the train window at a hillside where sheep were grazing. "Sheep around here are black."

"No," said the second. "At least *some* of the sheep around here are black."

"Not enough," said the third. "At least some of the sheep around here are black *on at least one side.*"

"Close," said the fourth. "At least some of the sheep around here are black on at least one side *at least some of the time.*"

Our imaginary scientist, if he were objective in looking at the results, would at the end of his apple experiment realize that he had not discovered anything of very much use. He would have a statistical analysis of that particular kind of apple on that particular day from that particular place. He now knows that some apples have worms and some do not, which is an improvement on his initial hypothesis. (If he were a modern scientist, he might well write a paper with all manner of graphs and gobbledygook and doubletalk and the claim that his research has produced "promising results," and he should therefore be awarded a huge research grant so that he might cut open more apples.)

The scientific method, having disproved his original hypothesis, would lead the truly inquisitive scientist to another question: What is it about some apples that they contain worms, while others do not? He might go back and take a closer look at the wormy apples and the pristine ones, and if he were careful he might find that the ones with worms display a blemish, a hole, whence the parent of the worm deposited her egg. From this he might establish a second hypothesis: By looking for such a blemish one can, without cutting it open, determine whether or not an apple has a worm inside. From this he predicts that he can diagnose apples. He puts it to the test, and this time he seems to be onto something. He might be disheartened a time or two upon biting into what he thought was an immaculate apple only to see half a worm wriggling where the bite had been taken. But more careful examination would show that the blemish, while not always obvious, seemed always to be present in apples that were the domiciles of worms.

From this he is able to establish a *theory:* There is an absolute relationship between the presence of the blemish and the presence of a worm. This is an objective claim, because anyone may test it. There is no special trick to his research that makes the theory appear to be

110

true. It could be tried out anywhere, using any apples, by any researcher, and if the theory is valid, the results will be the same. Over time, other things might be learned that would modify the theory and make it more precise. There might be some kinds of apples that are not vulnerable to worms, for instance, so the blemish created by the depositing of the egg might be present, but it would never hatch or grow into a worm. And there might be some other kind of worm that finds its way into the apple in a different way. The more observation that is done, the more is known. The generalization becomes narrower, but its accuracy nears the absolute.

The scientific method, needless to say, enabled careful and inquisitive persons to make sense out of the many scraps of random observation which otherwise would defy transformation into useful knowledge. *A priori* reasoning—thought without evidence—cannot do it alone. Nor can *a posteriori* appraisal—looking at the evidence alone. Examination of multiple snippets of observation might suggest relationships, but only when those relationships are put in the form of a hypothesis, the hypothesis used to make a prediction, and the prediction put to the test through repeatable experiments can a theory, the first useful derivative of observation, be formed.

That is how it works when it works properly. Today, it sometimes does not work properly. Too often, it is done backward, with a result settled upon and then a rush to cobble together experiments that support the foreordained conclusion.

Beginning in the closing years of the eighteenth century, the fledgling U.S. government took an interest in medicine. From a military start—it was at first called the Marine Hospital Service—we now have the U.S. Public Health Service and its commissioned corps. Public Health Service officials have military ranks and uniforms. The surgeon general holds the rank of, well, general, and appears at official functions in a white dress uniform similar to that of a naval officer. Lesser officials in the Public Health Service hold lesser ranks. The organization's purpose has in some ways paralleled that of the Army's Corps of Engineers in peacetime; but instead of draining swamps and building levees, the Public Health Service has been involved in matters of national health.

Over the years, the Public Health Service has done some very good things. It has fought epidemics that threatened the nation, often with considerable success. It also led to consideration of and interest in the subject of "public health," which is a sociological approach to medicine, covering epidemiology, vital statistics, and the like. The subject of public health is, too, where something called the "public health model" resides.

Science and medicine have achieved tremendous success over the last century through careful use of the public health model. It is based on a triad: agent, host, and environment. The "agent" is a living organism or toxin present in all who suffer from a particular disease—polio, smallpox, influenza. While it is possible under this model for persons who harbor the infectious agent to remain well, it is not possible for someone suffering from the disease brought about by the agent to lack that agent.

In recent years, however, there has been an attempt to apply the public health model in other ways, particularly toward substances. This attempt has been a failure scientifically, but as a way of rousing the news media and the plaintiff bar it has been a rollicking success. Unfortunately, because it is scientifically unjustified, it leads to the dissemination of erroneous information, the awarding of unjust judgments, and the diminution of funds that might otherwise be available for good research in many areas.

Like the scientific method from whence it came, the public health model is a powerful brake on the natural human tendency to jump to conclusions. And like the scientific method, it is straightforward and does not work in reverse. But more and more it has been employed as if the outcome is predetermined, with the search then on for evidence that supports the foregone conclusion. It is as if, when preparing an income tax return, one were to begin by deciding on the amount of payment to be made or refund to be received, then worked upward, adjusting the numbers to bring it about.

We have seen this happen in the hoopla over something called Acquired Immune Deficiency Syndrome, a panic that began in 1980 when a group of homosexual men in New York City suffered an abnormal incidence of a rare kind of cancer. A search was on to find a cause but, more than that, a cause which was behavior neutral. With tremendous fanfare but no commensurate application of either the scientific method or the public health model, it was decided that a retrovirus that was present in some—but not all—of those said to have AIDS was the culprit. There was tremendous political pressure brought to have this government-approved explanation accepted without question, and when inquisitive scientists did question it, their careers typically ended. The political clout attendant to the AIDS panic was given life through the awarding of grants. Academic scientists who wanted to have money for research quickly found that it would be forthcoming if the acceptance of the virus, HTLV-III (renamed HIV, for Human Immunodeficiency Virus) as the cause of AIDS were absolute. To this day, no one has *proved* that HIV causes AIDS, that HIV is harmful at all, or even that there is a distinct illness that can be called AIDS.

We have seen the public health model flung down and danced upon in consideration of tobacco products and their use. In 1964, the surgeon general issued the famous report that claimed to link cigarette smoking to disease. But, as anyone who bothered to read it quickly discovered, this report represented no new research but was instead a survey of other studies apparently picked to illustrate the conclusion that smoking causes to disease.

The academician who questions this conclusion, or the researcher who seeks to find out whether smoking is linked to illness and, if so how, would today be laughed out of the ivory tower or the government-funded lab. Yet some people use tobacco products their entire lives and remain in roaring good health, while others who have never touched the stuff suffer and die from the very illnesses for which smoking is blamed. This gave rise to the hypothesis of "secondhand smoke." The accidental inhalation of smoke from other people's tobacco products is blamed for thousands of deaths each year—yet no one has ever proved that secondhand smoke has ever killed a single person. This has not prevented the acceptance as if it were gospel that secondhand smoke is a killer, not in the scientific community and certainly not in the news media or in the carrion-feeding segment of the legal community. Governments have passed sweeping laws against what may very well at worst be nothing more than an odor that some find unpleasant.

The current popular panic has to do with the view that we as a society are too fat. Is there evidence to support this, commensurate to the attention it has gained? Well, no. The obesity "epidemic" in the United States came about with the stroke of a pen, when a U.S. government agency decided to recategorize its characterization of people's weights. A person who was said to be within a normal, healthy range of weights for his or her height one day was the next day, through no change in the person, suddenly deemed overweight.

Were there new studies that showed that such persons were less healthy than their thinner neighbors? No. It was a bookkeeping change. *Ah,* but were the media quick to glom onto the "epidemic," reporting it as newly discovered yet unquestionable fact and an issue of critical concern? Were opportunistic quacks quick to promote bizarre diets, some of which defied settled nutritional knowledge? Were lawyers ready to pounce, blaming not people who may have eaten too much but instead using those people as plaintiffs and blaming the people who sold them the food they may have eaten too much of? You betcha!

The examples of other such misuses are many.

For years, a growth hormone called Alar was used to strengthen the attachment of apples to the tree, so that fewer would fall to the ground and rot. News reports incorrectly called Alar, the Uniroyal chemical company's brand name for the hormone daminozide, a "pesticide" and uncritically parroted the claims of the Natural Resources Defense Council that the hormone caused cancer in children. The Environmental Protection Agency heavily criticized the NRDC's campaign, but as is so often the case, fear trumped fact. A television broadcast, relying on one study which would later be discredited, claimed that Alar was harmful to humans. The result was the withdrawal of Alar, a loss in excess of $100 million to the apple orchard industry, and higher apple prices for everyone.

In February 1990, Source Perrier S.A., bottler of Perrier sparkling water, was forced to withdraw more than 100 million bottles of the product due to reports that it contained minute amounts of benzene. Unreported was that to achieve even minimally dangerous amounts of benzene in his system, a person would have to drink a quart of the supposedly tainted Perrier every day for the rest of his or her life. Although Perrier had been at the time the leading provider of bottled water, it never again owned the market as it had prior to this revelation.

For decades we have heard about the crisis of "addiction." It is certainly true that there are substances some people find pleasurable to consume, and that after use of them some people may crave more. The public health model, though, tells us that for any generalization to be made about the addictive properties of a substance, that substance must create a physiological need within all those who consume it, or at least that all who crave it must have developed a physiological requirement for it. Yet evidence suggests otherwise: Numerous people have spontaneously quit using substances that are claimed to be among the most addictive in the world, while others have returned to those substances years after having given them up, long after any physiological need would have manifested itself. The generalizations about addiction, while convenient for those who would employ them to dictate the behavior of others, are just not true.

Are there people who have drug problems? Certainly. Are there behaviors that some people, under the influence of drugs, participate in that are not socially acceptable? Of course. Can the connection be made between the drugs and the problems people have? Beyond those who consume too much of a substance and die of its direct, toxic effects, no. The problem of drug abuse cannot be dealt with by society in any generalized way. It must be handled at the individual level, with a search for the individual's reasons for using those substances, whether those substances are harmful to that individual, and whether and how that individual ought to find a different expression of or cure for the things that led to drug use.

Consider caffeine, which may well be the next subject of a phony crisis brewed by those who like to tell others how to live their lives. Caffeine is a drug, a stimulant. Many people find it helpful to have a cup of coffee or more in the morning, while others have learned that its effects make them nervous or irritable or make it difficult for them to go to sleep at day's end. It is not possible to make a generalization about the effects of coffee on people—at least not to the extent that regulation of coffee would be sensible. A law banning caffeine would be as silly as one requiring people to consume it. Do not be surprised, though, one day to hear of lawsuits against "Big Coffee."

What? Certainly it is possible. And so is the notion of people being required to consume a drug.

Throughout the nation, unruly schoolchildren are forced to consume a variety of pharmaceutical products in order to make them more docile and pliable. Never is it considered that a child misbehaves ("acts out" in the current nonvalue vernacular; the old term, "acting up" seems somehow better to describe it) because the government-mandated curriculum, generalized in a one-size-fits-all way to produce no identifiable result other than docile children, might be bored to distraction—literally.

The drugs are administered to make things convenient for teacher and school, not to meet the needs of the child who has his or her mind altered by some substance that, later, he might go to jail for buying on the street. We preach that drugs are not the answer to our individual concerns, but then our children are taught—and parents willingly go along, almost as if having a drugged-up child bestowed bragging rights—that drugs may be forced upon us to achieve goals of societal convenience.

The difference? The person who "prescribes" his own drugs is exercising power over his own life. The person who has drugs forced upon him is under the control of those who would exercise power over him to achieve their ends, not his. If there is scientific evidence to support the compulsory drugging of children, it is evidence gathered with control over children in mind.

The real solution is found in self-respect. You know how much, if any, coffee is right for you. You know whether you are content with your weight. You know whether or not smoking is something that you find valuable. You even know whether or not you mind the smell of tobacco smoke. If you are a parent, it is your job, your duty as a parent if your child is troubled, to find out the source and nature of the problem. It could well be that there is an issue a pharmaceutical product could obviate. But this must be decided based on the best interests of the child, not on your convenience or that of the school system. (Isn't it funny how the homeschooling movement has grown; how home-schooled children, who are taught individually, are among the highest achievers; and how few homeschooled children need to be drugged?)

It is easy to fall into lockstep, to accept without question the prevailing view, to take your place in the mooing herd. But to do so is to abandon your self-respect, to vacate your own views and needs in favor of what is most convenient for someone else who may not have your interests at heart at all. The pressure to become a compliant herd animal is strong.

Of course, herd animals are typically led to the slaughterhouse from whence they emerge as hamburgers. After which, some lawyer sues the hamburger vendor.

11

DOCTORS ALWAYS GET IT RIGHT, RIGHT?

Surely medicine, with lives at stake, doesn't come to any conclusions of which it is not certain, or so one would think. But one who had those thoughts would be in error. While there have been a multitude of technological and scientific advances which let us know more and more about the human body, more often than not those new findings raise greater questions than they answer.

A recent collection of statistics taken from autopsies shows that the degree of misdiagnosis has not been reduced to any significant degree over the past seventy years, despite many wonderful new diagnostic tools. Much that has been publicized to the extent that it is now accepted as fact is anything but. As we have seen, the public health model fails when applied to the purported connection between Human Immunodeficiency Virus, HIV, and Acquired Immune Deficiency Syndrome, or AIDS. The reason? There are people who appear to have AIDS who show no evidence of ever having been exposed to HIV.

Even the agency that has been given the task of watching out for the purity of the food we eat and the safety and effectiveness of the pharmaceutical products prescribed to us can get so entangled in its own bureaucracy that products truly are safe and effective sometimes are held back in favor of ones that are less so, or that carry additional and unnecessary dangers.

An excellent example is that of Michael Zasloff, M.D., Ph.D., who through truly heroic efforts made a remarkable discovery that could have saved many lives and many thousands more from permanent disfigurement, only to see it cast aside by a government panel intent on examining everything *except* the obvious.

As chief of genetics of the National Institutes of Child Health and Human Development, Dr. Zasloff had noticed that the African clawed frogs used for experiments in his laboratory never got infected even though they were returned to bacteria-laden aquaria following surgery. Their wounds just healed—no swelling, no inflammation, no pus, no evidence of infection at all. He wondered why.

"The story of Zasloff's discovery of magainins is the kind of scientific detective tale seldom found in modern research," said a front-page story by Susan Okie in the *Washington Post* of July 30, 1987. "It is the story of how a single, elegantly simple observation led, with a speed rare in science, to the unfolding of a brand new area of animal biology. It vividly illustrates Louis Pasteur's dictum that in science, 'chance favors only the prepared mind.'"

In the world of scientific research, success is sometimes measured in much the way that in other professions the corner office with a view might be seen as evidence of having reached the top. At the NIH, laboratory chiefs such as Zasloff were not expected to roll up their sleeves at the lab bench and do the work themselves. Yet there he had been, in the lab late at night and on weekends, working on . . . something.

Of frogs that seemed abnormally healthy, most people would say,

"How nice for them," and get back to whatever else they were doing. Still more would probably fail to see a connection between robust wound recovery among strange, blank-eyed amphibians that have actual, bird-like claws on their webbed hind feet, and the genetics of child health and development, which is, after all, the purpose of the lab. But Zasloff had latched onto a question to which he demanded an answer.

He worked, on his own, designing experiments, then conducting them. He deduced that there was something in the frogs that turned away microbes, killed them, something. But what?

After many weeks of work, he had his answer. The frogs produced peptides—molecules that in the biochemical pecking order reside above amino acids and below proteins—that had unique properties. When a microbe paid a visit, the peptides would penetrate its protective cell membrane. The microbe would fill up with the surrounding liquid and pop like an overinflated balloon.

There was a tremendous allure to these peptides, which Zasloff named "magainins," after the Hebrew word for "shield" or "buckler." For one thing, they were effective against a very wide range of bacteria and protozoa, many of which infect people. For another, they were apparently nontoxic, unlike other powerful antibiotic agents. Of great potential importance was the fact that frogs had been around for millions of years and the microbes hadn't figured out a way to mutate themselves so as to become immune to the magainins, a phenomenon that drew much concern from scientists who believed that the overuse and improper use of antibiotics was over time creating a range of untreatable "superbugs." And of no minor consideration was that Zasloff had designed a way to synthesize them for just a few dollars a pound, no frogs necessary.

He published a scientific paper about his findings, and the National Institutes of Health patented his magainins. The general press got word of his work and inundated him with calls. The stories were some admixture of two themes: A scientist, working all on his own (unheard of in this day and age), makes an astounding discovery; and this discovery will cure many of man's most troubling illnesses. Almost as a footnote in the stories that mentioned it at all—and there were stories in publications from the *Post* to the *Star* supermarket tabloid—was Zasloff's comment that the most important part of his discovery was that the existence of those peptides in frogs is not the kind of thing that would get left behind in evolution—that it's likely that every creature had some form of them, too.

Something that made these molecules and the way they work so special is that their approach to invading organisms made it highly unlikely that the organisms could ever develop resistance to them.

Having made the discovery, Zasloff set about the task of translating it into something useful, a product that could cure the real-world diseases of men, women, and children. This, too, proved relatively straightforward. Then he made another discovery: The regulatory mechanisms governing such products make it extremely difficult ever to bring such a thing to market.

He founded a company called Magainin Pharmaceuticals. He believed that ultimately his miracle molecules would be helpful in many illnesses and injuries for which there are no effective treatments. For instance, victims of severe burns often succumb to dehydration due to the loss of the protection that skin provides. They are often immersed in water or saline baths to help preserve the liquid in their bodies. But this makes them vulnerable to infection—the very kinds of infection that frogs evolved magainins to combat. Blindness in much of the world is caused by terrible protozoan infections, and here, too, magainins seemed a likely choice.

But before approval could be gained for the use of preparations based on the molecules in situations such as those, it was best to get approval for something simple. The company chose the minor skin infection of children called impetigo. They did this in large measure because another drug for treating that condition had been approved, so the experiments were already designed and the company had a good idea of what the appropriate committee at the Food and Drug Administration was seeking. A large and expensive trial was conducted, including careful controls—some sufferers did not use the ointment containing a magainin derivative but instead what amounted to soap and water.

At the end of the trial, the peptide ointment was shown to be safe and effective—but so was the soap and water! Zasloff was perplexed, chiefly because he could not figure out how the earlier drug had managed to get approved. The company had spent a million dollars for nothing. But, being honest, it announced its findings rather than try to bluff its way through.

Magainin Pharmaceuticals, Inc., had not given up on Locilex, its name for the magainin-derived ointment. The impetigo fiasco had said nothing about the drug, really. A new disease for which it seemed appropriate was sought and found: infected foot ulcers among people with diabetes. These contribute to what the American Diabetes Association estimates are 80,000 amputations per year. There was no drug recommended for the treatment of these wounds; physicians typically treated them as if they were not infected, and if systemic evidence of infection appeared they would use a systemic antibiotic of the fluoroquinolone class (the most famous of which is Cipro). This can be problematic for several reasons: Some people have adverse reactions that cause them to stop taking the pills; the more people who use this kind of antibiotic, the greater the likelihood that microbes will develop resistance to it; and in the case of the foot ulcers, the medicine can be taken without the patient properly cleansing the ulcer, which is an important part of any treatment. Locilex, applied to the ulcer itself and not likely to induce microbial resistance, avoided these problems.

The company approached the FDA in hope of arriving at a series of trials which would be acceptable to the regulatory agency. Because infected diabetic foot ulcers are dangerous, a "double blind" trial, in which some participants would receive Locilex and others would receive tubes containing the petroleum jelly but no antibiotic, was ruled out. Instead, a "double-dummy" protocol was agreed upon. The only approved treatment available being systemic antibiotics, ofloxacin, a fluoroquinolone frequently employed in such cases, would be employed, too. Some patients would receive Locilex and placebo pills, while some would receive a tube of petroleum jelly and real ofloxacin pills. The goal was a result in which the Locilex patients did as well as the oxyfloxacin ones.

Locilex, being of a whole new class of antibiotic agents, was subject to closer scrutiny than would be a typical new drug. Thus the assemblage of the Anti-Infective Drugs Advisory Committee on the snowy morning of March 4, 1999, at the Silver Spring, Maryland, Holiday Inn. The committee, part of the Food and Drug Administration's Center for Drug Evaluation and Research, was to hear a presentation in support of approval of Locilex, the first real-world application of a whole new class of drugs derived from a whole new field of medical study. After hearing the presentation and discussing it, they would vote whether to recommend to the FDA that the new drug be approved for use.

"It was probably the worst day of my life," Dr. Michael Zasloff said later.

The proceedings began with a presentation by a consultant to the panel who was familiar in particular with uninfected diabetic foot ulcers, as many are. In such cases, said Dr. O. Fred Miller, debridement—the scraping or cutting away of dead material—was sufficient. This material, he said, often looks and smells infected but isn't.

Miller's presentation touched a poignant note with Zasloff, who was sitting among the spectators. His wife's grandmother had died from gangrene after infected diabetic foot ulcers led to progressive amputations—in the very hospital where Miller now worked.

Miller was followed by Dr. Kenneth Holroyd, Magainin's chief operating officer. He explained what Locilex was and how it was expected to work. He in turn introduced Dr. Benjamin Lipsky of the University of Washington, who had chiefly designed the trial and who reported on the results. Within the boundaries of statistical error, Locilex had performed as well as the systemic antibiotic had.

The panel of a dozen physicians and Ph.D.s had questions. The dropout rate among Locilex users had been higher—why? The test parameters, it was explained, excluded anyone who developed some other illness that required a systemic antibiotic. People already receiving one would be less inclined to develop such sicknesses. The illnesses, though, would have had nothing to do with foot ulcers, the subject of the study.

The committee was also concerned about physician competence at the prescription level, were Locilex to be approved. Could doctors treating patients correctly identify infected ulcers? Would they prescribe Locilex when it was not necessary? Would they prescribe it when a systemic drug was needed, because the infection had advanced beyond Locilex's reach? They were told that in the former case the drug would do no harm and that in the latter, symptoms would demand a systemic agent. The panel's comments suggested that they were unconvinced as to the former—the possibility of bacteria becoming resistant to antibiotics is a tremendous concern in the part of the medical community most interested in infections.

Following the lunch break, the panel's mood toward Locilex seemed darker. There was now talk, though only a few members had experience with diabetic foot ulcers, that there was probably no need for antibiotics at all unless the infection got so bad that a systemic remedy was required—something with which numerous amputees might not have agreed. These studies, in which Locilex had been shown to be as effective as the systemic antibiotic, were now being treated as if the foot ulcers were impetigo—that the results might have been the same if neither therapy had been used.

"Once you have taken out the infection and thrown it in the trash," said Dr. Julie Parsonnet, a committee member from Stanford University, "I am not sure that you need any antibiotic."

Several members suggested a placebo experiment, in which half the patients being studied would be given no antibiotic at all.

"That would be highly unethical and also highly ineffective," said Zasloff later. "The only wounds that physicians would feel comfortable exposing to such a treatment are so small that they probably *would* heal on their own when kept clean." Such wounds, too, are not likely to be infected. The only way to do a placebo test of substantial, infected wounds without running a risk of allowing the placebo patients to become much worse would be to provide daily care on a level that the company could not afford.

The committee's charge was to determine whether Locilex was safe and effective. They agreed that it was safe. They were divided as to whether it was effective.

"I think it probably does do something, but I don't think it has been demonstrated," said Dr. Robert Danner of NIH. The Magainin representatives gasped—it was almost as if their presentation were being graded, rather than a decision being rendered on a potentially useful therapy for people who needed it.

Four members of the eleven-member panel voted to recommend that Locilex be approved, while the other seven voted against it. A twelfth physician present, who would soon join the committee, said that were he allowed to vote he would vote for approval. Some of the votes against approval seemed unenthusiastic, as was Danner's.

Zasloff was crushed. He had spent close to a dozen years trying to convert a remarkable observation into something of practical use, but was learning more and more that there's many a disappointment 'twixt discovery and ointment.

The FDA formally denied approval to Locilex for the treatment of diabetic foot ulcers four months later. Magainin's stock took a further hit. The National Diabetes Center was outraged, accusing the FDA of going back on its word and pointing out that the regulatory body had approved the design of the trials before they were conducted.

Magainin quietly put Locilex to sleep. While there is laboratory work underway in connection with the discovery made by a lone researcher who was habitually observant, it is mostly overseas. The great promise of magainins remains unfulfilled, not because it lacked merit but because a self-important bureaucracy flexed its fickle muscles.

The advantage of a topical antibiotic over a systemic one is obvious: A topical ointment finds its way to the wound it is supposed to treat rather than throughout the system. It, therefore, deals only with the infection it is designed for. A systemic antibiotic goes after whatever it finds. This can include useful bacteria normally found in the body, creating adverse side effects. It can also include the microbes that would potentially bring on illness. If the infection for which the antibiotic is prescribed is cured before the other microbes are wiped out, those that remain are far more likely to have begun to develop resistance to the antibiotic. That alone would have suggested that the topical preparation was preferable to a systemic agent that produced identical or even a little better results. But the FDA said no.

This meant that persons who wished to use Locilex, who were willing to agree to dismiss any risks that might have been involved (though none had been shown), were prohibited from buying it. It was not just a lack of approval, it was a prohibition.

How many other good and useful pharmaceutical products are there which are not available to patients because the learned souls on some FDA committee lacked perspective of real patients, real diseases, and the real desire to get well? Plenty, but the FDA is not alone among groups who would protect us from our own choices as to our health.

The famous Center for Science in the Public Interest—which is the center of nothing beyond itself, which practices highly questionable science, and which can be said to be in the public interest only to the extent that it defines itself as the public—does much to lead the way in making sure that you are denied choices in how you live your life.

In a July 2004 article in *Reason*, writer Jacob Sullum detailed the organization's attack on foodstuffs of various sorts, the common denominator being that if you enjoy eating it, you probably shouldn't eat it at all. He quotes the CSPI book *Is Our Food Safe*, written by Warren Leon, executive director of the Northeast Sustainable Energy Association, and Caroline Smith DeWaal, CSPI's director of food safety: "In 1987, the Environmental Protection Agency (EPA) estimated that pesticide residues on food might cause cancer in as many as 6,000 people annually in the United States." Note the hedges—"might," "as many as." Sullum put it succinctly: "Given the uncertainties about extrapolating from huge doses of a chemical in rodents to tiny doses in humans, the actual number may be closer to zero."

Sullum quotes another CSPI book, *Restaurant Confidential,* on the artificial sweetener aspartame: "Some people believe that it causes dizziness, hallucinations, or headaches, but controlled studies have not confirmed those problems. In addition, aspartame needs to be tested better to confirm that it does not cause cancer." How's that for "science"? The fact that "some people believe" that the Earth is flat provides no evidence in support of the belief, and anyone writing about geography who wishes to be taken seriously probably wouldn't mention them or their belief at all. The argument—not that aspartame causes cancer but that nobody has proved that it doesn't—is risible, or would be if "some people" didn't take it seriously.

"*Restaurant Confidential* calls dishes that offend CSPI's sensibilities 'masterpieces of overwrought excess,'" Sullum continues, "which is also an apt description of the group's press releases. In CSPI lingo, which relies heavily on adjectives like artery-clogging and heart-stopping, a double cheeseburger is 'a coronary bypass special,' fettuccine Alfredo is 'a heart attack on a plate,' and a baked potato with butter, sour cream, bacon bits, and cheese is 'the culinary equivalent of a loaded pistol.'" Say what you will about the potential effects of fat-laden foods, the vast majority of people who consume them survive the experience without an intervening rush to the hospital. Such claims have no business in the work of a group that has "science" as part of its name.

Another CSPI target is salt. Sullum quotes CSPI as describing the substance—essential, by the way, to our existence—as "the deadly white powder you already snort." Yes, it is possible to consume too much salt. It is possible to consume too much of anything. People have died as a result of drinking too much water. But there is no evidence, none at all, that suggests that ordinary salt consumption is harmful to anyone. Clearly, whatever the Center for Science in the Public Interest has in mind, providing sensible information to people concerned about living a decent life while respecting their health is not it.

Who is watching out for your health? Just you.

Much has been made in recent years of prostate cancer, a disease that can be controlled in its early stages but which, untreated, results in many deaths. Its incidence increases with age. Conventional medical wisdom calls for early detection and treatment. Each year millions of men age fifty and over submit to a prostate examination, which no one has described as pleasant. Others undergo a PSA—prostate-specific antigen—test, a blood test that seeks indicators of prostate cancer, and of that group, some live in terror that an elevated PSA level might be the finding.

Now there is word—if you're a man over fifty, sit down, gently—that PSA tests may not be enough. To quote H. Gilbert Welch in the *Washington Post,* the only way to be *really* sure is "a more aggressive test—placing a probe through the rectum of normal men and inserting a biopsy needle six, maybe twelve times to search for cancer in various parts of their prostate." The question asked by Welch, a Dartmouth professor of medicine and author of *Should I Be Tested for Cancer? Maybe Not and Here's Why,* is this: How much *certain* pain and discomfort are we willing to endure to guard against the *possibility* of even greater pain and discomfort—and possible death—down the line? Should this kind of thing become standard procedure? (And, though Welch does not ask it, how many men would avoid going to the doctor at all if such draconian procedures were to become an expected part of the visit?)

"Millions of healthy Americans are being told that they are sick (or 'at risk')," writes Welch. More are undergoing invasive evaluations with needles, flexible scopes, and catheters. And more are taking drugs for early forms of diabetes, heart disease, osteoporosis, hepatitis, vascular disease, and cancer. "We need to start asking hard questions about whose interests are served by the relentless pursuit of disease in people who are well. Clearly it's good business—for test manufacturers, hospitals, pharmaceutical companies. And it's good for some doctors." But does it do us, individually or collectively, any good?

I mentioned above the study that showed that the rate of misdiagnosis has remained constant despite a revolution in the development of diagnostic tools. There are several possible explanations for this: Given the new tools, physicians may overreach, trying to put them to work doing things for which they were not designed and for which they are not of much use. They may be put to use sometimes when they are not needed as diagnostic aids because expensive equipment is otherwise underutilized, and the application of unneeded tests is a way to pay for them. And surely there is the fact that as protection from the burgeoning industry of malpractice lawsuits—in which a lawyer names all imaginable tests and demands to know if the plaintiff received all of them—physicians do not want to make it possible to make themselves look bad in front of a jury.

But I think that there is something more. The connection between patient and physician is not what it once was. Today's doctors may have new diagnostic tools, but do they *listen* to their patients? Or do they think of patient views and opinions as unfortunate annoyances in their practice? Do they think that they know more about their patients than the patients themselves do?

Doctors of old, lacking the latest marvels of diagnostic science, needed to listen, because what the patient had to say often provided the very best clues as to the nature of the illness. And a study done at Yale Medical School not long ago demonstrated that what a patient has to say may yet be the best diagnostic tool available—one that modern physicians overlook.

In that Yale study, a person's answer to the question, "Is your health excellent, good, fair, or poor?" was shown to be better at predicting the person's mortality over the next decade than was a detailed physical examination. Older people in the study who said that their health was "poor" were seven times as likely to die in the following twelve years than those who rated their health as "excellent." *Ah,* you say, but perhaps their estimation was informed by prior knowledge of their own physical conditions! Not so, according to the study, which measured the results within groups whose physical examinations had shown them to be in comparable health.

Norman Vincent Peale was on to something when he wrote of the "power of positive thinking." Consider the "placebo effect." This is the circumstance in which a group of people is given an inert substance in response to a complaint and told that the substance is medicine that will cure them. Some will get well—and the number is greater than the number who would get well on their own, given nothing. It is a terrible hobgoblin to the clinical researcher conducting "double-blind" tests, because always, or nearly so, some people who shouldn't have gotten better get better anyway. In some cases, the explanation may be as simple as the patient, now believing that the complaint is being treated, relaxes enough to get good rest and allow the body to do its job of getting well. But even this does not entirely explain the placebo effect.

So as the experts argue and study and conduct tests and in some cases do what they can to keep helpful medicines from you, you can be confident that you have a doctor within that will go a long way toward curing your ills and maintaining your health. And, based on what we now know on the nature of the science and politics involved, as well as the eagerness of organizations that claim to be in the "public interest" to function in the interests of their own power, that doctor within may well be worthy of your attention.

Though when looking for a doctor, it certainly doesn't hurt to look for one who takes time to listen and who appears to respect what you have to say.

12

CORRELATION AS CAUSATION

A friend tells of a phone call he received from a fellow with whom he flew airplanes and did computer work. The fellow had a young son, now two years old.

"He just said the word that every parent dreads a child learning," said the fellow.

My friend, searching his mind for words of profanity or obscenity that children occasionally and innocently latch onto, to the mortification of their parents, especially when company is around, finally gave up: "Oh my. What word is that?"

The response was unequivocal: "Why."

Every statement uttered to the tot, every instruction, was now answered by a tiny voice, "Why?" The father, who was at a loss to explain many things (and, truth be known, did not think he had the time to explain others), came to reply, "Because Daddy says so."

Not to criticize the fellow with the questioning son, but this is the way many of us are set up to accept insufficient answers to our most burning questions. "Daddy" gets replaced by other figures of authority: government, media, academicians, physicians, scientists, lawyers.

We are given all through our lives the moral equivalent of "because Daddy says so." Yet somewhere deep inside we know that that answer is insufficient.

It is true. We are by nature—well, most of us are, anyway—inquisitive. We like to know the *why* of things, of causes and their effects (though often the question is reconstructive: We know the effect and seek, now, the cause). Much of life is devoted to *why*, because so little of life provides easy, satisfying answers to that question.

We ask the question as a society, too, but as a society we too often do settle for the easy answer, even though it may well be the wrong one or an incomplete one.

The answer to *why?* is important because it allows us to come to terms with both ourselves and the world around us, to exercise some control. If the reason our head hurts is that the ladder slipped out from under us, we can reason our way to putting the ladder on firmer footing next time.

But because that question is often so difficult to answer, it can make us vulnerable to manipulation and open us to the machinations of those who want control not so much of the world around them but of us. One way of doing this is to answer the question not with a proof but with a statistical correlation which may suggest the path to a proof but which is not proof itself, even though it might be and probably is stated as one.

Here is a fact that you may not know: Of the thousands of people who contract the incurable, terminal, and painful disease of pancreatic cancer each year, almost all have at one time or another eaten celery.

Why, then, are there not huge campaigns urging people to live celery-free lives in hope of staving off this dread disease?

The reason is a very good one: Celery (probably) has nothing at all to do with cancer of the pancreas.

The above example, admittedly and deliberately ridiculous, but true, is to illustrate the danger of using correlation—two things statistically coincident at least to some extent—as a synonym for causation, which is a phenomenon in which one thing invariably leads to another, or in which one thing is invariably the result of another. Correlation is easy to establish; causation, very difficult. But researchers, the news media, and the legal profession have come to use the two almost interchangeably. This makes minor discoveries seem big, minor stories into headline grabbers, and law firm coffers bulge. It happens because we allow it to happen. We allow it to happen because we are urged to—by researchers, the media, and lawyers.

Let's start with the basics: Life ends in death. With the exception of those persons who are alive at this moment, every person ever born has gone on to die. We can reasonably presume that this is the fate, too, of those to whom it has not yet happened. The intervening details vary, but not the beginning and the end. Based on this *correlation* of life and death through history, we have reasonably concluded that we, too, shall die. We cannot, however, *prove* that this is so, nor shall we be able to produce such a proof for as long as there is one person alive. The statistical evidence is, of course, overwhelming, and the correlation allows us to make the assumption with some confidence. But that last little leap, from statistical near-certainty to absolute certainty does not exist.

There is very little having to do with human existence that can be proved, and a great deal that can *almost* be proved. Those things that can be proved get their proofs from scientific examination and under-standing of the mechanics involved, resulting in an experiment the results of which remain constant no matter how many times the experiment is done. Statistics can provide proof *only* when everything being measured is accounted for. If a little child has one hundred marbles and fifty of them are blue and thirty are red and twenty are green, it can be said with certainty that 50 percent of them are blue, 30 percent are red, and 20 percent are green. What cannot be said with any certainty at all is that these percentages have anything to do with other marbles or with the propensity of marble makers to favor one color or the other. It could be that the machine at the marble factory fills the marble bags at random. It could be that the machine is set to provide fifty of one color chosen at random, and thirty of another, and twenty of another. It could be that there are other marble factories that do things differently. It could be that the child received one bag of fifty blue marbles, one bag of thirty red marbles, and one bag of twenty green ones. It could be that he received 150 marbles, fifty of each color, and lost thirty green ones and twenty red ones. All we can learn from the spectral census of the marbles is how many are there, now, in just that group.

The first chapter of this book warned against overgeneralizing— and I generalize, correctly, I think, in saying that most generalizations are overgeneralizations. But correlations involving humans are just that: an attempt to take a limited body of data and to project it over the entire population or some subset thereof. This can be as misleading as an attempt to say something about all marbles based on those belonging to one child.

To carry the marble example one step farther before being done with it, there is, actually, something that *can* be learned about all marbles from that one bag. It comes when the observer learns what the marbles are used for, which reveals that marbles are spherical. This is not based on statistics but instead on observation of their characteristics and how well suited they are for what it is they are supposed to do. It is possible to err here, though, again through over-generalization. Glancing around the child's room and finding a variety of balls, the observer might incorrectly conclude that toys in general are spherical. The statistician might even come up with a correlation between toyness and spherical geometry, and, who knows, armed with the statistics, a toymaker might decide that it's a definite advantage in the toy world for things to be globular, which might be disproved when spherical teddy bears fail to catch on.

Human beings are not spherical—despite the current cries of an "obesity epidemic" that might leave one thinking so. We come in all different shapes and sizes, and we all work differently, have different thoughts, different values, and different propensities. We have differing physiologies, too.

Science has learned a great deal about human beings, about things that we have in common. Human anatomy is largely understood, as is a vast amount of human physiology. We know how the body absorbs and uses oxygen. We know how food is put to work. We know a great deal, but we do not know everything. About anybody.

Our science has taught us a great deal about infectious disease, too. There are diseases in which a particular microbe is invariably present.

But here we must pause, for here we hit a correlative bump. Everyone who has a particular disease also has a particular microbe (and by further research it might even be possible to determine, not by correlation but by observation, how the microbe brings about the symptoms of the disease). But does everyone who has been exposed to the microbe come down with the disease? The answer is almost always no.

Why not?

It might be possible, with observation, to determine why it is that some people are vulnerable to a particular microbe and some are not. But this poses some practical problems. How do you find people who are infected with a disease but who exhibit no symptoms? It can be done, with modern testing and a huge number of people to test. The obvious solution is to collect a group of volunteers, infect them all, and test the ones who don't show any symptoms. But for ethical reasons, there are many pathogens for which this is not possible.

So we do our best. First, we try to isolate and cultivate the microbe in a culture medium of some sort. Then, we try to infect laboratory animals with it, though as we have seen this is becoming more difficult due to the efforts of the animal rights crowd. From this we learn, perhaps, a great deal about the microbe's effects—on that particular kind of lab animal. We're still a considerable distance from knowing anything reliably useful about the microbe's relation to humans.

Or we take a different approach, which merges observation with statistics. A good example is the current concern over the West Nile virus. Blood tests on numerous people have shown that this microbe has a broad range of effects, from no symptoms at all, to a mild illness, to serious illness, to fatal disease.

Why? Why do some people die, some show no symptoms at all, and still others display symptoms covering the range in between?

Observational science and experimentation might provide an answer. Perhaps there is some other mild illness that produces varying levels of immunity to the effects of West Nile. Perhaps we have genetic propensities one way or the other. Perhaps is it the degree of exposure, as is the case with poisons, where a little exposure produces a little illness but a great exposure kills you.

At the same time, it might be useful to do a little supportive correlation by trapping mosquitoes. Do all of them carry the disease? Do relatively few? Is there some answer to be found by looking here?

One of the most important skills any researcher can master is the design of experiments. The purpose is to gain control over every variable, so as to isolate them, one by one, and determine which one or combination thereof leads to the results. It is not easy by any measure. Merely identifying all the variables is a daunting, often prohibitively difficult, task. Consider the mosquito traps mentioned above. How can researchers be sure that mosquitoes that carry West Nile are not more vulnerable to traps than other mosquitoes, or less so? Certainly, using different kinds of traps, which appeal to mosquitoes in different ways, is a possibility. But in the end, no one can be certain that all the variables have been adequately taken into account. And this is the great pitfall of correlational analyses of data: At best, correlations can provide a suggestion for further study, not an answer to the question itself. If every mosquito in every trap of every kind proved to host the virus, the suggestion would be a strong one, but even then there could not be an absolute statement saying that every mosquito, or even every mosquito in a given area, is infected. There are too many variables. And this is just mosquitoes we're talking about here!

Humans are an order of magnitude more difficult to grab by their correlational handle. There is an enormous number of variables in each of us. Reconstructive causality is far more easily suggested by statistical analysis than is predictive causality. That is to say it is easier to take a given effect and produce a statistically suggestive cause than it is to try to predict the incidence of something statistically. This only makes sense: Every woman who is pregnant experienced a sperm cell penetrating an egg cell, but not every incident of intercourse (even where no birth control is employed) results in pregnancy.

But experiments involving broad aspects of human life are almost impossible to construct, because it is almost impossible to account for every variable. Sheer chance plays a huge role in all our lives. We have difficulty enough keeping track of our own, singular existence. I know of two young people, both lawyers in big-city firms, who were married. Very much in love, they decided to devote some years to very hard work, to amassing enough money that they could retire at an early age and enjoy their lives together. They worked long hours, able to spend little time together, but they were happy because they were working toward their goal. These nice, bright, happy young people seemed to be doing it right, planning ahead, sacrificing now in hope of reward later. But then she was diagnosed as having a rare and virulent cancer. In the space of a year she was dead. In her final days, they anguished over how little of the time together they had so cherished they had actually allowed themselves to spend together. There is no statistical survey that can take that kind of thing into account, or even inform our decisions, because statistically that young couple had a plan that made sense, little comfort though that is to the grieving widower.

Statistics have their uses, but they are often put to use in ways for which they are not suited. The average temperature and other weather for a particular place on a particular date is an interesting datum, but it is nowhere nearly as helpful when going to the beach as are the current observations and short-term predictions. The average day, like the average person, doesn't exist. The moon's temperature at its equator varies from the boiling point to 200 degrees below zero, for an average temperature of zero. But the places where it is actually zero are few, and the time they are at that temperature is limited. By describing the average, we are providing no real description of the place at all!

So it is with people, and so it is with correlational analyses. First, it is impossible to take in all the variables, so we cannot be sure that we are measuring what we are trying to measure. Second, the results would apply only to the hypothetical average person. This means, simply, that for individuals—as we all are—correlations are of some use, but that use is to aid us in asking questions, because correlations are not and cannot be answers unto themselves.

Correlations are considered as proof of cause by the lazy, when there is always more work to do. For every statistical suggestion, a new *why?* is raised. Yet this is all glossed over as statistical findings are reported, and soon a correlational pointer is taken instead as fact by people living their lives, by the news media, and in courts. Inconclusive evidence becomes, effectively, proof.

But by its very nature—questions as to variables, the attempt to go from the over-general to the specific—correlational analysis is subject not just to error but to abuse. It is possible to cook up a statistical "experiment" that will provide very nearly any result that is desired. It is in this way especially that statistical analysis differs from observational experimentation.

So someone who seeks to prove a particular point sets up a survey seeking to support that point, skewed in that direction deliberately or not. The survey is taken, the results are as hoped, and the person seeking to prove the point publishes the findings, with certain hope that those findings will be reported with no disclaimers whatsoever.

We need to be on guard for this as we weigh the information we employ in deciding how we live our lives. Unfortunately, separating the useful information from the misdirected results designed to gain control over us is difficult and getting harder all the time.

13

BAD SCIENCE AND TOBACCO

When you turn on the television today, between the advertisements for lawyers who are hoping you will sue someone, you might find advertisements from tobacco companies.

Wait a minute! Tobacco ads were banned a long time ago. The Marlboro Man who rode through the rugged West accompanied by the theme from *The Magnificent Seven* is long dead. So to see tobacco company advertisements on television is curious indeed. Of course, these ads encourage you *not* to smoke! Yes, the tobacco companies purchase advertisements encouraging you not to use their chief product—cigarettes. These ads often point you to company Web sites which offer information on smoking cessation and on teaching your children not to smoke.

If this does not make sense to you, it is not your thought processes which have gone off-kilter. The antismoking campaign sponsored by the tobacco companies comes from—who else?—government and lawyers, supported by meddlers, do-gooders, and the ever-present group of people who are always willing to join the mob. It's part of the "tobacco settlement," in which the states and the federal government took on the (perfectly legal, by the way) tobacco industry, the idea being that tobacco use causes diseases that the states and federal government end up paying for. The settlement, it was argued, would cover the costs of these illnesses. (You might be wondering why, if cigarettes are so terrible, there is no outright ban on them. The answer is simple: Cigarette taxes are a huge source of revenue for government; indeed, there have been reports of state governments complaining that anti-smoking campaigns have been too effective and that tax revenues from cigarette sales have therefore been below expectations.)

While founded on a fiction (diseases attributed to smoking end up costing the government less than the cost of medical care for non-smokers) and the money didn't go where it was supposed to go (billions of dollars went to lawyers, while the rest was used for government projects that in many cases had little or nothing to do with health), the settlement was accepted uncritically, despite its many unforeseen effects.

But first a little history.

Smokers have been suing tobacco companies for their various cancers and lung disease since the 1950s. Juries had not been sympathetic to these suits, because the health dangers of tobacco have been widely assumed for many decades.

As long ago as 1892, for instance, the Senate Committee on Epidemic Diseases concluded that cigarettes were a public health hazard, rejecting a petition to ban cigarettes nationwide only because constitutional authority in the matter was seen as reserved to the states. The committee urged people who wanted cigarettes banned to seek redress from state legislatures. By 1909, fifteen states had passed legislation banning the sale of cigarettes. As with prohibition of the sale of alcohol nationally a decade later, these laws failed. Kansas did not drop its ban until 1927, the last state to do so.

On January 11, 1964, the surgeon general's Advisory Committee on Smoking and Health released a 387-page report that concluded that cigarette smoking is a cause of lung cancer and laryngeal cancer in men, a probable cause of lung cancer in women, and the most important cause of chronic bronchitis. The committee stated, "Cigarette smoking is a health hazard of sufficient importance in the United States to warrant appropriate remedial action." It was based on seven thousand articles in medical literature at the time. The original report has been followed by two dozen more, with the number of diseases now attributed to smoking so high, the scope so vast, that if the reports are to be believed, it is a wonder that anyone who has ever smoked is still alive to tell of it.

None of those reports has provided proof that justifies the conclusions. The majority of smokers do not get lung or laryngeal cancer, and an enormous number of victims of those diseases are not and have not been smokers. Thus, the public health model is grossly abused when it comes to smoking. There is, to this day, no proof that anyone has ever gotten cancer as a result of smoking. There is a statistical correlation which specifies that smokers are more likely to contract cancer (and suffer bronchitis, heart disease, and other ailments) than nonsmokers. We are asked to make the logical leap to the conclusion that because of that correlation, smoking is therefore the cause of cancer and other diseases. Recent years have seen an addition, the claim that the mere smelling of tobacco smoke causes cancer and other diseases. The correlation here is itself shaky, and there is no strong statistical evidence to bolster the claim.

Meanwhile, the correlation-equals-cause relationship between smoking and cancer is accepted as a truism (in what other area is the government's word taken without question?), to the extent that it is published as fact and to the extent that things such as the "tobacco settlement" have come to pass based solely on "proof" that doesn't really exist. And because of the secondhand smoke canard, smokers are now consigned to the social basement.

Nevertheless, it was decided that cigarette packages needed to carry warnings, so that smokers upon reading them might become ex-smokers.

The surgeon general's warnings have appeared on cigarette packages since 1966, explicitly preempting suits against the tobacco industry based on inadequate warnings. Juries, therefore, have repeatedly found that those who choose to smoke bear responsibility for the consequences of their choice.

In the 1990s, lawyers representing smokers in class action suits for damages against tobacco companies tried a new approach. They went to the attorneys general of several states. Because Medicaid budgets now cover much of the cost of treatment of cancers and respiratory diseases, and tobacco use is said to be a contributory factor in many of these diseases, they argued, tobacco companies should compensate the government for these expenditures.

This was a novel approach in law. The traditional rule was that a physician who provided services to a patient could not recover damages from another party if the victim had no cause of action against that party himself. If smokers were personally responsible for the consequences of smoking, the state-as-physician was not entitled to any damages not recoverable by the patient himself. But even if this precedent were reversed, the factual case is sorely lacking.

In fact, smoking imposes no net cost on government. Smokers pay

Social Security and Medicare payroll taxes, but the diseases attributed to smoking are diseases that shorten lives more than they lead to the need for prolonged, expensive care faced by sufferers of other ailments. Because most pension and health-care costs are concentrated in the late years of life, smokers are self-financing for every state as well as the federal government. Indeed, each pack of cigarettes sold saves over sixty cents in state and federal spending, according to W. Kip Viscusi of Harvard. When the existing taxes of fifty-six cents per pack of cigarettes are added in, smokers actually generate a net surplus of over a dollar a pack to government. Nonsmokers, in contrast, collect far more in Social Security and Medicare costs than they pay in taxes, thus imposing a net cost on government. Smokers thus actually subsidize the state health-care costs of nonsmokers.

Some lawyers took another tack, arguing that tobacco companies caused people to smoke who would otherwise not have done so, by denying the risks associated with smoking. If these people had known the real risk, they argue, they would not have smoked. Certainly tobacco companies tried to downplay the risks of smoking in the past, but they also (as long ago as the 1920s) made health claims that highlighted comparative health risks of their competitors—until prohibited by government from doing so.

What is more, surveys indicate that people tend actually to overestimate the risks of smoking. Anywhere from 6 to 13 percent of smokers will contract lung cancer due to smoking over the course of a lifetime, according to studies by the surgeon general, yet surveys indicate that Americans estimate that 38 to 48 percent will do so. Likewise, surveys show that people estimate that 50 to 54 percent of smokers will die from causes due to smoking, while the surgeon general's studies suggest that the actual proportion ranges from 18 to 36 percent. It appears that the attempt by tobacco companies to downplay the risks of smoking failed. If the logic of the antismoking litigation is sound, we must conclude that if people had a more accurate perception of the risks of smoking, the proportion who smoke would actually be higher.

Bear in mind, too, that nonsmokers also get cancer and other diseases that are attributed to smoking. While the incidence of these diseases is lower among nonsmokers, it leaves us with a public health model conundrum: The diseases appear among some who smoke but also some who do not, and some who smoke remain healthy as do some do not smoke. Even in the most pessimistic statistical analyses, smoking correlates to very serious disease in far less than half of smokers. All of which means that there is more, or less, here than meets the eye. Perhaps smoking contributes to an increased incidence of some diseases—but what, then, are the other factors? Perhaps some people themselves have an increased propensity toward certain diseases which is exacerbated by smoking. We do not know, and part of the reason we don't is that people with something to gain—power, money—stopped looking when a powerful and wealthy industry appeared in their sights. It then became less a search for scientific truth than a search for a legal way of separating that industry from its money, which it had legally obtained from willing consumers. In the research community, there is money to be made by pinning yet another disease upon tobacco and creating another class of plaintiff on behalf of which lawyers can enrich themselves by suing.

It seems likely that one reason why people overestimate the risks of smoking is the constant bombardment of antismoking propaganda. If that is the case, groups such as the Campaign for Tobacco-Free Kids, American Legacy Foundation, and Truth.org, who seek to increase the number of nonsmokers, are imposing net costs on the federal treasury. If tobacco companies were forced to pay for phantom costs attributed to smoking, perhaps these groups should reimburse the government for the costs of their own activities. Instead, these groups actually receive more than $1.45 billion from the tobacco settlement to increase their propaganda.

When the tobacco companies settled with the state attorneys general, the settlement was not in the traditional form of damages payments, but a negotiated penalty on future cigarette sales that amounted to an additional tax on cigarettes of thirty-three cents per pack. The penalty was to be paid not by tobacco companies, but entirely by future smokers. Because the "tax" is to be paid on all future cigarette sales, regardless of the risk of the cigarettes, it destroyed the incentive to develop less risky cigarettes, such as the Premiere brand, test-marketed in 1988, which was said to carry no cancer risk.

The $243 billion tobacco settlements went not to plaintiffs allegedly harmed by tobacco companies, but to the states, where it has been used for a wide variety of projects including, ironically, $42 million in new subsidies for tobacco farmers in North Carolina and a bailout of Florida tobacco companies. Additionally, the settlements restricted advertising and penalized new entrants to the tobacco markets in the various states, thus guaranteeing the market shares of existing firms. This revenue stream has greatly increased the government's interest in the continuation and expansion of smoking—which may explain why its heavy-handed antitobacco propaganda seems tailor-made to backfire upon youth who resent being told what to do by government. As humorist and former smoker Dave Barry put it, "The underlying moral principle of these lawsuits was: 'You are knowingly selling a product that kills tens of thousands of our citizens each year. We want a piece of that action!'"

Billions of dollars of the settlements went to plaintiffs' attorneys who were retained to represent the interests of state governments without any competitive bidding process. Among those who tried to cash in were the brother-in-law of the then Senate Majority Leader Trent Lott and Hillary Clinton's brother Hugh Rodham, who arranged to have then President Clinton videotape a tribute to the Castano Group of lawyers. They billed fees of $4.3 billion, which was reduced by one court to $1.25 billion, then thrown out altogether by another court. Six New York law firms received fees of $625 million, amounting to a rate of $13,000 an hour. They later came under ethics investigation by the New York Supreme Court.

This "tax" was not imposed by legislatures, but as a result of closed-door negotiations between tobacco companies and state attorneys general. As a result, the process lacked the checks and balances provided by the legislative process. It circumvented the public comment required for regulatory action, made an end run around "sunshine" laws requiring public disclosure of proceedings affecting the public, and avoided the involvement of legislatures accountable to the public for raising taxes. In short, it established an extraconstitutional precedent that could be used against any other industry.

It would be bad enough if it stopped there, but it didn't.

Emboldened by the tobacco settlement, numerous state legislatures added new taxes to the price of a pack of cigarettes, running the price well above five dollars in many locales.

There is an economic term called "price elasticity of demand," and what it states is this: Some products are more sensitive to changes in price than are others. If you raise the prices of some products, so many people will stop using them that you will end up losing money. Some products are so eagerly sought that a price increase will have little effect on sales, so the money will roll in.

It was long thought that cigarettes were so inelastic, as the economists term it, that unit sales would remain constant even with substantial increases in price.

But even a fairly inelastic product has its limits, and so it has been with cigarettes. It is possible to raise the price of a thing so high that people stop using it. The revenue expected from the new taxes on cigarettes has in no state met projections, because those taxes raised the price of cigarettes to a level where an unexpectedly large number of people simply stopped smoking.

There has been another unintended effect: The increased cost of cigarettes has disproportionately taxed the poor. The tax systems in most places in the country, and certainly at the federal level, is "progressive," which is to say that it is supposed to collect more from the rich than it does from the poor. Smoking has traditionally been among the "luxuries" that even the poor indulged in, because the cost of cigarettes was low. Now, with a carton of cigarettes costing in some cases $50 or more, the economic burden on people of limited means has become considerable, or else they are to be denied even this luxury, which is, after all, perfectly legal.

Cigarette smoking has been so thoroughly demonized that one would not be exaggerating to say that there are those who put forth not the view that a single cigarette will kill you but instead that *no cigarettes at all* will kill you, that even if you never smoked, you can still be killed by cigarettes. This, of course, is the story of secondhand smoke. It is proposed that tobacco smoke in enclosed environments—or, now, even in unenclosed ones—kills a certain number of people each year. And that number is high.

The National Cancer Institute published a monograph in 1999 that alleges that secondhand smoke is deadly, causing cancers of the nose, throat, and lungs, bronchitis, pneumonia, and even Sudden Infant

Death Syndrome. Reports in the journal *Circulation* say that second-hand smoke kills 53,000 Americans each year.

How do they know? They don't, because as with other diseases attributed to smoking, there is not a single case in which it can be proved that secondhand smoke was the *cause* of disease or death. There is statistical correlation, to be sure. But as we have seen, statistical correlation is an interesting pointer, not proof by itself. We are still stuck with this problem: There is no predictable, repeatable experiment in which it can be said that secondhand smoke is fatal (beyond one in which a person is placed in a room so rich with the stuff that he or she would suffocate as with any other smoke or, for that matter, any of many naturally occurring gases). The only health effect that can be certainly ascribed to smoking is that it is possible to burn oneself with a cigarette, cigar, or pipe. Beyond that, there are statistical suggestions only.

Now: Those correlations, those suggestions, are unquestionably worthy of interest. But they are a step on the path, not the destination. A study that stops with the news that there is a correlation between smoking and premature death has proved nothing except that correlation. It has not pinned down a cause.

Here's an example. There have been studies that show that drinking and smoking together are correlated to a higher incidence of certain cancers and other diseases than is either activity alone. That is an interesting datum, but it merely opens up new lines of inquiry: In that drinking and smoking are both widely perceived as having negative effects on one's health, might it be that persons who engage in those activities together live lives in which they do other things that might be unwholesome, that express little regard for their own health and well-being? More important, why doesn't everyone who both smokes and drinks contract these diseases?

154

It may well be that at some point a connection between smoking and disease, a regimen whereby it can be shown that for some group of people smoking always produces disease, will be discovered. But that hasn't happened yet, and until it does happen, the job has not been done—certainly not enough to accept it as a fact that smoking and even secondhand smoke are causes of death. Yet researchers have rushed into print study results that overstate their significance (which in the very competitive scramble for research dollars, plus the perfectly natural desire to be seen as doing important work, is not at all surprising), the news media are eager to pick up on studies the limits of which they do not understand and which in any case make better stories if they are overgeneralized; and, of course, lawyers are circling, eager to swoop down and collect money.

Oddly, while the government funds all manner of studies designed to encourage us not to smoke, it also collects taxes from us which are paid to tobacco growers as subsidies designed to make sure that tobacco growing is profitable. In June 2004, for instance, the U.S. House of Representatives approved $9.6 billion in buyout subsidies for tobacco growers. That comes to about $33 for every man, woman, and child in the country. Does that make any sense? Only in the odd world of Washington, where keeping the favor of special interest groups while also seeking to give individuals the impression that the government is doing good are both important to those who seek to remain in power.

The fact is that smoking is legal, and some people enjoy it. It may or may not result in the deaths of some of those people. But something causes the death of each and every one of us. People often die doing things they find pleasurable. A reporter friend points to numerous stories he has written about hobbyist fliers whose airplanes crashed, and the fact that in each of them the headline (which he didn't write) was a variation of "Dead Pilot Loved to Fly." That makes sense—if he hated to fly, he probably wouldn't have been flying.

Almost everything carries a risk, and the reason I say "almost" is that maybe out there someplace there is an activity that is entirely risk-free. But life always ends in death. Some people die in their sleep at age one hundred, while some drop dead while playing tennis at twenty-five. Some are killed while doing things they love, and others die at jobs they hate. It is not, in most cases, predictable.

What is predictable is that a lot of people would not care to live lives devoted solely to their own safety, to nothing more than extending the duration of their lives. Many people do things that they do not have to do that endanger their lives. That is part of our nature as people, part of our inquisitiveness and our desire for excitement and learning. It is among the natural rights that Thomas Jefferson recommended in the Declaration of Independence, because it has much to do with our liberty and pursuit of happiness.

Just under half of the marriages undertaken in the U.S. today end in divorce. There have been numerous studies conducted that show a correlation between divorce and illness and early death. Are we then to fear and avoid marriage? Is the surgeon general issuing reports advising us to do so? Are there warning labels affixed to marriage licenses?

It would be wonderful if it could be determined what circumstances invariably lead smoking to cause illness and death, just as it would be wonderful if it could be predicted with precision which marriages will end in divorce. If those things could be presented as repeatable, irrefutable facts, people would know what to avoid and when, unless disease or divorce or both were their goal.

Until such facts are determined and made available—and with the vast variation among people it is doubtful that they will ever be—it might be wise to wonder why it is that some life-threatening pursuits are widely praised while others are excoriated. It might make sense to become a little annoyed by the judgments attached to correlations. And it certainly makes sense that you are the one who needs to try to measure risks versus rewards and decide which activities, including smoking, return pleasures that make the bargain something with which you are comfortable.

All the while bearing in mind that you have no right to tell others that they must follow your lead, or that they are responsible for the results of your decisions.

14

ADDICTION

In well over half a century in the field, I have yet to encounter an addictive substance. Before you disregard that statement (and perhaps with it the other things contained in this book), let me explain.

In that the public health model is currently applied to substances, let us investigate what this would involve. Remember, the public health model requires a triad of infectious agent, host, and environment. Given these things, we are to believe that an effect invariably results. In the case of addiction, the substance itself is the agent, in the way that a microorganism is the agent in the study of infectious disease. The host is the user of the substance. The environment is the circumstance under which the substance is used. Though in the public health model not all those who have been exposed to an infectious agent necessarily come down with the corresponding symptoms—the environment is not right within those asymptomatic individuals—all those who have the disease are infected.

But this is not true of "addictive" substances. Not everyone who consumes those substances becomes "addicted," and not all those who show the symptoms of addiction do so as a result of some substance. For purposes of gaining power over people, authorities may well be assigning the ponderous word "addiction" to things that are, in many cases, merely matters of habit.

Why would they do this? One reason is obvious: No one would take very seriously government agencies and great medical institutions with the phrase "bad habits" in their titles (and even this would make a leap beyond evidence, for not all of these habits are necessarily bad for all people in all circumstances), while the word "addiction" implies a serious medical condition over which we should all be concerned. But there are other reasons, too.

In August 2004, French researchers announced the discovery that rats can become addicted to cocaine. The rodents were allowed to trigger a device that would inject cocaine into them over a three-month period. Then the cocaine was withdrawn. The triggering mechanism now produced no cocaine but instead electric shocks to the rats' feet. The researchers found that 17 percent of the rats continued to seek the cocaine anyway.

This, the researchers said, proved "addiction," because the rats continued to try to obtain something that had given them pleasure even in the face of adverse consequences. But by that definition, much that we do could be described as an addiction. Plain old observation suggests that a lot more than 17 percent of motorists, given the chance, exceed the posted speed limit despite the sense that going faster increases the likelihood of accident, injury, even death. Much that we do, from work that we do not especially love to eating food that we do not especially like, involves the acceptance of unpleasantness in exchange for a desired goal.

To say nothing of the 83 percent of the rats that *didn't* get "addicted."

Might this study just as easily be cited as evidence that some rats are not as bright, or perhaps some are more tenacious, than others?

It used to be said that wine makes one merry, that tobacco focuses the mind and calms the nerves, and that coffee wakes you up. The temptation to overindulge in such pleasures, like the temptation to overindulge in sexual gratification or overeating, it was taught, must be resisted.

For example, while the Torah teaches that "wine . . . cheereth God and man," and that God "causeth . . . to grow . . . wine that maketh glad the heart of man," it also says, "Put a knife to thy throat, if thou be a man given to gluttony," and, "The drunkard and the glutton shall come to poverty." Likewise, while the Gospels speak of Jesus making and sharing wine, Luke admonishes, "Take heed to yourselves, lest at any time your hearts be overcharged with surfeiting, and drunkenness."

Nor was this view specifically Judeo-Christian. The Greeks regarded the fierce struggle against desire to be the normal state of affairs. "Moderation in all things. Nothing in excess," said Socrates. Aristotle listed moderation among the moral virtues, and Paraclesus wrote, "The dose makes the poison."

The classical view was that pleasure should be temporary in order not to become painful. Socrates agreed with Protarchus's statement in Plato's *Philebus:* "Excess of pleasure possessing the minds of fools and wantons becomes madness." Pleasurable as the state of male sexual arousal is, for example, it becomes, when persistent, a condition known as priapism that is described by its sufferers as among the most painful experiences of their lives.

Typically, "addiction" is applied to the use of mind-altering substances, particularly ones that produce euphoria of some kind or pleasure, and which, therefore, may impart a desire on the part of the user to have more. But these mind-altering substances do not always possess qualities that cause users to immediately want more or to be immoderate in their use. Nor is moderation in the use of psychotropic substances a monopoly of the West. Many people labor under the misconception that hallucinogenic drugs owe their origin and manufacture to clandestine chemists. Yet fungi and plants are hallucinogen chemists *par excellence.* Every human culture save the Eskimos has used some botanically or mycologically derived hallucinogen. Such use typically does not produce what anyone describes as physical addictions but instead excites the brain, producing visions and emotional experiences of an intensity far beyond that of everyday experience.

The religious or spiritual use of hallucinogens in Africa, Asia, and the Americas was not associated with dependence on the drugs involved, because these substances were regarded as sacred, to be used respectfully, ritually. Such strictures built moderation into the use of these drugs in these various cultures.

This ethical approach, with its emphasis on personal responsibility for temperance, is today considered very old-fashioned, unscientific, and unfashionable. The current view is much more complicated, invoking such concepts as stimulus-reward, neurotransmitters, and endorphins. The individual is helpless before his genetic predisposition and such environmental factors as early childhood trauma and corporate advertising.

The chemical state of the brain, it is now assumed, determines one's mental state. Neglected is the fact that one's mental state itself has been shown to change the chemical state of the brain. That the individual possesses untapped reserves of power within himself, power to overcome tremendous adversity, to perform heroic feats, is seldom mentioned by the experts. For when people are aware of their own potential, what need have they of experts? Far better for the expert to persuade you of your powerlessness, the more to aggrandize his own power over you.

But there is more. If you are powerless over your tendency to improperly use substances, you can scarcely be held responsible for doing so. Political correctness here again is the handmaid of those who would exercise power over others. As a result, in the name of "helping" a "victim," control is gained.

Some people, the experts say, are genetically predisposed to have "addictive personalities"; others may have been conditioned to be that way by their upbringing or by advertising. Such people cannot help themselves, but must turn over their personal responsibility and power to the experts. In doing so, they also turn over their self-respect.

Present theories assume some pharmacologic property of a substance, or else some inbred genetic programming, turns a person into an addict, and that addiction is irreversible and follows the same inevitable course for everyone. Yet it is well-established that many people with a family history of addiction, and an early environment shaped by it, do not become addicts, while many others without any of these factors do become addicts. The "environment" portion of the public health model as applied to addiction here falls entirely apart.

Moreover, many addicts quit, and most do so without expert help. Heroin was once regarded as the most addictive substance known to man. Yet government surveys show that the vast majority of people who have tried heroin are not addicts; even people who have used heroin for years "mature out" by their mid-twenties—not because of disease or death, but because they just stop. Three years after the end of the Vietnam War, 88 percent of returning veterans who had said they were addicted to heroin had quit. Why? U.S. heroin was expensive and of poor quality, they said, and their parents and girlfriends disapproved. (Perhaps social stigma is not always a bad thing.)

Never was the doctrine of genetic and environmental determinism in addiction more loudly trumpeted than in the hysteria over "crack babies" in the 1980s. Yet follow-up studies of children born addicted to crack found that they did not have more severe problems than other, nonaddicted children born in similar circumstances. "Their average developmental functioning level is normal. They are no different from other children growing up. They are not the retarded imbeciles people talk about," said Dr. Ira Chasnoff, an original discoverer of fetal cocaine syndrome. "As I study the problem more and more, I think the placenta does a better job of protecting the child than we do as a society."

The truth is that individual, situational, and cultural variables are more important in addiction than genetic factors, environment, or the properties of the substance involved. Addiction is a way of coping, which an individual can change in time with a changing attitude to life and circumstances.

Addiction, though real, is not purely biological. Reactions to pharmacological experience involve a person's expectations: Experiments have shown that people who unknowingly consume alcohol show little sign of drunkenness, while those who think they are consuming alcohol (but are not) convince themselves they are drunk and act the part. This manifestation of the placebo effect, a bugaboo of researchers in many fields, demonstrates again the impossibility of accurately generalizing about human beings.

Even withdrawal and craving involve expectations: Many nineteenth-century narcotic users failed to become addicted because they did not know narcotics were addictive. When the local drug store served children Coca-Cola laced with cocaine for a nickel, and their mothers used laudanum (opium) to quiet crying babies, regular narcotic users held jobs, raised families, and were virtually typical citizens.

Perhaps the best-known example was Sigmund Freud, who was not only a cocaine user, but whose first scientific paper, *über Coca* ("On Cocaine"), published in 1884, hailed the drug as a panacea for fatigue, asthma, indigestion, morphine addiction, alcoholism, depression, autism, and especially lack of sexual appetite. (The trajectory of cocaine from panacea to demonized substance is one we have seen many times before and since. Even tobacco was once prescribed by European physicians for headaches, colds, rheumatism, asthma, ulcers, and giddiness. In London in 1665, Eton boys were required to smoke each morning as a defense against the Black Plague.)

Nor was the ability of people to live successful lives while using such substances limited to the nineteenth century. Much of the behavior ascribed to addicts is instead based on the search for the desired substance rather than its direct effects. "It doesn't happen often," said one doctor at a 1962 White House conference on drug abuse, "but once in a while, one of the so-called vilest addicts in East Harlem finds a doctor who gives him drugs or he gets an easy source from a friend. Under these conditions, he is likely to keep a job, maintain his family intact, and cut out his criminal activity. We see more of this kind of adjustment among middle-class and wealthy addicts who either have a medical disease which gives them a legal excuse for acquiring a regular supply, or who discover a brave doctor. With these people you see no social deterioration. I've yet to see a well-to-do addict arrested."

From its pinnacle as a wonder drug in Freud's day, cocaine is now reviled as the most addictive of drugs, far more addictive than heroin. Yet only one in five of the people who use cocaine actually become addicted to it. The recovery rate for cocaine users is about 90 percent compared to 40–50 percent for heroin.

Most drugs do not appear to be physically addictive. The evidence, so far, suggests that neither marijuana nor amphetamines is physiologically addictive. Nor is the theory that cannabis acts as a "gateway" to harder drugs supported by the data. "There is no conclusive evidence that the drug effects of marijuana are causally linked to the subsequent abuse of other illicit drugs," according to a 1999 report from the National Academy of Sciences' Institute of Medicine.

Marijuana, among the most readily available and commonly used of the illicit substances, has not been accused of causing physical addiction. So those who have decided that it must not be allowed (but that its use is not the bad act of someone who makes the decision to do it, and is instead the "disease" of its "victims") have declared that it produces "psychological dependence."

What is "psychological dependence"? It is habit. It is something one regularly does because one likes it or because it makes one feel more comfortable. I know someone who makes a point of organizing his pants pockets: the change and car and house keys go in the front right pocket, a small penknife in his front left pocket. It imposes a sense of order on his life, and when he needs any of those things, he automatically reaches into the appropriate pocket. If he does not find the sought-after item, he becomes alarmed to a degree, and his day is somewhat upset until the order of things—the proper placement of the items in his pockets—is restored. Is he "psychologically addicted" to having those items in their customary places? Is he a "victim" of those items? Of course not. Like all of us, he is a creature of habit, seeking to impose some order on his life in a terrifyingly random world. It is fine that we seek control over our own lives, even as it is not fine that others seek control over us.

In this case, as with many habits, my friend arrived at his arrangement of things out of perfectly sound reasoning. He did not like to have to search for his car keys, and if they were invariably in that front right pocket he would not have to do so; likewise a quarter for the parking meter or his knife when he needed to open a package. Most children are taught the slogan "A place for everything and everything in its place," and rare is the parent who would regret the child who adopted that slogan as a matter of habit, even to the point of not being able to fully enjoy play until the room is tidied.

As substances can be used to excess, to the point of abuse, so can habits be overaccented to the point of becoming obsessions. We might define this as the point at which a habit becomes so powerful that the habit alone remains after the (often very good, as we have seen) reason for it is pushed into the background. For example, I know of a family that is obsessed, or nearly so, with an aversion to what they call "clutter." Less is more, they believe, and their motto is "If in doubt, throw it out." That is a fine motto for some, but it can be taken to an extreme. And I know of someone who never throws anything away, the idea being that it might one day be of use or of value. Are these persons addicted? Let us return to moderation: Neither of these behaviors, in moderation, is anything more than a habit derived from a matter of taste, an approach that has perfectly sound reasoning behind it. But what happens when the fight against clutter or the desire to save everything that passes through our lives becomes an end unto itself? What happens when those matters of taste adversely affect our relations with others and make even our own lives less convenient—on one hand, throwing away something one needs in daily life; on the other hand, being unable to move through one's home without bumping into piles of things saved against the imaginary day when they will be needed? That is a problem, though whether it is an addiction depends on a very loose definition of the word.

"You sure have a lot of stuff," a person who saves everything might be told. To the person making the remark it is a criticism, but it is taken as a compliment. We are all different. The late Archbishop Fulton J. Sheen used to say that the effect of a stimulus or piece of information was dependent not only on the information or stimulus but also on the receiver. Mud hardens under sunlight, he pointed out, while wax softens, and so is it with people.

Now imagine if one point of view had power over the other. The anticlutter crowd could force the savers to divest themselves of their accumulations. Or the savers could force the clutter-averse people to keep everything. And imagine that there were a "zero tolerance" policy in effect—that this power were absolutely enforced. It would make their worlds miserable, though the faction in control would be pleased with the unfortunately natural human tendency to gain control over others, to impose one's will, even if the underlying reason for arriving at that will in the first place has in the process become obscured, and even if by following a different path no one is harmed.

Yet that is exactly what we have done in our declaration of addictions, even though in many ways our war on substances makes no more sense than would a war on clutter or a movement to keep everything whether it is immediately useful or not.

The markets that are most profitable to the vendors of illegal drugs are in affluent countries. Most people, under these circumstances, buy the drugs that have the fewest side effects and are least likely to cause "addiction." In this sense, drug users seem to behave as rationally as other consumers.

Pharmacological use and abuse is not simply a function of the substance, but of the individual's values, sense of self-worth, and alternative opportunities for gratification. A typical user is a risk taker, whose lifestyle involves bending the rules. In the U.S., drug use is 50 percent more common in households that are on welfare than in those that are not. Addictive behavior, like all human behavior, is an adaptation, however poor, to one's environment.

Nevertheless, the dominant view of addiction in the U.S. today is that it is a function of exposure to addictive substances; therefore, Americans need to be protected from themselves and their own desires. Do our very efforts contribute to and worsen addiction?

Larger social attitudes influence not only the view of addictions to a drug but a drug's very addictive potential. The more effort and money spent on drug and alcohol problems, the greater their magnitude. Just as there is a placebo effect, there is also an effect we might call "the lure of forbidden fruit."

Take a moment and imagine an itch somewhere on your body. Most of us experience such things, whether from the tickling of the label in a garment, a little patch of dry skin, or the natural physiological tendency to stimulate blood circulation. And usually we do nothing about them. Imagine now that you are concentrating on not scratching that itch. Really concentrate on it. It will drive you crazy—until something else gets your attention. Now imagine that advertisements on television remind you not to scratch that itch. Imagine that signs tell you that you have entered a zone where scratching of itches is prohibited. Imagine that you are constantly reminded that no matter what you do, you must not scratch that itch.

So it is with substances that those in power have decided you are not to use. A very popular belief held by persons who apparently have nothing better to think about is that children are zombie-like creatures who are dictated to by advertisements. I think that children are more sophisticated than we think and are capable of "tuning out" advertisements as well as adults can, and maybe they are even better at it. But let's suppose that the meddlers are right, and that children follow advertising as if it were some sort of religion. What is the effect when they see advertisements that tell their parents how to prevent their children from using drugs? What is the effect of advertisements that talk of children who died from using drugs? Remember, every child thinks that he or she is immortal. The lesson is that there is something dangerous and apparently interesting that someone wants their parents to keep them from doing. Human curiosity, not just childhood curiosity, would lead them to want to learn more, or at least some of them to want to do so.

Many government policies to deter the use of drugs are more harmful than the drugs themselves. Two million Americans are behind bars today, a higher proportion of our adult population than in any other nation. Four out of five inmates violated drug and alcohol laws, stole money to buy drugs, were high at the time of their offense, or were alcohol or drug abusers or addicts, according to the National Center on Addiction and Substance Abuse.

Today, one no longer reads that heroin or cocaine or crack is "the most addictive drug known": That distinction is now reserved for nicotine. Yet there are as many former smokers in the U.S. as there are current smokers, according to the CDC, and 90 percent of them gave up the habit on their own, usually by quitting abruptly.

If it is possible to quit, why do 50 million Americans continue to smoke? Surely they cannot be ignorant of the risks in the current political atmosphere. Bart Giamatti, who served as president of Yale and commissioner of Major League Baseball, was a lifelong smoker. A man of his education had to know the risks, yet he continued to smoke; isn't that proof that he could not quit?

Not necessarily. I myself continued to smoke for years, even while heading a government agency battling addiction. Some took this as evidence of my own addiction; yet when I tired of smoking, I gave it up without trouble. The diagnosis of addiction as a disease beyond the power of an addict, based solely on the behavior, is thus wholly unreliable.

The truth is hard to confront. We all have self-destructive impulses. Self-respect means accepting this in yourself, as well as your strengths. As mortal creatures, we must die, so we must each deal with the fear of death; we must test our omnipotent fantasies of invulnerability, of immortality. Without risk, there can be no failure, as one perceptive Spanish gentleman commented after one of my speeches. And without failure, there is no growth.

Does a risk-averse life mean no growth? Just living—or rather existing—a retarded life?

If addiction lies in the properties of certain chemicals, rather than in the culture and the individual, how are we to account for the phenomenon of "behavioral addiction"? The addiction-as-disease paradigm is spreading from its origins in chemical dependency to cover more and more areas of behavior and life.

Browsing any large bookstore's self-help section, one finds books on addiction, not just to substances such as alcohol or drugs, but to pastimes such as gambling, risk taking, pornography, television, and the Internet. We have books on addiction to such crimes as stealing, child abuse, and murder. One can be addicted, it seems, to the emotions love, rage, anxiety, sadness, and fear; to characteristics from incompetence to perfectionism; to everything from procrastination and forgetfulness to premenstrual tension.

Experts write reams explaining that we can become addicted to activities essential to life, including sex, relationships, marriage, eating, working, shopping, and fantasy. Even activities touted by experts, such as dieting and exercise, have their addicts, expert books, and twelve step recovery programs. Thus do experts beget experts.

No one argues that there is anything innately addictive in any of these things: no alcohol, no nicotine, no opium. The pleasure, excitement, or anxiety we feel from these things, it is said, causes us to become addicted to the rush of our own neurotransmitters and endorphins, produced by our own brains. Yet if we can become addicted to anything, what can be the reason for singling out certain chemicals for legal censure? Why not outlaw junk food, television, anything?

I have no doubt that one can become addicted to anything, but I have never come across such a thing as an addictive substance. The fact that it is now accepted that one can become addicted not just to chemical substances, but to behaviors, to emotions, to anything, demonstrates that the phenomenon of addiction is not fundamentally medical but ethical.

In my experience, no addiction is more dangerous than the addiction to expert "fixes," to self-help gurus, to twelve step programs. This addiction creates an insatiable appetite for more, ever higher doses, ever greater highs. Yet, because it rests on utterly false premises, this addiction always ends in a crash, when the addict gives up his self-respect in exchange for whatever "fix" is being pushed by the latest expert. Then it is time for the junkie to further degrade himself for the next fix, to sell a little more of his self-respect.

Indeed, throwing oneself into these programs, into the formulae proposed by self-help "experts," into acceptance of one's own actions as an "incurable disease" over which one is "powerless," is to cede control of one's own decisions to someone else. It is not merely allowing others to possess that power but is, in fact, serving it up on a silver platter.

Nothing is more addictive than power. The power that experts get over you when you allow them to medicalize ethical issues is a vicious drug. They are addicted to more and more research money, projects, and equipment—which is why we see scientists going public before research has been critiqued and replicated properly. Global warming? Endocrine disrupters? Electromagnetic fields? Science will save us.

Government agencies, universities, researchers, the legal profession, the media, and advocacy groups are addicted to revenue, notoriety, and power. And it is never enough. I well remember the thrill when I discovered that—whereas my scholarly work had received only polite notice from the research community—my casual utterances, once I became a government authority, were graven in stone, determining budgets, building empires. I remember the thrill of being mentioned in the press or appearing in the media. It is a feeling as addictive as any drug and far more dangerous.

If you want to help addicts and your society, there is no better place to start than the power junkies. They need to go cold turkey, and they cannot do it without your help.

James Thurber once wrote a book called *Fables for Our Time.* One of those fables dealt with the bear—for fables require the anthropomorphism of animals—who drank too much. This bear would get home from the bar, drunk, and would flail about, bumping into the furniture, knocking over the lamp, and troubling his children and wife. But there came a time when the bear "took the pledge," as it was once described, and swore to a life henceforth of utter abstemiousness. But it did not stop there. To demonstrate how much better he was now that he no longer drank, he would preach on the subject and even stand on his head—and come crashing down, bumping into the furniture, knocking over the lamp, and upsetting his family.

So it is with our approach to "addictive" things. Used immoderately, almost anything becomes more trouble than it is worth, and used moderately its influence does not extend beyond the user. If you reject the notion that people should be ceded power over others, then it follows that when an action affects no one else, it is also none of anyone else's business.

15

OBESITY

It is not likely that anyone who is fat has gained anything by the federal government telling him so. Yet the United States—and now, the entire Western world—is embroiled in a frenzy over what is generally referred to as "the obesity crisis." People sit in front of their televisions and munch cupcakes and potato chips and cluck to themselves over this crisis, and no doubt some of them demand that the *government* do something. Lawyers file lawsuits against vendors of foods that, misused by people who got fat and who apparently didn't want to be fat, are said to be the cause of our national chubbiness. *Time* magazine devotes most of an issue to fatness, never questioning the initial premise that we are obese and have no right to be.

Quack diets, always the subject of interest in grocery store tabloids and the topic of what passes for conversation at second-tier cocktail parties, became all the rage. The most fashionable of these, the subject of an advertising campaign and "news" coverage designed to play to that fashionability rather than impart information, encourages people to gobble up protein and fat and eschew carbohydrates. In our national panic over fatness, we are promoting a tacit policy that is likely to produce a lot of weary, cranky people who have heart disease—if other government statistics, the ones that tell us about diseases of the coronary arteries, are to be believed.

"Scarsdale diet, grapefruit diet, Beverly Hills diet, Cambridge diet, liquid protein diet, cabbage soup diet and, of course, Atkins diet and South Beach diet: The names change, the formulas alter, but the gimmick diet never goes away," began an editorial in the *Washington Post* on September 6, 2004, in the midst of what has become a national frenzy over weight. Or, more specifically, over overweight.

Yet at about the same time, the *New York Times* published an editorial in which the paper expressed its foursquare opposition to—sugar: "If your mother ever told you that eating sweets would spoil your dinner, she was right." The problem? "[T]he more sugar you consume, generally in the form of 'added' sugars like high-fructose corn syrup, the less likely you are to eat adequate amounts of nutritious food." The editorial went on to say, in a fashion typical of that newspaper, that the government ought to do more.

It is an established physiological fact that sugar tells the brain that you have been fed, turning off the hunger mechanism. It can, therefore, as the *Times* noted, cause you to eat less. It can cause you to eat less of the nutritional foods you need, yes, but it can also cause you to reduce your intake of fatty fare. While it is trendy to condemn carbohydrates, it cannot escape notice that bodybuilders and athletes consume carbs and avoid fatty foods. Five days after the *Times* editorial appeared, fifty-eight-year-old former president Bill Clinton underwent heart-bypass surgery. People had remarked in recent weeks how good the former chief executive looked, how slim and trim he was. He had been on one of the high-protein, high-fat, low-carbohydrate diets. Now his coronary arteries were clogged with fat. Nobody's arteries ever got clogged with sugar.

The government has told us that we should be obsessed with obesity, and there has been no shortage of opportunists eager to gain power over us by dictating the form that obsession should take.

In late July 2004, published reports championed the claim that we are too fat because we do not smoke enough. The reasoning went something like this: Government efforts to get people to stop smoking have worked. When people stop smoking, their appetites for food increase. So they eat more and get fat. Or so it was claimed.

Aside from the fact that if people want to be fat (or, for that matter, smoke) it ought to be left up to them, the ridiculousness of the obesity frenzy comes from the fact that it is in many ways a false alarm, brought about not by a change in our national girth but by a change in bookkeeping of vital statistics.

The story of the "obesity epidemic" is an excellent case of how questionable science unquestioned has led to a national panic, the enrichment of lawyers, and further erosion of your right to make your choices about how you care to live your life.

In late 2001, Surgeon General David Satcher released a "Call to action to prevent and decrease overweight and obesity," announcing, "The nation must take action to assist Americans in balancing healthful eating with regular physical activity." That was just the beginning. Within a five-month period:

- President Bush unveiled a "Health and Fitness Initiative," signing an executive order creating a "Personal Fitness Interagency Working Group" to report on ways the federal government can "promote personal fitness";

- Secretary of Health and Human Services Tommy Thompson launched a $190 million media campaign ("VERB: It's What You Do") urging children to get more exercise;
- Senators Jeff Bingaman (D-NM), Christopher Dodd (D-CT), and Bill Frist (R-TN) introduced the "Improved Nutrition and Physical Activity Act" (IMPACT) to allocate another $254 million to battle expanding waistlines, including another $125 million for a media campaign;
- The IRS reversed a long-standing rule to allow deductions for medical expenses undertaken for weight reduction.

This flurry of activity was the culmination of a campaign that had been building since 1998, when the National Institutes of Health announced that a majority of American adults were overweight. Public health experts, it seems, are unanimous on this judgment. Excess weight, declared NIH, is "a growing public health problem that affects 97 million American adults—55 percent of the population." The Food and Drug Administration agreed, calling obesity a "widespread, chronic disease." The Social Security Administration concurred: "Obesity is a complex, chronic disease."

Not only is obesity a disease, say the experts, it is an epidemic: "Overweight and obesity . . . have reached epidemic proportions in the United States," wrote Satcher. "Obesity in the United States is truly epidemic," testified William H. Dietz of the Department of Health and Human Services. "Obesity is an epidemic and should be taken as seriously as any infectious disease epidemic," echoed Jeffrey P. Koplan, director of the Centers for Disease Control.

Public health authorities have responded to various epidemics in the past by quarantine, draining swamps, improving sanitation, adding chlorine to drinking water, and vaccinating the vulnerable. The parallel drawn by the government in this case, however, is not to such epidemics as influenza or typhus, but to tobacco. "Overweight and obesity may soon cause as much preventable disease and death as cigarette smoking," said Satcher in a press conference accompanying the report's release.

New York University nutritionist Marion Nestle, author of *Food Politics: How the Food Industry Influences Nutrition and Health,* follows Satcher's logic to its conclusion: "Sellers of food products do not attract the same kind of attention as purveyors of drugs or tobacco," writes Nestle. "They should." In June 2004 she joined Yale psychologist Kelly Brownell, writing in *Time,* "Obesity is a global problem. Is irresponsibility an epidemic around the world?" (To which the answer might very well be "yes," because it has long served the purposes of those who exercise power over people to discourage personal responsibility in favor of doing what one is told to do.)

One suggested approach to the obesity "problem" is to restrict food advertising, as cigarette advertising is now restricted. "How different is Ronald McDonald from Joe Camel?" asks Brownell. "Maybe food ads should be erased from television the way cigarette ads were," suggests columnist Susan Ager in the *Detroit Free Press.*

Another frequently heard proposal is a "fat tax" analogous to taxes on cigarettes. "Congress and state legislatures could shift the focus [from personal responsibility] to the environment by taxing foods with little nutritional value," says Brownell. "We could envision taxes on butter, potato chips, whole milk, cheeses and meat," agrees Michael Jacobson of the Center for Science in the Public Interest. California has already considered such a tax—on soft drinks—but later dropped the proposal.

Some proposals go further: "Maybe the government should mandate nutrition standards for [restaurants] and supermarkets. . . . Maybe restaurant portions should be regulated," writes Ager. "Maybe vending machines should be banned unless they stock only low-fat snacks."

Yet another approach is class action suits like those by state attorneys general against tobacco companies. Already, tort lawyers have begun to go after large fast-food companies, hoping to add them to the herd they regularly milk.

When Congress was debating lawsuits against tobacco companies, Senator Phil Gramm asked, "Where does this end? If we don't hold people accountable for decisions they make, does it end with tobacco? Does it end with alcohol? Does it end with fattening foods?"

Gramm was attempting to make a *reductio ad absurdum* argument, to reduce the attack on tobacco companies to absurdity. Yet no sooner had tobacco companies settled their lawsuits than attorneys involved in these suits turned their attention to fast food. Indeed, when the Justice Department launched the tobacco suits in 1999, the Physicians Committee for Responsible Medicine recommended that it "also investigate preparing a case against major meat producers and retailers."

Lawyers fresh from the $242 billion tobacco settlements filed class-action suits against a number of fast-food restaurants on behalf of plaintiffs, including a four-hundred-pound fifteen-year-old in New York City. A federal judge threw out the suit in January 2003, but the lawyers filed an amended suit the following month. The case is significant in that it was the opening shot in a war of litigation that is likely to last many decades, as have various permutations of tobacco lawsuits.

Of course, much of it is a lie foisted upon us by the nanny state, which has taken responsibility for our own health away from us, and by opportunistic attorneys. The likelihood of reform is all but nonexistent, with lawyers making up more than half of the U.S. Senate and an impressive portion of the House of Representatives. Is obesity really a disease? Are Americans really in the midst of an obesity epidemic? How do we know if we are overweight? What is obesity?

"Overweight" is generally defined as weighing more than average for one's height, while obesity is defined as having 25 percent or more body fat for men, or 30 percent or more body fat for women. The National Institutes of Health bases estimates of the prevalence of overweight and obesity in the population on surveys taken through the years by the CDC.

From 1960 to 1980, according to these surveys, the proportion of American adults who were overweight stayed relatively constant at around 45 percent. Then something changed: From 1980 to 2000, the proportion said to be overweight increased to 64 percent, thus going from less than half to almost two-thirds of the total adult population.

For obesity, the reported increase for the period was even sharper: The percentage of adults who were obese more than doubled to over 30 percent, while the prevalence of extreme obesity rose faster yet, more than doubling in a decade, to just over 2 percent of all adults. The largest relative increase was for children and teens (six to nineteen years). The proportion of kids said to be overweight has tripled since 1980, reaching 15 percent of young people in 2000.

These startling figures are behind assertions of an "obesity epidemic." But the statistics underlying these figures should be examined with great skepticism. In recent years, the federal government changed its definitions of overweight and obesity, thus labeling a lot of people as dangerously fat, not by their having changed at all but by the standards having been altered. Nor was this due to new discoveries that produced alarming news about body fat—it was merely a bookkeeping change.

Up until 1998—under the old definitions—a man of average height (5 feet 9 inches) was considered overweight at around 190 pounds, and a woman of average height (5 feet 4 inches) at 160. But then the official standards were changed, so that now the average man is officially overweight at 175 pounds, and the average woman at around 145. With the stroke of a pen, more than 35 million Americans suddenly became overweight—without gaining an ounce.

The government changed its official thresholds of overweight and obesity in order to bring the U.S. definitions into line with those used by other countries and the World Health Organization, thus simplifying international comparisons of national health statistics. But the real, flesh-and-blood data actually go in the other direction!

Indeed, significant segments of the population in past years were losing weight, not gaining. For example, the average weight of women aged 25 to 69 fell substantially between 1954 and 1972, according to life insurance studies. These were extensive surveys, involving a base of nearly nine million people over nearly four decades. A 1987 review by the Harvard School of Public Health concluded that these were the most reliable of twenty-five major prospective studies that had been done, up to that time, on weight and longevity. Nor should that be surprising. Many studies are done by academicians who are funded by grants that require they show something, with the accuracy of that something being of secondary concern, but the life insurance industry lives and dies (so to speak) on the strength of its actuarial numbers. And the life insurance companies were not alone in noticing a trend. In addition to the statistics assembled by the life insurance industry, "The prevalence of overweight in white men in their twenties to forties . . . decreased from the early 1970s to the late 1970s," according to NIH. As we shall see, however, these data, derived largely from surveys by CDC, may be less reliable than insurance data, which are based on actual weights and measurements by doctors.

Moreover, neither males nor females in the U.S. population should be, on average, gaining weight, if government data on caloric consumption and exercise are accurate.

Officially recommended caloric intake levels for men of average size range up to 2,538 calories a day, while those for women range up to 1,982. (These recommendations are for "sedentary" men and women; caloric intake recommendations are higher for more active people.)

Yet according to the Department of Agriculture, American males consumed an average of 2,344 calories per day in 1994–96, while American females consumed an average of only 1,638—neither above the official guidelines.

If these figures are correct, even a sedentary average American man's daily calorie consumption fell within the recommended range, and thus his weight for the period measured should have been stable. What is more surprising, if these data can be believed, the average American woman—even if sedentary—must have been losing weight back in the middle 1990s.

According to these figures, the average American woman is consuming from 178 to 344 fewer calories per day than is recommended for her daily energy needs. That is an annual deficit of between 64,970 and 125,560 calories. At 3,500 calories per pound, that means that American women must be losing in the neighborhood of 18–35 pounds each, every year.

These results are obviously are questionable, because that which they predict is clearly not happening. If every woman in the U.S. lost even 18 pounds per year, we would notice it; in that not every woman loses that amount, it would mean that some lose even more. (The 35-pounds-per-year figure is abundantly ridiculous, for at that rate it would take only three years for a 105-pound woman to entirely disappear!) The surveys cited are compiled by sending interviewers out to knock on doors and ask people to recall what they ate over the prior twenty-four hours. Because the surveys are voluntary and unverified, people who eat a lot may refuse to participate or underestimate their consumption.

So how are these standards arrived at? What do they include and what do they leave out? What is actually being measured? Is weight really the key factor in determining human health, or are other variables as significant as weight, possibly even more so?

The main official measurement used in assessing the obesity epidemic is something called the "Body Mass Index" (BMI), a ratio of weight to height. BMI is calculated by dividing a person's weight in kilograms by the square of his or her height.

From 1990 to 2000, average BMI increased about 6 percent, from 24.9 to 26.5, according to an October article in the *Journal of the American Medical Association*. For our average woman, that represents a gain of 10 pounds in as many years; for the average man, 12 pounds in a decade.

Until 1998, the federal government defined overweight as a BMI of 27.8 or greater in men, and 27.3 or greater in women; it defined obesity as a BMI of 31.1 or greater for men, and 32.3 for women. Since changing the standards in 1998, the government now considers both men and women overweight at a BMI of 25 or greater, and officially obese at 30 or greater.

Because BMI is a ratio of height to weight, it cannot distinguish between fat and muscle. Muscle is much denser and heavier than fat, and skews BMI calculations upward. But health risks increase not with weight as such, but with the percentage and distribution of body fat. "One problem with using BMI as a measurement tool is that very muscular people may fall into the 'overweight' category when they are actually healthy and fit," as the NIH observed in 1996.

Thus Michael Jordan, Bruce Willis, Tom Cruise, Russell Crowe, and Harrison Ford are overweight under the new standards, while Sammy Sosa, Mark McGwire, Barry Sanders, and Sylvester Stallone are all officially obese—as is the governor of California, Arnold Schwarzenegger, whose previous career did not include any comedies that might have been called "The Tubby Terminator" or "Conan the Corpulent."

There is no consensus in the scientific community as to exactly where to draw the line between healthy weight and overweight. "[T]he health risks associated with overweight and obesity do not conform to rigid cutoff points," according to the NIH. "Health risks increase gradually as BMI increases."

These estimates are "based on a sample of only 1,446 people conducted over seven months in 1999," according to the *Wall Street Journal*. The paper quoted the director of the CDC's division of nutrition and physical activity as saying that "you need about three years [of data] for a confident estimate."

The CDC survey involves interviewers knocking on doors and asking some five thousand interviewees per year their height and weight (among other things), from which their BMIs are calculated. Interviewers also invite 10 to 12 percent of interviewees into "Mobile Examination Units"—tractor trailers containing clinics where participants are measured and weighed.

Because participation is voluntary, this survey may also suffer from self-selection bias. Very fat or very thin people may refuse to partici-pate, while very muscular or athletic types (whose high BMIs do not actually indicate excess body fat) may be overrepresented.

Even if the surveys present an accurate measure of BMI distribu-tion, the problem remains that BMI is only a proxy for true overweight or obesity defined in terms of body fat. BMI "is not a measure of body fatness per se," noted a 1997 paper by CDC researchers in the journal *Obesity Research*. "Because, strictly speaking, obesity is defined as excess adipose tissue [fat], there has been a conscious effort not to associate this term [obesity]" with the BMI *per se*. However, added the researchers, "at BMI levels in excess of 30, people are generally over-weight . . . and hence could generally be considered obese." The prob-lem comes in for people whose BMIs are between 25 and 30—official-ly "overweight" but not obese. In this range, BMI is much more likely to mistake muscle for fat, and so overstate the prevalence of over-weight. Also, while the health risks of obesity are well established, research suggests that the alleged health risks of this more moderate range of overweight are controversial.

"The risks of moderate overweight are almost negligible, especially for women, if they exist at all." says University of North Dakota School of Medicine nutritionist Frances M. Berg. "[T]he risks of being moderately overweight have been exaggerated by health professionals and the media, causing people to turn to diets that are more risky than the few extra pounds they carry." Indeed, actuarial data from the insurance stud-ies referred to above demonstrate that higher BMI numbers were actual-ly healthier than lower numbers as people aged. Above age fifty-five, a BMI below 25 actually increased risk of mortality. By age seventy, the low-est death rate was associated with a BMI of about 28, well into the gov-ernment's definition of overweight and approaching officially obese.

People in good physical shape may be more likely than fat or underweight people to participate voluntarily in government surveys asking one's weight. Fitter people tend to have high BMIs, without actually being fat at all. If such people are overrepresented in such surveys, the results tell us nothing about the actual fatness of Americans in general.

Because it cannot distinguish between muscle and fat, BMI is only a rough approximation of how fat a person is. To complicate matters further, body fat itself is only a proxy for poor diet and lack of physical activity, which appear to be the true risk factors for diseases commonly blamed on obesity or high BMI. Taken together, these caveats might give consumers cause to take assertions of an obesity epidemic with a grain of salt.

"[Y]ou do not need the BMI to find out if you are fat," writes Senior FAA Aviation Medical Examiner Glenn R. Stoutt Jr., M.D. "[J]ust take off your clothes and look in a mirror, see how your clothes fit, or see how much fat you can hold between your fingers."

Pause for a moment and let all this . . . yes, "digest" is the right word. Our society is more appearance conscious than ever before. Even small towns have health clubs, though small towns also are often populated by folks who engage in physical activity such that they are likely to have a healthy amount of dense muscle tissue. There is a national campaign, as there has been since the Kennedy administration, for physical fitness. Common sense tells us that to the extent we have gained national weight, a good portion of it is muscle. Part of the "obesity epidemic" could well be because people have followed the government's advice and attained a degree of fitness. A friend who in his late forties decided he was not comfortable with a "middle-age bulge" undertook an exercise regimen that included sit-ups, chin-ups, weight training, and outdoor exercise designed to stimulate his heart and lungs. Each day he stood on the scales. The pounds did not melt away. When he began, my 5'10" friend weighed about 190 pounds—within normal range under the old standards and a little overweight under the new ones. He wore pants with a 36-inch waist. As his exercise continued, his pant size dropped to 32, his physical abilities had increased, and he was noticeably more muscular—and he weighed 190 pounds and in all his rippling-muscle glory is still officially fat.

Aforementioned Arnold Schwarzenegger is the listed author, along with a writer named Bill Dobbins, of a book entitled *The New Encyclopedia of Modern Bodybuilding*. It is a remarkable book for many reasons, one of which is its recognition that people are not alike. It recognizes that some people tend to be lean, narrow-shouldered, with long arms, legs, and necks; some tend to be what one would describe as average build; and some tend more to store fat, have broad shoulders and short necks, legs, and arms. This, the book notes, is a function of their nature. To be a bodybuilder, the first group needs to work very hard to gain weight at all, never mind the effort in making that weight into muscle. The middle group has little dietary concern. The last group must work both for muscle and diet to be a successful competitive bodybuilder.

The observation in the book is an all-too-rare statement of the obvious. Some people are physically better inclined to be football players, while others are more naturally talented for basketball. This isn't to say that with hard work a member of one group cannot achieve success in the other. What it is to say is that one size definitely does not fit all—despite what the government, the circling flock of lawyers, and the Chicken Littles in the news media would have you believe in an effort to gain control over you or your money.

Nevertheless, according to the government, even moderate overweight is killing people. "Approximately 300,000 deaths a year are currently associated with overweight and obesity," claims Satcher. His source for this assertion was a 1993 study in the *Journal of the American Medical Association* that found "300,000 people die each year from illness related to dietary factors and sedentary lifestyle." Did the study list those 300,000 people for even one year? Of course not. As with all such statistics, it was a guess. An educated guess, most likely, but certainly a guess, as is just about any statistic that ends in five zeroes.

Satcher's substitution of "overweight and obesity" for "dietary factors and sedentary lifestyle" prompted a clarification from the authors of that study in a 1998 issue of the *New England Journal of Medicine:* "The [300,000] figure applies broadly to the combined effects of various dietary factors and activity patterns that are too sedentary, not to the narrower effect of obesity alone." Such as, perhaps, sitting home terrified while watching television news broadcasts that say you're too fat.

The following year, *JAMA* published a study that actually did conclude that obesity kills about 300,000 people annually. However, said the authors, "Our calculations assume that all excess mortality in obese people is due to their obesity," which is itself a powerful reason to go read something else. This study ignored such factors as diet, activity levels, and family history.

Furthermore, "the 300,000 deaths per year figure was derived without taking into account factors such as yo-yo dieting and diet drug use, both of which have been shown to have devastating effects on health," wrote the University of Colorado's Paul Campos. "Nor were variables such as class—poor people die sooner than the well-off—and social discrimination, which has been shown to have a very negative impact on health, taken into account."

In contrast, a 1996 study in the *American Journal of Nutrition* found that the best predictor of mortality was cardiovascular fitness independent of body weight, BMI, or percentage of body fat. Obese people by BMI or percent body fat standards who exercised had half the death rate of normal weighted individuals who did not exercise. The true risk factors were not BMI or even body fat, but activity and diet.

The study found that overweight or obese people who walked as little as a half-hour a day had lower death rates than people of normal weight who undertook less physical activity. "[L]ow fitness is a more powerful predictor of mortality than obesity," testified Tim Church, M.D., in 2004 congressional obesity hearings. "The proportion of deaths attributable to low fitness in many populations is higher than the proportion attributed to . . . obesity. . . . [D]eath rates for low-fit individuals . . . are two to three times higher than death rates in high-fit individuals. These results are seen in . . . the fat and the thin. . . ." Beyond that, found the *Journal of Nutrition* study, when diet and activity levels were controlled, "a high body mass index (BMI) did not have a significant effect on cardiovascular mortality."

"The data linking overweight and death . . . are limited, fragmentary, and often ambiguous," said the *New England Journal of Medicine* in an editorial. "Most of the evidence is either indirect or derived from [studies with] serious methodologic flaws. Many studies fail to consider confounding variables, which are extremely difficult to assess and control. . . . Thus, although some claim that every year 300,000 deaths . . . are caused by obesity, that figure is by no means well-established."

The story so far: The obesity epidemic we hear so much about is at least to some extent bogus; even the measuring system that determines the relative fatness of people is phony, lumping the fit among the fat and taking no account of differing body types—the sometimes true statement that a person is "big boned." And even if the epidemic were real, there is nothing particularly wrong with obesity alone.

There's more. Many medical conditions linked to obesity have actually been decreasing in prevalence. "Other conditions, such as hypercholesterolemia and hypertension, declined . . . at the same time that the prevalence of obesity was increasing," according to *JAMA*. "Total cardiovascular mortality and mortality from coronary heart disease and stroke have also declined over these years." These are the years during which we have become a nation of lard-laden citizens, supposedly.

"Although overweight and obesity are caused by many factors, in most individuals, weight gain results from a combination of excess calorie consumption and inadequate physical activity," according to the Department of Health and Human Services. "[T]he data are confusing, but the causes of the obesity epidemic most likely are too much food and too little physical activity," agrees Katherine Flegal, an epidemiologist at the National Center for Health Statistics.

Your level of physical activity is important in determining how many calories you should consume daily, according to a September 2002 report from the National Academy of Sciences. Are current Americans, as Satcher said, "the most sedentary generation in the history of the world"?

The data do not support this contention. Thirty-one million Americans now belong to health clubs, and 40 percent of these go to the gym at least twice a week. Since 1990—while obesity and overweight have apparently increased—the proportion of Americans who report no leisure-time physical activity has actually declined about 6 percent, according to the CDC. However, because the survey from which this estimate is derived is voluntary, people who do not exercise may refuse to participate. Because the data are self-reported and not independently verified, participants may overestimate the amount of exercise they get.

So, how much exercise is enough?

The National Academy of Sciences' Institute of Medicine recommends "sixty minutes of daily moderate intensity physical activity (e.g., walking/jogging at 4 to 5 mph)."

The American College of Sports Medicine is concerned that this recommendation may actually cause people to exercise less. "Focus on sixty minutes per day may cause Americans to be confused, and doubt that thirty minutes a day, or shorter bursts of activity such as three ten-minute walks, provides any health benefit," warns the group. "[A]dditional benefits can be obtained by greater amounts of activity, but . . . thirty minutes of moderate intensity activity each day provides substantial health benefits for sedentary adults."

The surgeon general agrees that "a minimum of thirty minutes of physical activity of moderate intensity (such as brisk walking) on most, if not all, days of the week" is adequate, adding that "greater health benefits can be obtained by engaging in physical activity of more vigorous intensity or of longer duration." The CDC concurs: "People of all ages benefit from moderate physical activity, such as thirty minutes of brisk walking five or more times a week."

Steven Blair of the Cooper Institute says that "thirty minutes/day [of physical activity] . . . reduces risk of early mortality, CHD, type 2 diabetes, and some cancers by about 50 percent. . . . Sixty minutes/day would drop morbidity and mortality risk by another 10 to 15 percent."

The most important factor for good health is not weight, but eating well and getting regular exercise. Consumers would do well to take some of the effort (and $33 billion per year) currently spent on weight-loss fads, and put it into eating a sensible, balanced diet and getting regular exercise. If more people did that, not only would they have better health, but many might find that they'd get a more svelte physique in the bargain. But what business is it of the government? (We know what business it is of the lawyers; it is their business to find or create the impression of problems, find someone to blame, shake down that someone, and grow, metaphorically if not literally, fat in the process.)

Obesity is now more common among the poor than the rich, according to government data—a startling reversal of the historical situation. This may be because those currently regarded as poor are able to consume as much, or work as little, as only the rich could in the past. If this is so, it suggests that the historical trend of generally increasing prosperity—if permitted to continue—will result in reversing the obesity epidemic, just as it has resulted in reversing population growth rates around the world.

Not considered in the studies of national trends is the national ethnic makeup. It is not a matter of prejudice but of fact that different immigrant populations tend toward different physiques, without that saying anything at all about their health or longevity. Over the years, different regions of the world have contributed more or less to national growth due to immigration. But in the name of political correctness and out of fear that someone will shout "racism" (as if nationality were a race), it is almost forbidden to take such things into account—which is itself too bad, in that different groups may well have special medical needs that honest studies could identify. Conversely, those different groups may well have physiological strengths from which we could learn.

But when you get right down to it, the study that matters is a study of one—you—or maybe a study of several ones, if you have children for whom you are responsible. Diet and levels of physical activity are matters of personal preference. The only justification for interfering in the personal preferences of others is that the government now bears the cost of health care for those who suffer illness due to their own choices. This is the rationale for regulation of drugs, alcohol, and tobacco. It is now put forward as a reason for the experts to dictate your diet and portion sizes.

In Maoist China, the government decreed that the people assemble each morning for mandatory calisthenics. This was regarded at the time in the U.S. as a paternalistic assault on the individual. Yet if lawsuits, regulations, taxes, and bans are justified in the interests of reducing obesity, why not compulsory exercise? If the idea seems farfetched, remember that the idea of suing McDonald's because some people who ate there are fat was only yesterday derided as ludicrous.

As the experts assume responsibility for more areas of life that were once the province of the individual, the individual gives up responsibility. In surrendering responsibility, we surrender freedom. In becoming the wards of paternalistic experts, we trade our self-respect for their protection, and they obtain increased power over the most personal aspects of our lives.

But it is more, even, than that. Yes, the government says that many of you are fat, even those of you who followed other government decrees that you become fit. The government says, itself and through studies funded with your money, that you should walk four or five miles each and every day. (One wonders when a parent—asked in his or her fat kid's lawsuit against the donut shop why it was the parent didn't notice the kid was getting fat—will offer the following defense: "I was out doing the government-mandated, hour-long walk instead of being a parent, which any good parent will tell you provides plenty of exercise on its own.")

Again we see that generalization is not possible, that the range of possible humans and actual humans is so vast that any study of any group larger than one has a built-in problem. Even among the studies cited here, which deal with varying sizes of groups, we see that "overweight" is a healthy condition past a certain age. More than that, were you to ask the author of any study to specify with certainty when a person who weighed twenty-five pounds too much would die as a result thereof, that author couldn't. How about fifty pounds? Nope. Well, one hundred pounds, then? One hundred fifty pounds? Two hundred? Still no answer. We are too different to make any hard and fast rules in such things.

As this book was going to press, another revealing new report was released. After years of the most dire forecasts about the danger of being overweight and the hundreds of thousands of people killed by obesity each year, the Centers for Disease Control issued a startling new report that might well have been entitled "Never mind." The report stated that obesity kills about 26,000 Americans annually— not the 365,000 the CDC had estimated only three months earlier. What's more, the CDC found, being moderately "overweight" by the government's standards actually causes people to live longer. The CDC estimated that about 85,000 people who would otherwise die each year continue to live as a result of being overweight. Whether this set of statistics is any more reliable than the earlier ones remains to be seen.

Nevertheless, fat people have a right to be fat, if that is their choice. The description above of the dubious science in connection with the health effects of the issue merely illustrates the slipshod process whereby a questionable conclusion was reached and taken as mainstream fact. It is intended neither to justify fatness nor to denigrate it. Your life is up to you, or ought to be, so long as your choices do not make you a burden upon others. Unfortunately, by seizing more and more the burden of responsibility for the health of the nation, the government has more and more taken, too, the "right" of telling you how you may or may not live. We have seen the proposals whereby it would become more expensive to be fat—with the additional money going to the government. Taxes designed to change your behavior are called "sin taxes." They are why so much of the cost of a bottle of liquor or a pack of cigarettes—the vast majority of the cost in the latter case—goes to the government. (This produces a bizarre paradox: If everyone in the country stopped smoking and drinking today, tomorrow the government would be in big trouble, so much has it come to rely on our doing things it officially wishes we didn't.) When the government begins to tax fatty foods, it will rake in even more of your money, which it believes it can spend more wisely than you can.

Not only do you have a right to be fat, you have a right—with one caveat—to do unhealthy things. The one caveat is the extent to which you are responsible for others, whether, for instance, you are a parent. If you are the parent of a child who is so fat as to be unhealthy, the chances are very good that you are a bad parent. If you are so fat that you cannot be a proper parent, you're a bad parent, too. Rights invariably carry responsibilities, and self-respect demands that both be embraced equally.

16

REVOLT AGAINST THE MACHINES

One day in June 2004, the *New York Daily News* carried an article from which we were supposed to be scandalized over the easy availability of samurai-style swords at stores in that city and over the Internet. Anyone, the story told us, could buy one. The horror!

The article was a follow-up to an item the previous day in which a teenager had hacked an acquaintance to death with such a sword. It was the kind of story editors love: It took a specific incident and broadened it into a general comment on society—a "trend piece." In this case, the trend was fashioned from a solitary incident.

It may be that a teenager dismembering another teenager does indeed have broader societal implications—the specifics of the story, accurately reported, would determine that. But that implication probably has nothing to do with the choice of implement for the murder. People are regularly stabbed in New York, yet the easy availability of sharp objects is not the kind of thing that normally results in newspaper stories. People have been beaten to death in New York with rocks, pieces of pipe, and bricks, but the *Daily News* is silent on the failure—

of who? the government? manufacturers?—to make them less easily obtained.

The fact is that somebody intent on killing will do so. The Bible tells us that Samson slew a thousand men with "the jawbone of an ass" (a term that might also be applied to the mandible of whomever at the *Daily News* decided that there was scandal not as much in the killing as in the implement employed in bringing it about). But samurai swords are special, or so we would be led to think. This probably has to do with the belief that there is someone to blame other than the actual murderer, someone who lawyers can sink their beaks into.

Today, the guilty party is the object and, by extension, its manufacturer, not the person or persons who put it to improper use.

Beginning with Ralph Nader's attack on the Chevrolet Corvair nearly forty years ago, the combination of scientists and engineers who will testify to whatever a plaintiff wants, lawyers eager to blame "deep-pocketed" manufacturers for the shortcomings of their clients, and news media who will uncritically parrot the claims made in lawsuits has resulted in many items being withdrawn from the market entirely, and others loaded with "safety" features and warnings that in some cases actually make them more dangerous. The science-lawyer-media axis has managed to add a large percentage to the cost of just about everything you buy.

More and more, new products are designed as much by lawyers as by engineers, in an effort to prevent liability lawsuits.

From automobiles to firearms to hair dryers—no product is immune.

Have you purchased any electrical device in the last decade? Have you cracked open the owner's manual and other literature that came with it? Have you noticed how much of that manual and that literature are devoted to things that you are not supposed to do with that item? (And have you actually read any of those warnings?)

In the late 1980s and early 1990s the light aircraft industry in the United States was nearly driven out of business due to lawsuits that had nothing at all to do with the quality and reliability of its products. Incompetent, inattentive, or impaired pilots would get into airplanes, some of which were decades old and some others improperly maintained and improperly checked preflight. They would take off and then they would crash. Their survivors would find lawyers (or the other way around) and file suit.

Often these lawsuits involved the "divide-and-conquer" approach. The aircraft maker would be sued, but so would be the makers of the parts aboard the aircraft, from tires to engine to radio. The theory is that when this approach is taken, the various defendants will try to prove their innocence by showing how it is one of the other defendants that is really to blame. This is a smart legal move but anathema to justice—one of the many places where the law and any notion of justice are at opposition. In one notable case a carburetor maker was added to the list of defendants, even though the carburetor in the crashed airplane had been made by someone else. Yet it was only after the expenditure of $25,000 in legal fees and a signed agreement that the company would not attempt to recover those fees from the plaintiff's lawyers, that the company was dropped from the suit.

Several of the best-known makers of light, general aviation airplanes suspended their manufacture of airplanes likely to be purchased by hobby pilots and other individuals. One that did keep cranking out light planes announced that about half the price of one of their new planes went to cover the liability insurance premium.

It is certainly possible that some shortcut taken by a manufacturer could result in a faulty product, and that fault could cause harm. It is reasonable to wish in the worst of these circumstances that the victim have some recourse. But the provision for that in the law has been terribly abused, with no reform in sight. Now every bad event is looked upon as a winning lottery ticket in which the lawyer gets 40 percent of the award, plus expenses.

A friend was a reporter at about that time for one of the "tabloid" television shows which were for several years all the rage (and which greatly influenced more "respectable" long-form news programs on the major networks, such that their behavior today is little distinguishable from those tabloid shows of more than a decade ago). She has pointed out that among the formulae for producing compelling stories quickly, easily, and inexpensively was to find a lawyer who represented the plaintiff in an interesting lawsuit. The show would then present his case for television viewers, complete with weeping plaintiff or survivor thereof. (A tip for would-be television reporters: The surest way of drawing on-camera tears from a survivor is to ask, "What do you remember most about [dead person]?") The story was told from the point of view of the "victim." Never was it suggested that the lawsuit might be utterly without merit; never was the other side fairly presented. To the extent that the defendant appeared, it was through some hidden-camera interview known in the trade as an "ambush." These techniques are very effective and had they been available at the time could have made Pontius Pilate appear to be the real victim of the crucifixion of Jesus. These techniques are employed today in mainstream media in an effort to subtly persuade you to favor one side of an issue over the other, especially in matters involving tort lawsuits.

This is all well and good, from the broadcaster's point of view. It presents a vague morality tale in which the little guy is victimized by and decides to take on the big, powerful industry, with the noble lawyer in shining armor there to champion the cause (and collect 40 percent plus expenses). Lawyers who regularly serve up usable lawsuits are considered heroes by the broadcasters. Justice be damned—the plaintiff is always right. Never is it heard that "one possible cause of the crash is that the driver was stinking drunk," though in an extreme case there might be a lawyer for the survivors saying, "The car maker should have known that its vehicles would be popular among those who tend to get stinking drunk and therefore they should have built into their cars safeguards that make it impossible for anyone who has had a drink to start the thing," or words to that effect.

The worst part of the ugly triumvirate of lawyers-media-science is the prostitution of science. We all know that lawyers tend to be shady and newspeople a little dim, but scientists are supposed to seek truth within the limits of their testing procedures. This is not always the case, though. While there is room for debate about the validity of scientific findings—and as we have seen, there ought to be more of it—our suspicion ought to be tickled by the fact that every big-money lawsuit involves "expert" witnesses on both sides, giving contradictory testimony. There is a whole industry of expert witnesses for hire. (I must disclose that I have myself served as an expert witness, but I testified as to what I knew to be the case rather than asking counsel how my testimony should be shaded. I was chosen because my work supported what the party wished to present to the jury. And I never put up a shingle as an expert witness for hire.)

While there has been a tremendous effort to bring about such lawsuits—and there is still the possibility of something heretofore seen only in the atrocity known as "the tobacco settlement"—for some reason lawyers have not yet been able to gain wide judicial acceptance of the proposition that plaintiffs did not know that guns send forth projectiles at high velocity that tend to make holes in whatever they strike. Even so, in an effort to sway opinion and alter the interpretation of the Second Amendment to the Constitution, researchers have undertaken to shade things to support their positions.

Often the experts overwhelm us with statistics. These arrays of numbers, tables, and regression analyses give an air of scientific objectivity that laymen are ill-equipped to dispute. But experts are only human, with all-too-human passions. Sometimes this air of objectivity masks such passions, particularly in areas of research that are what experts call "policy-sensitive." No area of research today is more policy-sensitive—and prone to passion—than the question of gun control. Two recent incidents in this area demonstrate how passions can lead even the most respected of experts into behavior that is not merely deceptive but downright bizarre.

In September 2000, Michael Bellesiles, associate professor of history at Emory University and director of Emory's Center for the Study of Violence, published *Arming America: The Origins of a National Gun Culture.* The book purported to disprove the myth that gun ownership was widespread in early America. The book claimed to demonstrate, using probate records, that, until 1850, fewer than 10 percent of Americans owned guns, and fully half of those weapons were non-functional.

Respected scholars including Edmund Morgan, Garry Wills, Fred Anderson, Roger Lane, and Richard Slotkin praised the book fulsomely. In 2001, Columbia University awarded Bellesiles the prestigious Bancroft Prize for History, and Chicago's Newberry Library awarded him a $30,000 Newberry fellowship, funded by the National Endowment for the Humanities.

Bellesiles had published an earlier article on the subject in 1996, in the *Journal of American History.* That article won an award for "Best Article of the Year" from the Organization of American Historians and was cited in a decision by the Ninth Circuit Court of Appeals. Anthony Ramirez of the *New York Times* noted that probate records were the author's "principal evidence." John Chambers, a military historian from Rutgers, reviewed the book for the *Washington Post,* saying that the probate records were Bellesiles's "freshest and most interesting source." Edmund Morgan, one of the country's leading historians of colonial America, followed suit, exclaiming in the *New York Review of Books,* "The evidence is overwhelming. First of all are the probate records."

But then came the question: Did Bellesiles make up his data?

Not everyone went along with the accolades. James Lindgren, a Northwestern University law professor and probate specialist, found significant errors in Bellesiles's work. In his book, Bellesiles reported a national average of 14.7 percent of probates listing a gun in 1765–90, a period in which other published probate researchers found three to five times as many.

Lindgren "utterly devastates Bellesiles's research," said University of Chicago law professor Albert Alschuler. "Lindgren's data show that Bellesiles was not correct," agreed UCLA historian Eric Monkkonen.

"Bellesiles fails to provide even basic information about the probate figures that form the basis of his claims for the rarity of guns," commented Joyce Malcolm, a history professor at Bentley College. "And he repeatedly makes general statements that are extreme. But if you check his footnotes, a more disturbing pattern emerges. It is not just an odd mistake or a difference of interpretation, but misrepresentation of what his sources (if they exist) actually say, time after time after time."

In 2001 the American Historical Association and the Omohundro Institute of Early American History and Culture came to Bellesiles's defense, passing a resolution reading:

> Although it is appropriate to subject all scholarly work to criticism and to evaluate that work's arguments and its sources, the Council of the American Historical Association considers personal attacks upon or harassment of an author, as we have seen directed at Michael A. Bellesiles following publication of *Arming America: The Origins of a National Gun Culture,* to be inappropriate and damaging to a tradition of free exchange of ideas and the advancement of our knowledge of the past.

In the Organization of American Historians newsletter in November 2002, Bellesiles explained why he could not more fully substantiate his findings:

> [M]y notes on these probate records had been destroyed when the pipes in Emory University's Bowden Hall burst and flooded the building, doing serious damage to nearly every office. . . . The ceiling of my office collapsed and the ensuing flood turned most of the legal pads on which I had taken notes into unreadable pulp. At this point I suppose that I could have withdrawn *Arming America* from publication, since the notes for these five paragraphs were ruined. Perhaps I should have then removed those paragraphs from the text or devoted the ensuing summers to recreating the material before allowing the book to appear several years from now. I must admit that this thought never crossed my mind. I deeply regret losing this material in the flooding of my building, a contingency for which I was unprepared.

Many of these records are on microfilm from the Genealogical Society of Utah (GSU), which is affiliated with the Church of Jesus Christ of Latter-day Saints. . . . However, I completely forget in which of several California archives I read what I recall to be twelve probate records from 1859 and 1860 with San Francisco as the stated location.

Bellesiles claimed to have counted guns in the probate records of people who died in 1849–50 and 1858–59 in San Francisco, and he embellished his story with a location: the Superior Court.

"I used county probate records from the Superior Court," he told one reporter. "I had to go the courthouse—the San Francisco Superior Court." Yet Clark Banayad, deputy clerk of the court, said, "Every record at the San Francisco Superior Court predating 1906 was destroyed by fire, or other causes, in the 1906 earthquake."

The probate records cannot be found at the History Center of the San Francisco Public Library either. Librarian Susan Goldstein said that the center has "no record of the number of guns owned in the city of San Francisco prior to the 1906 earthquake." Kathy Beals, author of three books on San Francisco's early probate records, says, "To my knowledge, there are no official probate files in existence for years prior to 1880, and only scraps from 1880 until 1905."

When a reporter told Bellesiles that the probate records could not be found at the San Francisco Superior Court, he changed his story: "Did I say San Francisco Superior Court? I can't remember exactly. I'm working off a dim memory. Now, if I remember correctly, the Mormon Church's Family Research Library has these records. You can try the Sutro Library, too." But according to Martha Whittaker, a reference librarian at San Francisco's Sutro Library, "All official probate records were destroyed by the San Francisco earthquake and fire because the city hall burned down." At the Family Research Library, Elaine Hasleton, supervisor of public affairs, says the index does not list information about gun ownership. "The index only lists names and the locations of the actual probate records. It does not list possessions."

When confronted with these disclosures, again Bellesiles changed his story: "The probate records are all on microfilm in the National Archives. I went to the East Point, Georgia, federal center to read these microfilms."

When this story, too, proved false, Bellesiles changed his story yet again: He did most of his probate research in over thirty different county or state archives around the country—from original records, not microfilm, as he had claimed.

In September 2001, Bellesiles told the *Chronicle of Higher Education* that he had located the records and that he had sent for them himself. But in November, Bellesiles changed his story again, writing in the newsletter of the Organization of American Historians that he forgot where he viewed the San Francisco probate records.

Writing in the Emory University journal *Academic Exchange,* Professor Bellesiles said he had finally located the mysterious San Francisco probate records. "They are housed in the California History Center. (Complicating matters is that fact that the center, where I read these files in 1993, moved last year [to Martinez], and it does not have a Web site.)"

Bellesiles was referring to the Contra Costa County Historical Society History Center. Bellesiles e-mailed colleagues that the records he cited could be found there, reported the *Chicago Tribune.* However, the center's director, Betty Maffei, said there is "no evidence that such a cache of San Francisco County records exits at the History Center. We are a Contra Costa County archive; we hold Contra Costa County records, not San Francisco records."

The allegations eventually forced Emory to appoint an external investigative committee. Bellesiles was suspended with pay pending the committee's report.

The investigative committee, comprised of Stanley N. Katz, professor of public and international affairs at Princeton; Hanna H. Gray, professor of history at the University of Chicago; and Laurel Thatcher Ulrich, professor of history at Harvard, reported in July 2002 that portions of the book reflected "unprofessional and misleading work" and showed "serious deviations from accepted practices in carrying out and reporting results from research," including "exaggeration of data," "egregious misrepresentation," and "evidence of falsification." It concluded that Bellesiles's "scholarly integrity is seriously in question."

The committee published its findings July 10, but the university withheld the report pending an appeal Bellesiles filed in September. Upon losing his appeal, Bellesiles submitted his resignation from the university faculty. While defrocked, he is not downcast.

Bellesiles began preparation of a second edition of his book for Vintage, the prestigious paperback arm of Random House, at the Newberry Library in Chicago, but that edition was withdrawn, only to be published by Soft Skull Press, a small New York house which also published a seventy-four-page tract, *Weighed in an Even Balance,* in which he took issue with his critics. After Emory began its investigation into Bellesiles's work, the NEH demanded that its name be removed from Bellesiles's research. In December 2002, Columbia revoked Bellesiles's Bancroft Prize.

"One could only imagine the outcry if a conservative scholar, fabricating evidence to prove a pet conservative point, had been found to be careless (to say the least)," wrote Melissa Seckora in *National Review.*

One does not need to imagine, however. It appears to have happened.

John Lott, a University of Chicago economist, wrote the best-selling 1998 book, *More Guns, Less Crime.* Analyzing FBI crime data, the book purported to find a correlation between concealed weapons laws and reduced violent crime rates. On the strength of the book, Lott was appointed to a position at Yale University Law School and later became a resident scholar at the American Enterprise Institute.

On page three of the book, Lott wrote, "If national surveys are correct, 98 percent of the time that people use guns defensively, they merely have to brandish a weapon to break off an attack." The year before, in the *Wall Street Journal,* Lott had attributed this figure to a number of sources: "There are surveys that have been done by the *Los Angeles Times,* Gallup, Roper, Peter Hart, about 15 national survey organizations in total that range from anything from 760,000 times a year to 3.6 million times a year people use guns defensively. About 98 percent of those simply involve people brandishing a gun and not using them."

In 1999, retired University of California at Santa Barbara professor of sociology Otis Dudley Duncan sent Lott a draft of an article stating, "The '98 percent' is either a figment of Lott's imagination or an artifact of careless computation or proofreading."

Lott replied with a letter, like Bellesiles, changing his story dramatically. He now attributed the figure to a study he had conducted himself: "The information of over 2 million defensive uses and 98 percent is based upon survey evidence that I have put together involving a large nationwide telephone survey conducted over a three-month period during 1997." In the second edition of his book, published in 2000, Lott changed the wording to read, "If a national survey *that I conducted* is correct, 98 percent of the time that people use guns defensively, they merely have to brandish a weapon to break off an attack" (emphasis added).

In March 2000, Lott again changed his story, attributing the figure to Florida State University criminologist Gary Kleck: "Kleck's study of defensive gun uses found that 98 percent of the time, simply brandishing the weapon is sufficient to stop an attack," wrote Lott in an article published by the Independent Institute.

In fact, what Kleck had written in the journal *Social Problems* in 1988 was:

> [T]here were about 8,700-16,600 non-fatal, legally permissible woundings of criminals by gun armed civilians [annually, and] the rest of the one million estimated defensive gun uses, over 98%, involved neither killings nor woundings but rather warning shots fired or guns pointed or referred to.

Lott had apparently overlooked the warning shots fired or simple misses, counting all defensive gun uses that do not involve killing or wounding as "mere brandishing."

Nearly simultaneously with this article, in an article in the January/February 2000 issue of the journal *The Criminologist,* Duncan publicly challenged Lott's 98 percent figure. Replying in the journal, Lott again changed his story, returning to the explanation that he himself had conducted the survey from which that figure was derived: "The survey that I oversaw interviewed 2,424 people from across the United States. . . . My survey was conducted over three months during 1997."

But this time, Lott added a twist reminiscent of Bellesiles's flood: "I had planned on including a discussion of it in my book, but did not do so because an unfortunate computer crash lost my hard disk right before the final draft of the book had to be turned in."

In September 2002, on an online discussion board, Australian computer programmer Tim Lambert raised the possibility that Lott had fabricated the existence of the survey. James Lindgren, the same Northwestern University law professor who had exposed Bellesiles, offered to investigate the question. "I thought it would be exceedingly simple to establish" that the research had been done, Lindgren wrote:

> Lott claims to have lost all of his data due to a computer crash. He financed the survey himself and kept no financial records. He has forgotten the names of the students who allegedly helped with the survey and who supposedly dialed thousands of survey respondents long-distance from their own dorm rooms using survey software Lott can't identify or produce.
>
> Assuming the survey data was lost in a computer crash, it is still remarkable that Lott could not produce a single, contemporaneous scrap of paper proving the survey's existence, such as the research protocol or survey instrument.

But let us give Lott the benefit of the doubt: Let us assume that he actually conducted a survey of 2,424 people and actually lost all evidence of it. As Lindgren writes:

> [T]hat would mean that about 25–26 respondents reported defensive gun uses out of his 2,424 people surveyed. Thus, only 1/2 of a person (2% of 25 people) reported firing a gun—and that 1/2 of a person breaks down further into 3/8ths of a person firing warning shots and 1/8th of a person firing at someone.

Questions raised, certainly, but while the origin of the data seemed clouded in mystery, it is not desperately different from that of Kleck and certainly not as strangely absent as the data of Bellesiles. But then things grew stranger.

Julian Sanchez, a staff writer at the Cato Institute, was discussing the Lott controversy on his blog, when a responding comment was posted from someone named "Mary Rosh." Rosh took Sanchez to task for commenting on the controversy without first contacting the parties involved. Sanchez wondered how Rosh knew whether he had contacted Lott or not. What was more, Lott himself had repeatedly complained about the same issue in e-mails to Sanchez. Sanchez did some cybersleuthing. He soon discovered that the e-mails from Lott and Rosh originated from the same Internet Protocol address. (While this in and of itself proves nothing absolutely untoward, it does show that Rosh used Lott's computer or one that entered the Internet through the same gateway, as might be the case with a home network or small network in an office that got Internet access through a common local router.) What is more, he found large numbers of posts by Rosh on many different Web sites, all defending Lott and attacking his critics.

Rosh posted that Lott was "the best professor that I ever had." On one blog, Rosh commented: "Critics such as Lambert and Lindgren ought to slink away and hide." She posted a rave review of *More Guns, Less Crime* on Amazon.com: "It was very interesting reading," she said. "Lott writes very well. He explains things in an understandable commonsense way. I have loaned out my copy a dozen times and while it may have taken some effort to get people started on the book, once they read it no one was disappointed. If you want an emotional book, this is not the book for you."

She added praise for Lott personally:

I had [Lott] for a Ph.D. level empirical methods class when he taught at the Wharton School at the University of Pennsylvania back in the early 1990s, well before he gained national attention, and I have to say that he was the best professor that I ever had. You wouldn't know that he was a "right-wing" ideologue from the class. . . . There were a group of us students who would try to take any class that he taught. Lott finally had to tell us that it was best for us to try and take classes from other professors more to be exposed to other ways of teaching graduate material.

Finally, Lott admitted that "MaRyRoSh" were the first letters of his sons' names.

"The account was set up for his children years ago, and kept around as a way to respond to points in online discussions, he said, without the time commitment posts under his real name might have required," wrote Sanchez. Lott claimed that one of his sons had used the "Rosh" account to post the Amazon.com review.

"I probably shouldn't have done it—I know I shouldn't have done it—but it's hard to think of any big advantage I got except to be able to comment fictitiously," said Lott.

We are most vulnerable to sloppy or intentionally misleading statistics when they are used in the service of a cause we already support. The National Institute for the Humanities, Columbia's Bancroft Prize Committee, the Newberry Library, and the American Historical Association fell for Bellesiles's fraud because they *wanted* it to be true. In the same way, the Independent Institute, American Enterprise Institute, and others accepted Lott's numbers uncritically because they supported their cause. While we must be most on our guard against hoaxes when they buttress our prejudices, it is difficult to establish equivalence between Bellesiles's apparent fabrication of data and Lott's peculiar explanations for his, which were available to some extent also in Kleck's work. The use of a pseudonym for online posting is an artifice used by many well-known persons who slip into their digital mufti when they wish to be part of the online world without creating the uproar that their real-name presence would produce (though using that alter ego to promote oneself and one's work, though tempting, would in the minds of most cross a line that oughtn't be crossed, no matter how tempting it is). Indeed, examination of the Internet's Usenet newsgroups and popular online policy discussion sites illustrates the fact that even nonnotable people seldom post under their own names. This is not to excuse a lapse by someone who should know better if he expects to be taken seriously, but to note that offenses vary as to their significance.

The good news is that nonexperts like the humble blogger can expose the misbehavior of experts, if one remembers to approach their numbers-shrouded pronouncements with the proper skepticism.

The bad news is that these methods are not available to us in many circumstances. In a lawsuit, it is legal procedure, not right and wrong, justice and injustice, that rules the day. Jurors do not get to investigate "expert" witnesses. Lawyers do, but they are interested in legal procedure and winning the case for their client, not justice. The voices that are heard are greatly outnumbered by the voices that must remain silent. The skilled and careful pilot who wants to achieve his dream of airplane ownership must pay extra for that plane, the result of the lawsuit brought by the survivors of the irresponsible pilot, supported by an effective lawyer interested only in winning.

What can we do about it? If we are so inclined, we can demand better, though better is hard to come by. We can write letters to the editor, and we can write letters to advertisers on television programs that we do not believe covered issues fairly. But we cannot always know, and this right is even more easily abused than is the right to use legal leverage to treat a tragedy as a ticket to riches, whether the facts warrant it or not.

We can certainly be skeptical in nearly all things, and we can bolster our self-respect by making the unbreakable vow to ourselves that even if a lawyer assures us we could sue and collect big money, we do so only if our case is not just legally viable but just, and then collect only an amount commensurate with our real losses.

Presuming we can find a lawyer who would take such a case.

17

THE ATTACK ON BUSINESS

Unless you are self-employed, you work for someone; even if you are self-employed, you probably have clients. You are reliant in many ways on businesses, the formal entities whereby groups of people get things done through application of the profit motive. The United States achieved its wealth and position in the world today because of the strength of its business.

Yet somehow business has been transformed in the public mind into the enemy. While the roots of this can be found in the working conditions and wages paid a century ago, today business is purported to be "evil" because it has money. Jurors, being presented a monolithic picture of business, think nothing of awarding the allegedly wronged plaintiff millions of the business's dollars—never pausing to think that the loss of that money could mean that people will be laid off by the business, or that the business's value will drop (perhaps reducing the value of the jurors' own retirement nest eggs), that the price of the business's products may well rise to make up for the loss, or, often, even that the plaintiff is responsible for his or her plight.

Time was when you could buy a cup of coffee from the drive-through window at McDonald's on the way to work, and the coffee would still be hot enough to enjoy when you got there. No more. In 1994, McDonald's reduced the temperature of its coffee from 170 degrees to 150 degrees. The change came after a New Mexico jury ordered the company to pay $2.7 million to an Albuquerque woman who spilled McDonald's coffee on herself while trying to remove the lid in order to add cream and sugar while sitting in a car.

A judge later reduced the award to $640,000 (the case was subsequently settled for an undisclosed amount), even though, according to the plaintiff, her medical expenses were only $11,000—and she, not McDonald's, spilled the coffee. Not surprisingly, this case spawned a number of "copycat" suits by people claiming to have been injured by hot coffee, tea, or cocoa. In England, thirty-six people sued McDonald's for such claims, but the British judge, unlike the American jury, would have none of it.

"I am quite satisfied that McDonald's was entitled to assume that the consumer would know that the drink was hot, and there are numerous commonplace ways of speeding up cooling, such as stirring and blowing," the judge said.

In his decision, this judge upheld the ancient common-law principle of "assumption of risk." Classic precedents maintain that a person who, for example, breaks a tooth on a pit in a cherry pie or chokes on a bone in a fish fillet has no cause of action. Because cherry pies often contain pits and even filleted fish often contains bones, consumers assume such risks in consuming them. The judge applied the same reasoning to coffee.

The difference between the outcomes of the British and American cases is a microcosm of the differences in the two countries' legal systems. As a portion of Gross Domestic Product, U.S. tort costs are now more than triple those in England. Over the last half-century, the share of U.S. GDP consumed by tort costs nearly tripled, according to the insurance consulting firm Tillinghast-Towers Perrin. Even adjusted for inflation, the tort cost per American is now more than six times as great as in 1950.

This estimate does not include indirect costs: the cost of unnecessary and duplicative tests ordered by doctors as a protection against potential malpractice litigation, the reduction in the number of people seeking medical degrees, or the disappearance of certain products, companies, or entire industries due to liability costs. Such costs can be ruinous to investors in or employees of the companies involved. But the biggest cost is borne by consumers, who often are deprived of valuable products. The only beneficiaries are the lawyers, the media, and the experts who contrive such suits.

In his book *Galileo's Revenge: Junk Science in the Courtroom,* Peter Huber gives several examples of how such junk suits harm consumers.

One example involves the pertussis (whooping cough) vaccine. Following its introduction in 1949, this vaccine virtually wiped out whooping cough, formerly a major childhood killer. Then, a 1981 U.K. study indicated that the vaccine might be linked to brain damage in immunized children. U.S. lawyers jumped on the claim, charging the vaccine with causing epilepsy, mental retardation, and other types of brain damage.

In response to this pressure, Wyeth Laboratories, a major supplier of the vaccine, withdrew it from the market. Then, in 1990, the *Journal of the American Medical Association* published a review of studies of vaccinated children, finding no evidence of serious neurological complications or deaths from the vaccine. "It is time for the myth of pertussis vaccine encephalopathy to end," concluded *JAMA*. "We need to end this national nonsense."

Not to be put off, the lawyers came back with a claim that a preservative commonly used in vaccines, because it contained mercury, caused autism. This promised to be the winning lottery ticket for the researcher ready to hire himself out as an expert witness in cases where parents of autistic children sought big money in lawsuits against anyone who had had anything to do with the vaccination of their children.

The original claim came about when a British researcher made the unsurprising discovery that a few autistic children showed evidence of mild measles infection after they had received a combination measles-mumps-rubella vaccine. Oddly, that vaccine contained none of the mercury preservative. While few would expect lawyers to prefer truth over money, there was a time when this could not be said of researchers.

A lengthy study was undertaken by National Academy of Sciences' Immunization Safety Review Committee at the Institute of Medicine. It could find no connection between the preservative and autism or any other disease or dysfunction.

Another of Huber's examples concerns the morning sickness drug Benedictin. In 1979, the *National Enquirer* ran a story claiming that the drug was responsible for the birth defect of a young boy. The only "experts" it interviewed happened to be the two expert witnesses of Melvin Belli, the famous attorney suing the drug maker, Merrell Dow Pharmaceuticals, on behalf of the boy. His witnesses' "expert" opinions linking Benedictin to birth defects were based on a single Australian study using a small number of rabbits. Nevertheless, the "mainstream" media picked up the story, and soon 1,500 lawsuits were afoot, eventually consolidated into a single class action suit. Never was the confluence of weak science, lawyers, "experts," and the media better illustrated.

After spending tens of millions of dollars defending itself, Merrell Dow in 1983 offered a $120 million settlement and withdrew Benedictin from the market. Although numerous studies since the 1950s have failed to find any more birth defects among women who used Benedictin than those who did not, the drug can be obtained now only in Canada. The real losers in this case are American women, who must suffer with morning sickness, deprived of a very effective treatment, for which there is no replacement—victims of lawyers, the media, and the experts.

Some experts paraded before juries have little credibility in the eyes of their peers. Even when such experts do not deprive the public of important products, they can impose substantial costs. For example, in 1985, according to Huber, a jury in Sedalia, Missouri, ordered Alcolac Inc. to pay $49 million on behalf of thirty-two people suffering from everything from nerve damage and heart disease to brain damage, vomiting, kidney infections, and headaches. This judgment was based on the testimony of a pair of "clinical ecologists" who testified that trace levels of pollutants were responsible for all these afflictions. The culprit, they testified, was Alcolac's nearby plant, which manufactured specialty chemicals for soaps and cosmetics.

This opinion was based on the experts' claim that they had found "pervasive abnormalities" in the immune systems of all thirty-two people they tested. Most of the tests they used had been developed by a team at Harvard Medical School, headed by Stuart Schlossman, chief of the Division of Tumor Immunology at the Dana Farber Cancer Institute.

"The expert testimony in Alcolac was not only outside the mainstream of science," wrote Schlossman in 1989, "it was outside its widest perimeter." Nevertheless, on the basis of these "expert" opinions, the jury's judgment had been upheld by the trial judge as well as an appeals court.

Huber shows how such expert testimony is procured: "You get a professor who earns $60,000 a year and give him the opportunity to make a couple of hundred thousand dollars in his spare time and he will jump at the chance," says one personal injury lawyer. "They are like a bunch of hookers in June." Procuring such expert witnesses has become a very cynical business. Huber quotes the Medical Legal Consulting Service of Rockville, Maryland: "If the first doctor we refer doesn't agree with your legal theory, we will provide you with the name of a second."

Consumers may be grateful that coffee has not been withdrawn from the market, although McDonald's coffee cups now bear a warning label. Such warnings, now ubiquitous in the U.S., have become a great source of international amusement, supposedly highlighting the imbecility of Americans. But what they really illustrate is the fear of litigation Americans now confront in every aspect of life. Indeed, many such warnings are so absurd, it is hard to imagine that anyone who needs them is capable of reading them. Consider the following list, all reported as actually appearing on products marketed in the U.S.:

- Box of staples: "Caution: Staples have sharp points for easy penetration so handle with care."
- Electric carpenter's router: "This product not intended for use as a dental drill."
- Package of AA batteries: "If swallowed or lodged in ear or nose see doctor."
- Baby stroller: "Remove child before folding."

- Sleeping pills: "Warning: May cause drowsiness."
- Public toilet: "Recycled flush water unsafe for drinking."
- Sled: "This product does not have brakes."
- CD player: "Do not use . . . as a projectile in a catapult."
- Marbles: "Choking hazard. This toy is a marble."
- Ladder: "Do not overreach."
- Handheld massager: Do not use "while sleeping or unconscious."
- Child's play helmet: "This is a toy."
- Aerosol deodorant: "Do not spray in eyes."
- Rollerblades: "Learn how to control your speed, brake, and stop."
- Laser printer cartridge: "Do not eat toner."
- Electric iron: "Never iron clothes while they are being worn."
- Blow dryer: "Do not use in shower. Never use while sleeping."
- Wheelbarrow wheel: "Not intended for highway use."
- Car sun shield: "Do not drive with sunshield in place."
- Self-defense pepper spray: "May irritate eyes."
- Shin guards: "Shin pads cannot protect any part of the body they do not cover."
- Manufactured fireplace log: "Caution—Risk of Fire."
- Birthday candles: "DO NOT use soft wax as ear plugs or for any other function that involves insertion into a body cavity."
- Mechanical massage chair: "Do not use massage chair without clothing," and "Never force any body part into the backrest area while the rollers are moving."
- Snowblower: "Do not use . . . on roof."
- Dishwasher: "Do not allow children to play in the dishwasher."
- Smoke/Carbon Monoxide alarm with "silence" button: "Do not use the Silence Feature in emergency situations. It will not correct a CO problem or extinguish a fire."

In addition to ridiculous warning overkill and the loss of useful consumer goods and services, such suits impose a heavy cost on corporations, which must come out of investor funds, employee wages, and consumer prices. As Walter K. Olson relates in his book *The Rule of Lawyers,* some of these verdicts have actually run into the billions of dollars.

For example, on Christmas Eve 1993, a drunk driver in California rear-ended a car stopped at a red light, at a speed of 70 mph. The six survivors suffered severe burns when the gas tank exploded in the crash. Lawyers for the survivors argued that the fault for these injuries lay not with the drunk driver, but with the manufacturer of the victims' 1979 Chevy Malibu, General Motors. The National Highway Traffic Safety Administration does not regard the Malibu's gas tank as defective; nevertheless, the jury ordered GM to pay the plaintiffs $4.9 billion, which was later reduced to $1.2 billion.

Staggering as a billion-dollar judgment may sound, it gets worse. In October 2002, a California jury found tobacco giant Phillip Morris liable for a woman's lung cancer. This despite the fact that she testified that she knew the hazards of smoking, that her doctors had been telling her to quit smoking for more than ten years, and that she was aware of the surgeon general's and public health organizations' warnings that smoking could cause lung cancer. The jury ordered Phillip Morris to pay $28 billion. To put this judgment in perspective, that sum is greater than the GDP of eighty-four countries listed by the World Bank.

In addition to his books, Olson operates the Overlawyered.com Web site that details abuses of the legal system, and he is a senior fellow at the Manhattan Institute. Perhaps the most damning publication other than Olson's site is *Trial Lawyers, Inc.,* a report on the nation's biggest tort law firms put together in the form of an annual report by the Center for Legal Policy of the Manhattan Institute. The 2003 report is sobering:

> [T]he classic conception of a plaintiff's lawyer is an advocate who waits until he is approached by a client with a grievance to be resolved—by negotiation, if possible, and by court action only as a last resort. But that conception is far from the current reality, at least for the big plaintiffs' attorneys running Trial Lawyers, Inc.
>
> These leading plaintiffs' lawyers run complex, multi-million-dollar organizations that use sophisticated and expensive marketing to pursue clients through every commercial avenue, including the Internet. Like any business expanding its market presence, Trial Lawyers, Inc., uses sales tactics such as no-cost, no-risk offers. As one lawsuit-industry-sponsored Web site declares, "Seek justice NOW by submitting your class action information online to be considered for a FREE case evaluation!" These tactics are often designed to launch mass tort cases of the sort that have all but replaced the principle of fair and impartial justice with a new governing principle: winning through intimidation.

It is an enormous problem, the report continues:

> The impact of predatory litigation is staggering. Asbestos litigation alone has driven 67 companies bankrupt, including many that never made or installed asbestos, costing tens of thousands of jobs and soaking up billions of dollars in potential investment capital. Moreover, the negative social costs of Trial Lawyers, Inc., can be measured in more than just dollars and cents. In 2002, a dozen

states experienced medical emergencies because doctors and hospitals could no longer afford malpractice insurance. Women scrambled for doctors to deliver their babies, seriously injured patients had to be airlifted out of some locations because there were no practicing emergency room physicians available, and hospitals closed maternity wards to protect themselves.

And thanks to Trial Lawyers, Inc., the babies that do get delivered are vulnerable to deadly and thoroughly preventable diseases. Why? The litigation industry has used specious theories lacking scientific support to sue vaccine manufacturers for alleged harmful effects caused by vaccines and vaccine preservatives. Recognizing that vaccines provide enormous public benefit but inevitably cause side effects in some recipients, Congress in 1986 saved the few remaining vaccine manufacturers from near bankruptcy by shielding them from lawsuits and setting up an alternative no-fault compensation system for those harmed by vaccinations. The lawsuit industry's recent end run around this legislation, in an age of potential bioterrorism, threatens not only public health but also homeland security.

Trial Lawyers, Inc., the report says, is among the biggest businesses in the nation, even though it produces nothing and instead leeches off the production of others. The tort lawyer industry in the U.S., it notes, has revenues half again as great as Microsoft Corp. and twice the income of Coca-Cola.

Harmful as they are, none of these effects—loss of products, loss of companies, loss of industries—is as serious as the impact of runaway litigation upon the medical field. Never before have Americans faced a health care crisis as bleak as that looming today. The litigation explosion threatens literally to destroy the U.S. medical system. If current trends continue, Americans will soon face a system of triage like that in Third World countries.

As recently as 1972, there were 10,000 more doctors than lawyers (including judges) working in the U.S, according to the Bureau of Labor Statistics. Yet by 1999, the country had in excess of 200,000 more lawyers (not counting judges) than doctors. And this imbalance is growing. The number of medical degrees granted annually in the U.S. has dropped since the mid-1980s, while the number of law degrees granted each year continues to climb, according to the National Center for Education Statistics. For every two new doctors, the U.S. now gets five new lawyers.

This has not been good news for health care.

Only 3 percent of medical malpractice trials went before judges in 1996, the other 97 percent going before juries, according to researchers at the National Center for State Courts. This is significant, because average awards are higher in jury-tried than in judge-tried cases, according to a study of data from the Civil Trial Court Network. That is perhaps because plaintiffs' attorneys are able to use peremptory challenges to dismiss potential jurors, something they cannot do with judges. Just since 1995, the average award for jury malpractice trials has doubled to over $3 million in 2000, more than twenty times greater than in 1978—even after adjusting for inflation. At the same time, the plaintiff win rate nearly doubled, from one-quarter to nearly half of all jury trials.

In 2001, for every dollar they collected in premiums, medical malpractice insurers paid out $1.40, according to the Insurance Information Institute. Since 1976, malpractice premiums nationwide have quintupled, according to a 2002 report by the Department of

Health and Human Services. Premiums can run as high as $200,000 a year for a neurosurgeon or obstetrician. As these words are written, doctors in West Virginia are on strike—a first in American history. Nor are doctors alone facing this problem. In just two years from 1999 to 2001, medical malpractice premiums increased by a quarter, but product liability premiums jumped by a third, while "other" liability premiums grew by a quarter.

Since 1977, the number of civil cases filed in federal courts has increased by nearly half, according to the Administrative Office of United States Courts. Of these, the share tried before juries rather than judges has more than doubled since 1978, according to the Judicial Statistics Database at Cornell University Law School. By 1996, over 85 percent of tort cases were tried before juries rather than judges, according to the Department of Justice.

Law in the United States is being transformed. It is no longer a search for truth: It is now a process of recruiting victims and making excuses for culprits. It is becoming a process of devising ingenious ways of vilifying parties with deep pockets, hiring expert witnesses who will play along, and carefully selecting jurors who lack the skills of critical thinking. When we blame the car maker rather than the drunk driver, when we blame the tobacco seller rather than the smoker, when we use the law to excuse the guilty and plunder unpopular targets, we abandon personal responsibility, we betray justice, and in doing so, we lose yet more self-respect.

The experts, the media, and the lawyers now form an iron triangle of greed, ratcheting us ever more tightly into tyranny. In the 2000 elections, according to the Center for Responsive Politics, the single biggest industry in terms of campaign contributions was "Lawyers/Law Firms," with more than $32 million in political donations. As the legal lottery continues to siphon an increasing share of our nation's wealth into the pockets of litigators, they will be able to enhance their position of dominance. (In Chapter 19 we will see how the politicians join this unholy triumvirate to make certain that it will get worse, not better.)

The American people are at a crossroads: Either we will reign in the legal profession and return the law to its role as an instrument of justice, or we will become a nation ruled not by law, but by men called lawyers. The prospects do not look good.

This is not to say that businesses are always in the right. Businesses can go wrong as surely as individuals can. Instead, it is an example of how, in attempt to exercise power over people, lawyers, expert witnesses, and news media demonize business by giving only one side of the story. For us to believe ourselves well-informed and capable of forming an opinion, we need to seek out both sides.

That is made all the more difficult by the way in which news accounts portray businesses. When a business is successful, it is feeding off the labor of the little guy—there being no mention of the millions of "little guys" who earn livings, many of them quite good livings, by working for businesses, except when there are layoffs, whereupon it becomes coverage of greedy businesses willing to let loyal employees starve in order to save a buck. When was the last time you saw mention of trial lawyers in a similar negative light in the mainstream media?

And when a business goes wrong, as some have done, the wails of outrage from the media are—literally—not to be believed.

18

TERRORISM AND OTHER WORRIES

Had you seen in 1999 a story describing the events of September 11, 2001, you probably would have thought it was a compelling, if somewhat far-fetched, tale of the post-Cold-War world.

Had you seen at that time—or any time up to and including September 11, 2001—a description of our and the world's response to the events of that day, you probably would have dismissed it as a hopelessly impossible, absurdist fantasy.

In those tragic events and our response to them lies a very important lesson: While the government and various well-meaning groups do all they can to exercise control over us, it is obvious that they sometimes trip over their own attempts at omniscience and politically correct "fairness." From this it can easily be seen that your first and last line of defense is your own common sense.

Let us recount those events and what we as a nation did in response:

On the morning of September 11, 2001, nineteen young Islamic men boarded airliners in the United States. While some of them were in the United States illegally, the laws they had broken were not ones that the government much enforced. They carried weapons, but the weapons they carried were neither particularly fearsome nor illegal. Had the crew and other passengers aboard the planes any inkling of what was about to unfold, the nineteen young men would have been stopped before they had an opportunity to carry out their plans, so limited in power were those weapons. But the crew and other passengers did not know, nor could they have known, nor did anyone else not involved in the plot.

After takeoff, the nineteen young Islamic men brandished the weapons and in some cases demonstrated that they were serious by slitting the throat of a fellow passenger. In so doing, they gained control of four airliners, all heavily laden with fuel for cross-country flights. Our country had experienced hijackings before, and all hijacking threats were taken seriously, no matter how ridiculous (as in an incident in January 1979 when a woman threatened to blow up an airliner at New York's Kennedy airport unless she were introduced to Charlton Heston; her "explosive" later turned out to be a bottle of perfume). Because of our experience with this kind of crime, it had been decided that the safest course of action was to acquiesce to the hijacker's demands, even if they hadn't killed anyone and even if their weapons were insufficient to force the crew to relinquish control. As a result, the nineteen Islamic men gained control of the four airliners.

Things took a stunningly unexpected turn when the hijackers gained access to the airliner cockpits and killed the flight crews, taking physical control of the airliners themselves. They changed the planes' courses. They then flew two of the planes into New York's World Trade Center and one into the Pentagon, killing all aboard the planes and many in the buildings. The fourth plane crashed in a Pennsylvania field. Some of the passengers on the fourth plane had learned of the other crashes through conversations via cellular telephone. While it was already too late for them to save themselves, they were able to prevent the airliner from crashing into its target, thought to be either the White House or the U.S. Capitol. (Had it hit the former, while there would have been substantial loss of life, the president and many of those closest to him would have been safe because they were in Florida. But had the plane hit the Capitol, a substantial portion of the House of Representatives and the Senate, as well as the first lady, who was at the capitol that morning, might have been killed.)

That morning was filled with fear, rumor, and shock. First one, then the other of the World Trade Center towers collapsed, something that had been thought so unlikely that it was not considered by those reporting on the event and even by emergency services who had responded. There were reports of additional planes headed for Washington, bombings at the State Department and elsewhere, a plan to strike Air Force One with the president aboard, and many others. Looking not at what was known but instead at how very much was not known, the president ordered the Federal Aviation Administration to ground all aircraft flying over the United States and to require them to remain on the ground until further notice. The president was taken to a semi-secret underground bunker in Nebraska.

In the following weeks and months, numerous actions were undertaken in hope of punishing the Islamic movement that had sponsored the attack and in hope of making a repetition less likely. Afghanistan, whose Islamist government had shielded the al Qaeda Islamist organization, was attacked. (An aside: While we may think of the al Qaeda terrorist group as angry men in robes who live in caves, it is in fact a very sophisticated organization; indeed, its very name means "the base," from the computer database of Islamist fanatics assembled by Osama bin Laden during the Afghan war against Soviet occupation in the late 1970s and early 1980s. The group is highly computer literate, with access to a vast knowledge of weapons and the weak points of the hated Western world.) A new government department was established called the Department of Homeland Security.

New security measures were enacted, most of which made no sense at all. Following the attack, people were nervous about flying, not without good reason. The airline industry, which is important to our commerce and recreation, as well as being an important employer and tax-paying segment of the economy, had taken a disproportionate hit as a result of the attacks. And, clearly, there was cause to undertake an intelligent effort to keep such a thing from happening again. But the government didn't simply overreact, it overreacted to no sensible end.

There are a few things we know about the terrorists who carried out the attacks of September 11, 2001. One is that they were all Middle Eastern men, particularly natives of the Islamist monarchy of Saudi Arabia. Did we, then, subject Middle Eastern men to heightened scrutiny? No, we did not. That would have been "profiling," the politically incorrect act of concluding, with evidence or without, that a particular group is more likely to be responsible for certain acts than is the public at large. So we instead put everyone who cared to fly through a gauntlet of foolishness. Sometimes Middle Eastern men were questioned, but just as often it was a seventy-five-year-old grandmother from Springfield, Missouri, who was called aside for scrutiny. Entire airports were shut down when "security screeners," who owed their jobs to union membership rather than job performance, lost track of some potential passenger. The government utterly disregarded the commonsense fact that anybody brandishing a pocket knife on an airliner would be beaten to death or nearly so by other passengers before there was the opportunity for him to relay any demands to anyone, with the result that would-be passengers had their fingernail clippers and knitting needles confiscated, and airport restaurants now use only plastic eating utensils.

Did the government take a look at the flow of Islamists into the United States? Did it call on the Islamic community to denounce the extremists from their ranks who supported the attacks and hoped for more? Did the government even tighten the immigration loopholes that allowed the attackers of September 11 to enter the country? The answer is: none of the above. That would have been politically incorrect. It might have offended someone. And today, making any kind of moral judgment—such that being offended is not as bad as being murdered—is not allowed; giving offense has become the worst possible crime.

It should be noted that none of this is to say that all adherents to Islam are terrorists. It is to note, though, that all of the September 11 terrorists were Islamic and, more than that, Islamist—the particularly militant, strict Islamic sect.

The United States is not dependent on many regions of the world, but it is dependent on the Middle East, because it is from the Mideast that much of the petroleum that we use flows. In that we were now at war—and it is a real war, declared by our enemies if not wholly declared by the U.S.—with a movement centered in the Middle East, it might make sense for us to do what we can to minimize that foreign dependence, don't you suppose? Did we? No, again. Because of the immense power that the pseudoscience environmentalists, the animal rights extremists, and the blame-America-first crowd possesses, efforts to exploit domestic American petroleum reserves were shot down in Congress. Indeed, many of the silly things that the administration did following September 11, 2001, might have been less silly had the administration been able to count on a less silly Congress. It is too bad that the administration did not have some better way to bring pressure on that august body, for history tells us that there is no end to the silliness of which Congress is capable.

Instead, we made it more difficult and expensive to use the airlines, we made it clear that the "security" measures that were imposed were unlikely to be of much use, and we did nothing to relieve our dependence on Middle Eastern oil. The result was a terrified public taking to its automobiles, a relatively inefficient use of that petroleum. As this book went to press, the price of crude oil and, more important, gasoline reached record levels, which promises to have vast economic effects.

The political and social opposition to the administration, which is to say the minority in Congress and the news media, sought to assign blame to the administration, to put political advantage ahead of the security of the people it allegedly serves. There are so many examples of this that it would take a book longer than this one just to list them all. But the most public of these spectacles was the commission established to "investigate" the attacks.

There is not a lot of fertile ground here because the attacks were straightforward, as outlined above. The Islamist sect seeks to destroy the way of life that we enjoy, and we, a fairly free and open society, are vulnerable to that kind of thing. An imaginative terrorist who is not afraid of losing his own life could choose from an infinite number of ways to harm America and kill Americans, and it is impossible to anticipate most of them. Yet the commission sought to prove that the administration was to blame for the attacks because it had not anticipated them. And herein lies a problem.

The commission was able to discover some vague, disparate memos from widely separated agencies which, if cut apart, shuffled, and carefully pasted back together in a different order, suggest an attack that very broadly resembles the one that took place, minus any specifics such as the date, the people involved, the places whence the terrorists would begin their actions, or the targets (though the World Trade Center was admittedly a likely one; it had been targeted before and, as a symbol of the commercial West, it was unparalleled). Only by extensive manipulation was the commission able to come up with even this much. What, a sensible person might ask, would any administration be able to do with such information, even if it had been able to assemble it in the way that the commission, with the benefit of hindsight, did? What would have been the right thing to do? Ground all the airlines? Close all the cities and, most especially, the World Trade Center?

Later, the commission blamed the administration for failing to get military aircraft into the sky in time to shoot down the airliners. And how, exactly, was *that* supposed to have worked? Can you imagine a president coming to the people of the United States with the announcement that American fighter planes had shot down several American airliners because there was the belief, based on snippets of possibly unrelated information, that they might be headed for terrorist crashes into important American buildings? Is there anyone who would want the government to begin shooting down airliners based on that kind and amount of information? Even if those planes had been shot down and the World Trade Center saved, the administration would have been excoriated for having done so, the information denounced as insufficient—and the criticism would have come from the same people who have since criticized the administration for *failing* to shoot down those planes. Which is to say that much of the "security" concerns of the post-September 11 world have nothing to do with security and everything to do with politics, the acquisition and maintenance of power over others.

Our national response to the events of September 11 tell us a great deal about ourselves, and it is not all stuff of which we can be proud. The idea that we look to the government as some kind of omniscient, omnipotent being is a misguided one and a frightening one. For government to have enough power to do all that we expect of it in the way of keeping us safe, we would need to cede to government all our freedom: to admit that we are too frightened and foolish to be trusted with any control over our own lives—the ultimate surrender of self-respect.

Worse, some of the families of those killed on September 11 turned to the government expecting that it was the government's responsibility to "make them whole," to use the legal term. The government was supposed to compensate for the lost loved one. It gives one pause to wonder, standing back and looking at it all. A husband, wife, mother, father, sister, or brother was lost. Government lacks the ability to bring back the dead. And because people are not interchangeable, that lost person cannot be replaced. So the government was supposed to "compensate" the families for their loss. What is the value of a human being? What would you accept as payment for the brutal murder of the person you most love? The very question is an insult, yet it was decided that money would make it all better, as if it were some kind of divorce on a grand scale.

Terrorism is real. There are people in the world who wish us dead, who believe that everything we stand for—such as the notion of self-respect—is detrimental to their vision of the world. They want to exercise the ultimate power over us, the power to kill us. We quite reasonably disagree and quite reasonably hope that those who come round seeking killing end up the guest of honor at such killings as take place.

There will be more terrorist acts. The bombing of the World Trade Center in February 1993 and the bombing of the Murrah Federal Building in Oklahoma City a little more than two years later, added to the atrocities of September 11, demonstrate that. It is simple for even a lone individual—consider Theodore Kaczynski, also known as the Unabomber—to bring about death and mayhem on a broad scale. Terrorism is the crime of the new millennium, even as serial murder was the crime of the last part of the last one. It is with us, and it will remain.

But terrorism, by definition, is designed chiefly to incite terror, to frighten us. Following September 11, there came to be a cliché to the effect that if this or that thing happens, "then the terrorists will have won." The fact is, if we are terrified, the terrorists will have achieved their goal, because their goal is to terrify us, to cow us, to make us lose our resolve to live the best lives we can fashion for ourselves.

It does not detract at all from the tragedy of September 11 to note that on that day about 3,000 people were killed as a result of the Islamist attacks, while 2,416,425 people died in the U.S. in 2001, or about 6,620 per day, every day. Though terrorism is, and rightly so, a cause of concern, even in that fateful year terrorism accounted for slightly more than one-tenth of 1 percent of the deaths in the U.S., which statistically means that a person who died in the U.S. in 2001 had a 99.9 percent chance of dying for a reason other than a terrorist act.

For instance, in the U.S. during that year, 700,142 people died of heart disease; 553,769 of cancer; 101,537 from various accidents, and so on. More than 60,000 died from the flu and pneumonia. More than 30,000 died from systemic infections.

These statistics are to enable some perspective; you have to provide the perspective yourself. Consider the extent to which you have been concerned about terrorism since 2001. Have you been 233 times as concerned about heart disease? Have you been 185 times as concerned about cancer? Have you worried 34 times as much about having an accident, 20 times as much about the flu, and 10 times as much about developing some sort of fatal infection? Has your concern about other causes of death held a 999-to-1 ratio over your concern about terrorism?

Of course, the statistics are not utterly valid—statistics seldom are—because the concern over terrorism includes the fear that it might happen again and that, indeed, the next time or the time after that the death rate might be much higher. That is a possibility. It is a historical certainty, though, that heart disease kills two-thirds of a million people each year, that cancer kills a half-million, and that 100,000 people die from accidents. In many cases these deaths could be prevented, were we willing to go to sufficient lengths to do so.

We do not go to sufficient lengths, though, and not without reason. Sure, we all have something inside of us that says we will live forever, that the effects of actions will happen to someone else, not us. Still, we know that some activities are more dangerous than others, and we engage in them anyway, having decided that the pleasure is worth the risk, even when that risk is relatively high.

On August 29, 2004, the *New York Daily News* provided something more for those who like to worry to worry about:

A tsunami triggered by a volcanic eruption on an island off the coast of Africa could result in mountainous waves up to 75 feet high crashing into New York and other East Coast cities, scientists are warning.

A 12-mile-wide chunk of the Cumbre Vieja volcano on the

Canary Islands rattled loose during a previous eruption and is at risk of smashing into the Atlantic Ocean, triggering what could be one of the largest tidal waves in recorded history, researchers told Britain's Royal Institution earlier this month.

This alarming datum may well be of use to an insurance company guarding buildings on the east coast, but what are the rest of us to make of it? One supposes that a preemptive evacuation of that part of the country might create upheaval far in excess of the tidal wave multiplied by its likelihood. And lest readers in California chortle over the report, there is also a theory that much of one of the Hawaiian islands is due to slide into the sea, producing a tidal wave so immense that it would nearly create beachfront property in Nevada—never mind the California earthquake that we have heard for years will have the same effect. What are we to do: Create a city of 300 million people in the neighborhood of Topeka, Kansas, and, once there, worry about tornadoes?

(Persons in the United States who tuned in to the news late the evening of Christmas 2004 heard the first reports of the Indian Ocean earthquake and subsequent tsunami that killed many thousands. They were probably not surprised when days later the chorus of second-guessers began their song. The first verse had to do with the fact that the Pacific Rim countries have an elaborate tsunami warning system, while the less-developed countries of the Indian Ocean do not. They did not bother to mention that this is because Pacific Ocean tsunamis are common, while they are rare in the Indian Ocean. The second verse was even more foolish: It was argued that industrialized society had somehow caused the earthquake itself.)

Benjamin Franklin famously said, "They that can give up essential liberty to obtain a little temporary safety deserve neither liberty nor safety." How much liberty do you suppose is the right amount to give up in order to be safe from terrorism? As much as you give up to be free of heart disease? As much as you give up to be free from cancer? As much as you give up in order to avoid accidents, or contracting the flu, or getting an infection? And this assumes that death from terrorism is as likely as death from those other things, even though statistically it is not.

Something further to ponder—the most important thing—is this: There is nothing you can do to make yourself entirely safe from any of those things. Yes, you can reduce the statistical likelihood of any of them visiting you, but too much reliance on statistics eliminates consideration of pure chance, which is a very big player in all our lives.

Look: By all measures, Jim Fixx was a remarkable man. His 1977 book, *The Complete Book of Running,* did much to popularize the sport of distance running as both a competitive endeavor and a way to improve cardiovascular health. In July 1985, while he was out running, he fell to the ground stone dead of a heart attack. He was fifty-two years old.

Lance Armstrong loved to race on a bicycle, and he was very good at it. In 1996, the twenty-five-year-old bicyclist was ranked number one in the world when he was diagnosed as having testicular cancer that had metastasized to his lungs and brain. It would almost certainly prove fatal—but it didn't. He went on to become the first person ever to win six Tours de France.

Two very talented, trained athletes. But they have something else in common: They defied the best opinions of the experts and more statistical analyses than there is space here to repeat. If the experts and their numbers were accurate, Armstrong would have been dead in 1996, while Fixx, now in his seventies, would be a marvel of geriatric fitness, with heart and lungs as clear and strong as those of most men half his age. Perhaps Fixx listened to the experts and paid no attention to warning signs that might have led him to some course of treatment or action that could have prolonged his life. Armstrong was certainly unmoved by the dire "proof" offered by the statistics. Perhaps if the treatment or action had precluded running, which he loved, Fixx would have chosen to live the shorter but more rewarding life that turned out to be his fate. If he had, he, too, would have been going against the experts, though different ones now than those who could have "proved" statistically that he would not drop dead at fifty-two.

What would you do were you in the position of Fixx before his death, or Armstrong before his recovery? It's not just an academic or philosophical exercise, because you are in their position, to large and small degrees, dozens of times every day.

Returning to the matter of terrorism, we have all heard stories of people who would not normally have been in the World Trade Center but who just happened to be there the morning of September 11, and stories of those who missed their buses, or who went to a dentist appointment only to learn that they had not checked the message on their answering machine which told them the appointment was canceled, who would normally have been in the World Trade Center that day but weren't. Pure, sheer chance kills, and pure, sheer chance saves. If you are religious, you might think of this as some kind of divine intervention, the "Hand of Providence," as it was once called; perhaps like many you have a vague, amorphous spiritual sense that talks of "fate." Those things are far beyond the scope of this book, which is fine— they're perfectly adequately discussed in hundreds of other books.

The point is twofold. The first part is that it abrogates your self-respect for you to expect anyone to protect you entirely from anything, including the acts of terrorists. The second is that the (generally over-stated, so far) risk of terrorism is like other risks. It is up to you to decide how concerned you are and ought to be with it and what actions or changes in your life are appropriate, what *measures* to take—the word "measure" being something that is a response that is in pro-portion. Only you can decide what the right measures are for you.

Some of them would seem nonsensical to most of us: cowering in a shelter, breathing bottled air, drinking specially purified water, and dashing out only occasionally to replenish the supplies. Some of them make more sense, as with a person I know who, when his family grew too large for their home in the city moved to a suburb. This person was willing to endure a long daily commute in exchange for the belief that if there were even an enormous terrorist attack reducing the entire city to rubble, his family would be safe, but it turned out that this was-n't necessary. He talked with his bosses, and they decided that his work was such that he could do it from home, via computer. He actually gained extra time for work, and extra time with his family, by telecom-muting. He thought it prudent to make sure his household was stocked up on food and even had plenty of bottled drinking water. This hasn't protected them from any terrorist attacks so far, but it cer-tainly came in handy when a snowstorm left them without electricity for nearly a week, with roads largely unplowed and travel, even to the store, all but impossible. People where there is a regular threat of bad weather often lay in such supplies anyway.

Some people have done little or nothing, concluding that terror-ism is no easier to predict than the possibility of getting conked on the head by a meteorite. (Interestingly, the *New York Times* once ran an article that stated that your chance of being killed by an asteroid is greater than your chance of dying in an airplane crash. This is statistically sound, which chiefly serves the purpose of showing how misleading statistics can be. Yes, it has been determined that over the history of the Earth, the planet has been devastated by a collision with an asteroid a few times every million years or so, and the effects of such a collision would kill so many people that the total would exceed the total killed in plane crashes between asteroid collisions. As a practical matter, on a scale consistent with even very long human lifetimes, most people live their entire lives without anyone anywhere being killed by an asteroid, while thousands die in plane crashes.)

Terrorism is frightening, in part because of the coverage it receives and the human tragedies it brings to light, and certainly because we are horrified to be reminded that there are people in the world who would see us dead and are willing to do terrible things to bring our deaths about. But the bottom line is that every life ends in death, and many of those deaths are tragic. Spending a disproportionate amount of time worrying about it may prolong our lives, but in another way it allows death to enter and take control of our lives before its time.

Self-respect demands that you take the measure for yourself, and that you do not count on others to do it for you or criticize them if the measures that they find right are different from your own. That applies to terrorism. It applies to everything else, too.

19

THE MONEY FACTOR

Follow the money." That famous quote, attributed to the source called "Deep Throat" by Watergate scandal reporters Bob Woodward and Carl Bernstein, has proved to be wise advice in unraveling other relationships and actions which might otherwise defy explanation. Another saying worth keeping in mind is, "The Golden Rule: Whoever has the gold rules," not so much because it is true—it isn't always—but because it is true among those for whom money seems to be the only measure of value.

Much of the phony science, bad law, and erroneous reporting is, in addition to gaining power over people, formulated in pursuit of money. Scientists seek research grants and other funding, some of which comes from appearing as expert witnesses. Lawyers, many of whom advertise on television in search of plaintiffs for personal injury and class action lawsuits, employ physicians and scientists in hope of winning those suits—which often end up paying far more to the lawyer than to the plaintiffs. The scientists, physicians, and lawyers all appear on television news programs, which serves their purposes—achieving fame that aids their pursuit of grants and clients—and serves the purposes of the media, providing controversial topics for discussion, thereby increasing ratings and circulation and allowing the media to charge more for advertising.

Cheap, prepackaged reports make it easy for the news media to appear to do their jobs while avoiding actual hard work. The splashier the headline, the better. Thus we have groups such as the Center for Science in the Public Interest (mentioned in Chapter 11) becoming real media darlings. "CSPI is a hit with journalists largely because of its inflammatory rhetoric and dependable alarmism, which make for eye-catching stories," writes Jacob Sullum in *Reason*. Does anyone bother to find out if the claims made by such groups are accurate? No. It's easier to hedge by stating that this group with its impressive-sounding name has made the claim; all the better if the lead paragraph can end with the magic words: "a new study shows." The reporter then has the out of saying, "I'm just reporting what I heard—I am not responsible for whether or not it is true." So much for the trendy "news you can use."

Writing in OpinionJournal.com, Orson Scott Card takes it even further. "[T]he reporters covering science in America today are so wretchedly miseducated that they don't even know what questions to ask when interviewing biased sources," Card writes. "And they are perfectly willing to make ridiculous statements—which would include any sentence beginning with 'scientists believe.'

"This is the postreligious equivalent of a fundamentalist preacher starting a sentence with 'The Bible says.' It invokes authority without context, without understanding, and without admitting the possibility of error. (Most self-respecting fundamentalist preachers would at least tell you which book in the Bible they were quoting.)"

In September 2004 the country witnessed the spectacular results of media, science, and politics coming together in a particularly alarming way. A CBS television program broadcast a report centered on several documents which the network said it had acquired and which cast the president of the United States, then seeking reelection, in a bad light in connection with his military service more than three decades ago. The network further claimed that it had received the documents from an "unimpeachable source" and had employed document experts who had confirmed that the documents were genuine.

The story would have ended there were it not for ordinary people who, looking at the documents, realized that they were phony on their face. Before even considering the contents, they noticed that the documents had been created on a computer that had not existed at the time they had supposedly been created. Because the people questioning the authenticity of the documents were themselves connected by the Internet, they were able to combine their voices in an ever-louder cry that the documents were fraudulent. The network at first defended the documents and their experts' appraisals. But the shouts of outrage did not diminish, and over a period of weeks it came out that the documents were in fact fake and even that the network's own experts had refused to authenticate them. What's more, the "unimpeachable source" turned out to be a man active in opposing the president.

Assigning motives for what was clearly a breathtaking lapse of reportorial judgment is difficult. At the very minimum, CBS did not allow serious doubts to prevent the airing of a story that, if true, might have been a coup for the network. It was governed by what it wanted to believe, rather than by gaining its beliefs from the evidence before it. But the network was scarcely unique in establishing the conclusion first, then seeking evidence to support it. (At one point, CBS even tried to find, within the experts' reports that did not verify the documents, language that the network said did verify them.)

Many, perhaps most, of us have engaged in this kind of behavior from time to time, and many, perhaps most, of us have learned that it seldom leads to the desired outcome. Perhaps it is something as modest as looking for reasons to believe that a sports team will win—when what is really being said is that one likes that team and hopes it will win. The lesson is driven home a little more vividly if evidence gathered in support of a hope leads one to, say, bet twenty dollars on the game.

But this phenomenon lies at the heart of more than news reports and sporting events. It is fundamental, for instance, to the way many lawsuits are undertaken.

Chapter 17 dealt with the assault on business, primarily as manifested through the plaintiffs' bar. But that is not the end of it nor, really, the beginning. The legal profession has established itself as controlling the only branch of government that wields true power over how we live our lives. That may seem like a very strong statement, but it's true.

The American Bar Association says that as of April 2003 there were 1,058,662 lawyers in the U.S.; that is before the number was increased by that year's law school and bar class graduations and, of course, before subsequent years' hatches. There are more lawyers in this country than there are total residents in each of seven states, eight by now. There is one lawyer for every 290 people in the United States, compared to one physician for every 350. This represents a substantial growth in the lawyer population: 627 people had to share each lawyer in 1960; by 1988, there was a lawyer for every 339 people. Remember that the total population has grown, too; growth in the lawyer supply has exceeded population growth by a substantial margin. By comparison, there are about 690 people per lawyer in Great Britain; 2,450 per lawyer in France; and in Japan, 8,150 have to somehow squeeze by per single lawyer.

There were about 300,000 lawyers, total, in the U.S. in 1960. The lawyer population having more than doubled relative to the population over the last forty years, there is a need for them to have something to do, or at least they feel a need to have something to do. The ABA says that 3 percent of American lawyers work in some capacity in the judicial branches of federal and state government. An additional 8 percent work in nonjudiciary jobs in government. (For those fascinated by numbers, this means that in the United States the governments alone employ more than 116,000 lawyers. That's more than the total population of many cities—and, oh, what a city it would be, if they all lived there!) That leaves almost 950,000 lawyers. What are they all doing?

Some serve, either in-house or with law firms, as counsel for companies. Some are in general practice, putting together wills, dealing with closings in real estate transactions, and the like. (Interestingly, in other countries many of these functions are performed by what amounts to a clerk, a licensed paralegal who charges less than a lawyer does.) But even these duties do not require more than 900,000 attorneys. What are these lawyers to do? Sue people.

"America has deregulated the business of litigation. In a series of lamentable legislative and judicial changes over the past few decades, we have encouraged Americans to sue each other," wrote Walter K. Olson in *Medical Economics* in September 1991. "The unleashing of litigation in its full fury has done cruel, grave harm and little lasting good. It clogs and jams the gears of commerce, sowing friction and distrust between the productive enterprises on which material progress depends and all who buy their products or work at their plants and offices. It seizes on former love and intimacy as raw materials to be transmuted into hatred and estrangement. It sets parent against parent, doctor against patient. It exploits the bereavement that some day awaits the survivors of us all and turns it to an unending source of poisonous recrimination. It torments the provably innocent and rewards the palpably irresponsible. It devours hard-won savings and worsens every animosity of a diverse society. It is the special American burden, the one feature hardly anyone admires of a society that is otherwise envied the world around."

To some lawyers—and we all know or have heard of them—the law is a true profession, a place of learning and scholarship and the proper handling of such conflicts among men as are unavoidable. But to many others, the law is a machine that prints money and they get most of it. Turn on the television. Look at the advertisements. Where once there were come-ons for pornographic 900 numbers there are now lawyers encouraging you to sue someone. Sometimes these advertisements are seeking plaintiffs for a class action lawsuit the firm is already undertaking. There are, certainly, differences between the services offered by the lawyer ads and those offered by the old 900 numbers, but there are similarities, too. But these outfits are small time compared to the big law firms devoted to tort actions, class action, or otherwise. Like a flock of vultures they pick a likely victim, swoop down, and soon there is little remaining but bones and fattened vultures, with the purported plaintiff(s) given whatever was left over after the birds were sated. Companies employing many thousands of people have been driven out of business by this kind of litigation, something to be remembered when a political candidate who is also a lawyer holds forth on the subject of job creation.

This kind of law practice is very much like the problem at CBS: A conclusion is reached, then evidence to support it is sought or, often, victims of the preconceived offense are canvassed for. It is almost like trying to find cookies that fit the cookie cutter.

As noted, not all lawyers are in tort practice (though of those who aren't, many are employed in either prophylactic or courtroom defense against them—there are at least two lawyers per lawsuit).

The need for sweeping reform of tort law is largely unquestioned outside the legal industry. So why hasn't it taken place?

The coterminous Town/Village of Scarsdale, New York, has an unusual system of selecting local officials. A slate of candidates—one candidate per position to be filled—is chosen by an entity called the Town and Village Civic Club. That slate, with rare exception, comprises all the candidates on the ballot, and is elected. Scarsdale points with pride at how smoothly things have run since the adoption of this system, the catalyst of which was the rancorous election of 1909 in which the Democrat candidate went back on a handshake agreement not to run, enraging the Republican candidate. As the years unfolded, both parties' town committees agreed to the "nonpartisan" system. Scarsdale's elections since then have been mere afterthoughts, the real decisions having been made by a quasi-official organization. It is interesting and appears to work, but it does not closely resemble most people's idea of democracy.

The judicial branches of the federal and state governments are populated in much the same way. But instead of the Town and Village Civic Club the governing body is the bar association. Bar associations may be thought of as the lawyers' trade union, and the practice of law as a closed shop.

Bar associations, much like the craft guilds of centuries past, were formed to oversee the training of lawyers and, in a day when the number of lawyers was easily controlled, limit that number. While state associations and the American Bar Association today serve those purposes to some extent (though limiting the number of lawyers is a lost cause), they chiefly serve to promote the legal profession and to regulate it, making lawyers, literally, a law unto themselves.

The self-regulation of the legal profession has drawn attention and been criticized, and defended, as when in the May 2002 *Virginia Lawyer Register* Virginia Bar Counsel Barbara Ann Williams proffered a claim: "Comparing the number and resolution of complaints against attorneys with the number and resolution of complaints against professionals who are not self-regulated dispels the notion that attorney self-regulation serves lawyers at the expense of the public." Well, no, it doesn't. The only valid comparison would be one involving self-regulated lawyers versus non-self-regulated lawyers. But she does provide some statistics that are enlightening in a fashion she probably didn't intend: In the fiscal year 2002, complaints were filed against almost 15 percent of Virginia's lawyers, compared to less than 6 percent of its dentists, less than 4 percent of its physicians (including surgeons), and less than 0.5 percent of its nurses. What this tells us is open to debate, but the possibilities do not obviously point to the ability of the legal profession to keep its clients—who, after all, *filed* those complaints—happy.

At the swearing in of new lawyers on a steamy late-summer 1996 afternoon in Brooklyn, New York, the presiding officer delivered a little homily in which he warned the group against—what? Failing to adhere to the law as written? Failing to provide the best possible representation for their clients? Failing to buck the trend and bill only hours actually worked? No. He warned them, these recent graduates of, mostly, very good law schools who had only recently passed the bar examination: *not to dip into the till!* Appropriating money belonging to clients before a lawyer has clear title to that money, he said, is very likely to get one disbarred. He didn't couch it in terms of right and wrong—sadly, justice is not as important to the machinery of the law as we might hope and believe, as when the killer goes free because his lawyer has gotten the videotape of him doing the killing ruled inadmissible at trial. Still, it was probably a useful reminder, if for no other reason than to point out that it *is* possible to get disbarred in New York, something they might not have believed after, say, looking at what is known as the Matter of Delaney, from February of that year.

Delaney was a lawyer in New York when he *pled guilty* in federal court to witness tampering, tax evasion, and mail fraud. As a result, he was suspended from practice, then disbarred. He appealed, citing a belief that his guilty plea had not constituted a conviction. (He won, because he had not yet been sentenced.)

But the question of whether the legal community is capable of regulating itself is a side issue. Bar associations exist today mainly to promote the legal profession, which is to say create as much work as possible for lawyers. For instance, the ABA House of Delegates passed a resolution on same-sex marriage on February 18, 2004. The resolution opposed any federal measure that would prohibit states from defining marriage. Timothy Walker, delegate from Colorado, said that the resolution was silent on same-sex marriage but was "about states' rights." In the same session, the ABA voted to oppose extending to states and municipalities the authority to enforce the nation's immigration laws.

It takes little imagination to realize the land-office business that fifty different marriage and domestic partnership laws would create for lawyers. Add to that the fact that the Defense of Marriage Act does not require states to recognize other states' innovative marriage laws. In a fairly mobile society, all kinds of legal mischief could come to pass.

Divorce, however, is divorce. The all-lawyer National Conference of Commissioners of Uniform State Laws sought to establish a national standard for marriage *dissolution* when it followed California's example in establishing a model "no-fault" divorce law. As is customary, the law was passed along to the ABA for its approval before being distributed to the nation's state legislatures, most of whom approved it in one form or another. There's no particular advantage to lawyers in having vastly different divorce laws from state to state. What emerged is the lowest of low common denominators, setting marriage apart from all other contracts in that it may be unilaterally broken, and no evidence other than the allegation itself—that a marriage is "irreconcilable"— by one party is required. This allows lawyers to make good livings merely doing the paperwork.

Promotion of the legal profession does not typically involve selling lawyers to the public. For most people, a lawyer is not a discretionary expenditure, and when one needs a lawyer it is not a happy event resulting from one *wanting* to have a lawyer. Certainly, bar associations and their members like to think of it as a public service when they advise people to get their affairs in order ("pay a lawyer today or your survivors will pay a lawyer a lot more tomorrow, especially if they had your respirator unplugged and parted you out for transplants because you did not hire a lawyer to draw up the document telling them not to"), and there *is* some sense to it. But the real, hard-core promotion of the legal industry, the special interest that is the legal community, comes in the country's legislative bodies. The more lawyers in the state house, they argue, the better.

"[I]n the recent past, there have been bills introduced to eliminate the South Dakota Bar Association altogether," wrote James S. Nelson, president of the South Dakota Bar Association, to his membership in December 1996. "Lawyer legislators have historically been instrumental in saving our profession and the legal system from certain disaster. That is why it is critical for lawyers to continue to serve in the legislature. . . . Ideally, every lawyer should have the opportunity to serve in the legislature. I urge all of you to seriously consider serving several terms."

Writing in his state's bar journal in the November/December 2003 issue, William M. Corrigan Jr. spoke of the Missouri Bar Association's efforts to gain greater sway in Jefferson City. "I am delighted to report that, thus far, 10 lawyers have contacted me to express varying levels of interest in running for the legislature," he said. "Remember, only 26 lawyers currently serve in the legislature. Thus, the bar's initiative is off to a great start. . . . There are a number of steps that the state bar is undertaking to increase the number of lawyers in the legislature."

David Beckman, president of the Iowa State Bar Association, wrote during his tenure of something that nonlawyers might be disinclined to see as a problem: "Lawyer-legislators have become an endangered species. There are a total of 12 lawyer legislators in Iowa, six in the House and six in the Senate. That is 12 out of 150. Eight percent. Thirty years ago there were almost three times as many lawyer-legislators in Iowa." It is unlikely that 8 percent of Iowans are lawyers, so some would argue that even at the low figure Beckman lamented the legal special interest was disproportionately represented on the high side.

In the spring of 1998, William G. Scoggin, director of governmental affairs for the North Carolina Bar Association, commented on an earlier plea by Betty Quick, president of the association, for more lawyers to seek elective office.

"It is encouraging to note that some members of the bar heeded Quick's call (or perhaps anticipated it), both at the state and federal levels," he said. Among them was a fellow who had made a tidy little fortune for himself as a trial lawyer. His name was John Edwards. Six years later, he hoped to move a trial lawyer—himself—into the White House. Had he succeeded, lawyers would have gained control of all three branches of the federal government, as was the case during the litigious 1990s.

In numerous states, the representation of lawyers in the legislature is dropping, and the state bar associations intend to reverse the trend. The reason, if not already obvious, is that it is nearly an article of faith that a lawyer's first duty is to promote the legal profession. They sometimes let that fact get in front of themselves, as happened in the Georgia legislature in 2002. Writing in the *Macon Telegraph,* reporter Andy Peters described a mistake made by Rep. Tom Bordeaux: "Bordeaux, a Savannah trial lawyer and chairman of the House Judiciary Committee, told the House that legislation he authored was complicated, and lawmakers in the chamber who weren't attorneys probably wouldn't understand it." He was jeered for the remark. In Florida in 2001, Senate President Tom McKay said a new ethics bill probably would not come to a vote because four senators who were lawyers had looked at it and pronounced it "bad."

"I can't tell you why it's terrible; I don't have the educational background," he told the *St. Petersburg Times.* The issue of whether legislatures should be considering laws they do not understand is of less concern to the bar than that laws which only lawyers can understand be enacted. It means work for lawyers when only a lawyer can tell you what a particular law means.

But it is at the federal level where things become frightening, and where the unholy special interest alliance all but controls the country.

In Washington D.C., "law firm" and "lobbying firm" are nearly synonymous. Lobbyist lawyers move freely into and out of government jobs and government chambers. Yesterday's—or tomorrow's—agency or committee counsel is today's lobbyist. It's all very incestuous.

In the executive branch, lawyers are everywhere. Agency lawyers produce agency regulations that only other lawyers can even hope to understand. The tax code, produced largely by lawyers and in tax courts populated by lawyers, is so convoluted that it is beyond the ken of any one attorney—ask any business executive who has come up against it, or any of the smiling lawyers who, after payment of a substantial retainer, will put their firms to work helping to sort it out. Forget trying to sort out employment or pension law on your own. The maxim, "ignorance of the law is no defense," has been turned by Washington's regulators into "you'd better hire a lawyer."

Of course, many of our presidents have been lawyers. The first was John Adams. The last three were Richard Nixon, Gerald Ford, and Bill Clinton, of whom one resigned under threat of impeachment and was disbarred, and one was actually impeached and suspended from the practice of law. Gerald Ford is the third.

Then there is the legislative branch.

From all the howling you might suppose that Halliburton, or at least the "oil interest," controlled a third of the House of Representatives and three-fifths, say, of the Senate. But that is not the case. The legal special interest does, including those howling loudest about "special interests." Nor is the legal industry content with that degree of influence.

"I note that the electoral process produced the biggest drop in lawyers in Congress in at least 14 years, according to the American Bar Association," wrote Detroit lawyer Lamont E. Buffington in January 1997. "Compared with the previous Congress, there are 12 fewer lawyers in the House and three fewer in the Senate. In the previous six elections, the number in Congress had never dropped by more than five.

"Since 1981, lawyers have accounted for 46 percent to 48 percent of the members of Congress. This year, they constitute 43 percent. Lawyers headed about half of the committees in the old Congress; this year, they lead only one third." What a nightmare!

Buffington is no doubt heartbroken that today only 158 members of the House of Representatives are also members of the bar. He might rally upon learning that fifty-three of the one hundred senators are also lawyers. Of these, twenty-nine are Democrats, including such persons as John Kerry, John Edwards, Ted Kennedy, and Hillary Clinton.

For those of us who are not Buffington, there is something worth keeping in mind when considering relative power: Though we have more than a million lawyers, they still comprise only a little more than one-third of 1 percent of the population, and 53 percent of the Senate.

While of the fifty-three senators who are lawyers a mere twenty-nine—a bare majority—are Democrats, the political proclivities of the legal profession are clear: In the 2002 election cycle, 74 percent of the $95,408,115 donated by lawyers and law firms to Congressional candidates went to Democrats; during the first eighteen months of the 2004 cycle, 68 percent of $42,049,316 went to them. It should also be noted that among the Republican lawyers are several who seem devoted more to the legal profession than to representing their constituencies in a deliberative, representative body.

In the autumn of 2003, word leaked out about some memoranda on the Democrat side of the Senate Judiciary Committee. The coverage of it mostly had to do with the persons who found and leaked the memos, in which coverage Chairman Orrin Hatch was perfectly complicit. He's a Republican, but he's a lawyer, too, and he spent more time apologizing over staffers having seen the memos than he did discussing their explosive contents.

Those contents detailed complicity between Judiciary Committee Democrats and a litany of far-left interest groups to block the president's nominees to the federal bench. Despite a Republican president and Republican majorities in both houses of Congress, the president could not get his judicial appointments confirmed, because Senate Democrats, a majority of whom are lawyers, filibustered them.

But why?

The president's nominees were mostly of the "strict construction-ist" philosophy, a term which means that they believe the job of the courts is to interpret laws, not create them. While this is a generally good thing for the notion of representative government as set forth in the Constitution, it does not give lawyers all the power that they believe they can acquire.

The philosophy held by Democrat lawmakers (and this appears to be simply how it came to pass, in that there is no special part of the Democrat philosophy of big, centralized government that particularly supports it) is for what is called "judicial activism." This is the idea that the courts can actually create laws where none existed, and is the *reductio ad absurdum* result of an 1803 case, *Marbury v. Madison,* in which the court gave itself the power to declare acts of Congress unconstitution-al. As a result of judicial activism, the court has "found" in the Constitution such things as a right to privacy and a right to have an abortion, even though no such rights are specified. The court has writ-ten in gold some parts of the First Amendment, e.g., "Congress shall make no law respecting an establishment of religion," which has come to mean that religion may not be recognized in any public circum-stance, ever, while flinging down and dancing upon another part of the same amendment, "or prohibiting the free exercise thereof," which the court itself has in effect done. No matter your view of reli-gion, you cannot dispassionately believe that the court has come down evenly toward these two clauses. The Second Amendment has been virtually gutted by Congress and the states, and the courts have remained silent—judicial activism can take the form of acquiescence.

That amendment rules inviolable the right of the people to keep and bear arms; it was written as a line of defense against the seizure of tyrannical powers by the government, so it is easy to understand why the government might want to sweep it under the rug.

An activist judiciary is a system in which one branch of government, which is not responsible to the people of the country, effectively seizes control. It is therefore subject to abuse. Today, it means that lawyers in fact run the country. Through a majority of lawyers in the Senate, who favor judicial activism that grants ever-increasing power to lawyers, that power is being consolidated.

It is all about money and power for lawyers. Think about that the next time you see a television commercial begging you to sue someone. Or the next time you see a lawyer running for political office.

Ah, but surely the news media, also mentioned in the First Amendment, serve as a check on the unbridled power of the legal cartel. If you think so, think again.

And while you're thinking, do a little research. Scan up and down the television dial during commercial breaks. If you do this over a fairly long period of time you'll get a better sense of it, but even a brief survey will show you the extent to which television broadcasters rely on advertising revenues from lawyers. There was a time when lawyers were prohibited from advertising; the lifting of that prohibition opened the floodgates to much of the abuse—and it is exactly that—which we see today. Broadcasters rely on lawyers, especially tort lawyers, for much of their income.

Now watch an all-news channel for a while. Take note of the number of lawyers who appear. (Bear in mind that not all lawyers are identified as such, so the actual percentage of faces you see that belong to lawyers will be even higher than your survey will indicate.) Note the bias in coverage, which nearly without variation supposes that the legal profession is a good thing almost worthy of our awe. We are all to a lesser or greater extent prisoners of our biases, but we do not all own television stations.

The relationship goes very deep. Lawyers are very good at self-promotion. They would not have achieved the control they have without it. One of the things they do is serve up very appealing stories to newsrooms that are happy to have them. Why? Because the lawyer has done all the work, so they are very easy to report—from the lawyer's perspective. This results over time in a terrible skewing of reportage and of the perceptions of people silly enough to believe what they read in the paper or see on television. Businesses are always the bad guys. Why is this? Because it is businesses that lawyers sue. Why is this? Because, as the relatively more honest bank robber Willie Sutton famously said, that's where the money is.

In television news coverage, the employee, the tenant, the consumer is a victim. Business is almost always in the wrong. When the toolmaker Stanley Works of New Britain, Connecticut, sought to move its corporation to Bermuda in 2002 to escape oppressive taxation, the move was reported by media in the state as a betrayal of workers. When Stanley Works, forced to remain in Connecticut, announced that the oppressive taxation would force it to lay off a thousand employees and close warehouses and plants, the move was reported by media in the state as a betrayal of workers. The issue of oppressive taxation was never seriously considered.

The legal system provides entertainment and distraction, too, which helps to fill up the broadcast day. In late 2003 and early 2004, hour upon hour of "news" coverage was devoted to the case of one Scott Peterson, a California fellow who was accused of murder in the death of his wife and their unborn son, who had apparently been ripped from her womb and strangled separately. An interesting, even compelling, case. But not a case of national importance. Nor was it covered because it was important. It was covered because Peterson's pregnant wife disappeared on Christmas Eve. The broadcast media are desperate during Christmas for any story that does not have to do with Christmas, the most sought after of which are tragedies that provide a counterpoint. The reason that you have heard of Scott Peterson and his murdered wife is solely a matter of timing. (This is true, too, of preteen beauty queen—and isn't *that* an obscene phrase—JonBenet Ramsey, whose fame resulted from her having been found strangled on Christmas Day.)

These cases are reported almost as if they were athletic events, with varying "experts"—always lawyers—cheering on each side. Oops, the prosecution fumbled. Hurray, the defense gained valuable yardage on that play. People get sucked into it, the ratings rise, and broadcasters make money. The relationship between lawyers and the news media—the broadcast media, especially—is symbiotic, and is about power and money.

Nor are the more respectable media exempt. All the media believe, but the print media especially believe, that they have a far better idea of what is good for you than you do. On the morning of June 30, 2004, the *New York Daily News* filled its front cover with an attack on a man named Joel Steinberg. By all accounts, Steinberg (a lawyer) was a man whose life has not been well spent. In his trial in the 1980s, it was determined that Steinberg had severely beaten his girlfriend over a long period of time and had done the same to his adopted daughter, Lisa, resulting ultimately in her death. By the standards employed by the media and the courts in measuring the culpability of businesses, the coverage at the time might well have focused on what monstrous perversion of the system had resulted in the six-year-old girl being adopt-ed by Steinberg, but it didn't. Now, having been convicted and having served seventeen years in prison, Steinberg was to be freed. Labeling him "New York's Most Hated," the *Daily News* published a front-page editorial in which it sought to make sure that the nation's largest city devoted itself to hatred of Steinberg:

> Stare at him.
>
> Wherever he goes, stare at him.
>
> Up the street, down the subway, into the corner deli—stare at him. Unflinchingly and unrelentingly and unforgivingly, stare at him. Let him feel every New York eye burning straight through his rotten soul.
>
> Joel Steinberg doesn't like to be stared at. That rattles him. That's why he broke apart a baby girl with his bare hands. She was staring at him, he thought.
>
> So stare at him.
>
> Do not touch him. Do not do him harm. Do not spit on him. Do not curse him aloud. Say nothing. Just stare.
>
> Just stand back, give him room, and stare at Joel Steinberg, every hour of every day.
>
> Let him never forget how much he is despised, forever.

How about that? A supposedly responsible newspaper seeks to gather the frustrations and dislikes of an entire city and focus them on one man. The *New York Daily News*, which knows better than you do, has now undertaken to tell you whom to hate! Had Steinberg been driven to suicide by this campaign, the *Daily News* would have perhaps rejoiced.

Nor is the *New York Times* much better. Beset itself by scandal—one of its young, rising star reporters was found to have made up all or part of hundreds of stories—that august newspaper still seeks to control your life; its editorial board, don't you know, is far wiser than you are. Oh, how much better the world would be if the editorial board of the *New York Times* ran everything, or so the *New York Times* editorial board seems to say. Wherever and whenever possible, that newspaper's editorial page has come out in favor of judicial activism, almost of the establishment of a controlling "star chamber" to rule the nation. Despite pretenses to the contrary, the *New York Times* does not believe that you are smart enough to govern yourself. Those duties should be turned over to those who agree with it.

Added to it all are the "experts" who enable all of this. These are persons who might well be joined together in a new institution, the American Academy of Opinion Whores. Their expert opinion is for sale. Some appear in the newspapers; for instance, an adviser to the failed and apparently corrupt corporation Enron, Paul Krugman, appears on the editorial page of the *New York Times*, denouncing aspects of government in which mere citizens still have any control, up to and including those who were elected to office, and demonstrably feeling no loyalty to the truth in so doing, at least in the opinion of some—the conservative Web site *National Review Online* even established a continuing feature called the "Krugman Truth Squad" to correct his columns. But he is just one example. There are thousands more, hired opinion slingers where once hired gunslingers were brought in to do the dirty work. Where the Hippocratic oath begins, "First, do no harm," their motto might begin and end with, "What's in it for me?" They come in all political stripes.

You can be assured that that is the motto of all these institutions, this unholy alliance. Some of them believe they know better than you do, and some do not care so long as there is a way whereby money can be transferred from you to them—as is the case whenever you buy anything, whenever you pay a bill, whenever you purchase a service.

But of one thing you can rest assured: They do not give a damn about you.

20

THE ASSAULT ON PERSONAL RESPONSIBILITY

Why do you do the things you do, and refrain from doing the things you don't do? Is it because you have thought things through and arrived at a decision with which you feel comfortable, or is it because you are relying on the judgment of others, perhaps fearing their disapproval, maybe even fearing that you will be punished? It is very likely that most of your decisions are derived from a combination of external and internal influences, and it is certain that some of your decisions are. It is impossible to be an expert on everything (and in some fields it is impossible to be an expert on *anything*), so we come to rely on those whose knowledge of a particular subject is greater than our own.

The problem is that objective information is often difficult to find. We tend, rightly, to form our opinions based on our time, place, and needs. We tend, then, not so necessarily rightly, to offer those opinions to others, whose time, place, and needs might be entirely different.

Suppose, for instance, that you have won a contest in which the prize is money for the purchase of a vehicle, any vehicle, but you may purchase only one. You sensibly would like to get the very best vehicle in the world—after all, there is no reason to think that an opportunity like this will ever come along again. So you ask around. And you are probably surprised at the answers.

Get a fast corporate jet, one person tells you, because there is no greater status symbol, nor anything that will get you from place to place so quickly.

Nothing is as good for the soul as a sailboat, a big, well-outfitted one on which you can live during leisurely cruises from continent to continent, says another.

A fine, new, high-end tractor will let you get the crops in with speed and comfort, offers someone else.

The hottest Italian two-seat sports car will really lure the babes and make you think highly of yourself, says yet another.

There are now fine, luxury minivans that offer performance, safety, and the ability to carry the whole family, someone else suggests.

The paperboy (there still are paperboys, aren't there?) mentions that he has been saving up for something that you, too, might want to investigate—the latest in skateboards.

And at the end of the day, all you have learned, really, is what other people would choose, what they think is right for them. If you think about it for a minute, there is something else you've learned, too: Those people all assumed that whatever was right for them is right for you, too.

Those people don't even have anything at stake in your decision. Imagine how much more fervent the pitches will be by those who do believe they have something at stake and who believe they know what's right for you. The problem is, whenever someone tells you what is right for you, they are also telling you that you do not have sense enough to figure out what's right for yourself.

Those who seek power over you do so by claiming that you are not bright enough to have power over yourself. They wrap that dark message, though, in an enticing sugar coating: You cannot be held responsible for anything you do. From the stripping of all meaning from marriage vows to easy bankruptcy to lawsuits against companies by persons who misused the companies' products, from poverty to substance abuse to crime—the current trend is to absolve you of responsibility for your actions and, often, to place the blame elsewhere.

This is offered in the name of allowing you to feel good about yourself. Well, sometimes you shouldn't feel good about yourself. And you certainly shouldn't if you buy in to the belief that you bear no responsibility for your life.

Consider: Do you believe that you are entitled to payment for what you do? Would you be angry if that payment were denied you? Of course you do, and of course you would. You work long hours, do your best, have gone to the trouble of obtaining some skill, and quite rightly feel that for this you should be compensated. Or perhaps you have decided not to work so hard, or for as many hours, or you made the decision to explore facets of life other than those involved in gaining a saleable skill, in which case you have made the decision that income is not what's most important to you. That is your right, and no one has any business taking it away from you.

If you have decided to be a bank robber, you've earned something also, and it is something that you should not be denied: jail time. And the payment for murder in many states is the privilege of being strapped to a gurney and receiving through a needle whatever is behind Door No. 3.

It is continuous. Action equals result, the nature of the result depending on the nature of the action. This is so simple that it is not even much of a philosophical concept, because it is so much a part of the physical world around us.

The words "rights" and "responsibilities" are so intertwined that it is really a shame that there are two words for what is really one idea. They are not the opposite sides of the coin; they are the same side of the coin. It is your right to walk across the room, but as you go, you might want to watch where you are going, because that is what will determine the payment you receive for the action—a cold beer from the refrigerator or a stubbed toe and a reacquaintance with language usually not allowed on television. They are not separate things but all aspects of the same thing.

Yet there is a move afoot to upset this, to spin a fairy tale in which it all can be dissected apart and pieces removed—where actions are separated from consequences and where rights are divorced from the responsibilities that give them much of their meaning. If diamonds were all over the ground, they would have little value; it would be automobile tires capable of driving over them that would suddenly become the item held dear. It is what it takes to get a diamond that makes it special. Just so, it is the responsibility that gives value to the right. They cannot be divorced if the value is to be retained.

Likewise, if work receives no pay, that careful walk across the room results in no cold beer, or if pay requires no work and the beer is delivered without you ever having even to take the walk, then something is lost. The connection is broken, and what is really nothing less than an immutable law of the physical universe has been thrown into confusion. And so has your hope of self-respect.

Human beings, among all the creatures of the earth, are alone in thinking that we can change that law. Every time we have tried, the result has been a little short-term gain in exchange for long-term misery.

The mention of all of this as a law of the universe is not metaphorical. An example from the extremely physical will begin to explain.

Some highly skilled pilots fly acrobatic maneuvers with their airplanes. One of the most popular of these maneuvers is the loop, where the airplane is flying straight and level, then noses up and over to where it is going the opposite direction and is now upside down, then the nose is pointed down (though this is still "up" from the airplane's point of view; the controls do not really change throughout the maneuver) and it dives toward the ground, finally nosing "up" to return to the place where the maneuver began. You might think that at the beginning the pilot feels the same force of gravity as he does on the ground, then feels it slowly move to his back; at the top of the loop he's hanging there, upside down, still at the same weight he is on the ground; as the plane dives toward the earth, his weight—still constant—presses him forward against his harness, and, finally, when the maneuver is over, he is back to sitting in his seat as if in a chair on the ground, weighing apparently the same.

But that is not so. The weight, or feeling of weight, is the force of gravity, which is referred to as 1g. Depending on how the loop is done, there can be periods of apparent weightlessness, or 0g. But if the loop is done in that fashion, it will include a corresponding portion of the loop in which the pilot is pulled with the force of twice his weight on the ground, or 2g's. This is inescapable. No way around it.

The supremely skilled pilot Bob Hoover (and others, too; it is not the ultimate test of Hoover's skill) has perfected a loop in which he employs the centrifugal force of the loop itself to maintain a constant 1g throughout, with the orientation of his weight constantly toward the cabin sole, as if in straight and level flight. There is even a film of coffee being poured aboard his plane as the maneuver is being conducted. Not a drop is spilled. From all sensations, persons aboard his plane might well think that he is not doing a loop above the Earth, but

instead the Earth is doing a loop around the airplane. But the point is
that no matter how it is done, the average g-force on those aboard the
plane is a constant 1. A few seconds of 0g flight here means a few seconds of 2g flight over there. Or 1g flight can be maintained throughout. The way the maneuver is conducted is up to the pilot, but the law
of the universe remains the same.

So it is with what we do. Yes, there is chance—blind, dumb
chance—that inserts a degree of unpredictability, but being chance it
by definition averages out to zero over time, and over enough lives.
And by definition there is nothing we can do about it. But beyond
chance, we can fairly well predict the results of our actions, the responsibilities which engaged can alter those results and make them more to
our liking.

Why, then, would anyone want to remove responsibility from the
equation?

Doing so, it is thought, gives us something which we have not
earned. But it also denies us something we have earned. The former is
always accented; the latter scarcely ever mentioned at all. When the
consequences are removed from sexual activity, for instance, then sex
loses all its meaning beyond brief physical pleasure; and to the extent
that one partner feels powerful as a result of the conquest, the other
feels cheapened. When that activity results in pregnancy, a belated
right to control over one's body is invoked and a consequence is
washed down the drain—often to the anguish of the woman involved
later.

When divorce laws are rewritten—as most in this country have
been—to make marriage nothing more significant than going steady
with property rights, that once-sacred state between two people
becomes worthless. It means land-office business for lawyers, for mar-

riage counselors who, in order to stay in business, now offer "divorce counseling" in which for $100 per hour you are told to "get on with your life." But the cost is greater than that—far greater. The law's view toward marriage today is that you are incapable of making a vow and meaning it. By embracing that view, you make it true. And everywhere you turn there are people urging you to do just that.

All through society, there are movements afoot to eliminate responsibility and consequences. And all through society, there have been people ready to lower themselves to the occasion. It goes far beyond personal relationships.

When it is said that some groups of people should not be held to the same standard as others, a responsibility is removed. But the cost is a steep one: That group is forever labeled as not quite as good as everyone else. Members of whatever group it is might rightly be outraged at the mere suggestion of such a thing. But there are always demagogues who seek power over them and who are ready to urge them on by feeding them the lie that they are "owed" special treatment. That special treatment is nothing special at all. It is true that there are groups of people who, due to some handicap, cannot and will not ever possess the same abilities as most people have. There is nothing wrong with recognizing and allowing for this. It is when manipulative persons seeking power apply such a standard in encouraging groups to achieve less than their best that any hope of that group gaining respect for itself and from others is lost.

When misbehavior is diagnosed as a disease, the person might get away with the misbehavior, but at the price of being labeled "defective." There are people who truly cannot be held to account for their actions, and it is surely just that they not be punished. But those who claim a disease in nothing more than an effort to get off the hook deserve to think of themselves as inferior, as unable to function by the rules that others live by. Their claim of disease can turn into disease— the haunting knowledge of having cheated. Those persons cannot hold their heads high or claim any self-respect, and if they think the people who aided them in getting free of the wages of their actions respect them, they have another think coming.

So it is, all down the line.

There is no escaping the immutable laws of the universe. At best, their effects can be briefly postponed. Anyone who tells you otherwise is not your friend.

21

DEALING WITH GUILT

You know more about yourself than anyone else does. Period. And most of us have an ingrained sense of right and wrong. When we do something that we believe to be wrong, we know it and feel bad about it—as we should, because it provides a powerful incentive not to do things we believe are wrong.

No person, no group, no study can take that away from you. If you do something that you think is wrong, rationalizing that some person, group, or study says it isn't wrong will not relieve your feeling of guilt. Nor should it.

It is, after all, you who will face the consequences if your feeling of guilt turns out to be accurate.

Confession, they say, is good for the soul, and guilt is your guide toward self-respect. When you have a bad feeling in anticipation of an action, it is one of two things: You think that the anticipated action might not work, or you think that it is wrong. Or both.

Perhaps you remember having gotten away with something. Maybe you once cheated on a test, for instance. If you are at all introspective, this probably comes back to haunt you. It does so at times of its own choosing—which are usually when you can least afford self-doubt, when you are most trying to summon inner stores of courage. And when it does push itself into your mind, it probably does so out of all proportion to the significance of the actual event. It comes back to remind you that you once did something that you knew was wrong, and it robs you of self-respect.

I do not offer this as popular psychobabble but rather as a truism: You need to be your own best and worst critic, for above all others, you have to live with you. You might be able to make excuses to others, but it takes a real skill at self-deception to make excuses to yourself.

The reason this is in this book is that all around you there are powerful forces seeking to prod you along toward actions and beliefs that you probably feel deep inside are wrong. Those forces make it easy to go along with the crowd and difficult not to. It might help you to remember that when the crowd has dispersed, you will still be there to live with your actions and beliefs just as if you were the only one who took or held them.

A quick survey of your own life may well help describe the majority of things about which you feel guilty: actions designed to provide short-term relief without any thought as to the long-term consequences. Do not feel alone—if this were not a fundamental human failing there would not be so many politicians holding office after campaigns which offered precisely that. We live in an instant gratification world. Marketers of all sorts have learned that from their perspective the goal is to part you from your dollars/vote/influence as quickly as possible, leaving you to repent alone at your leisure. Surely you have seen the advertisements for strange kitchen gadgets and other geegaws on television that inform you that "this amazing offer" is available "for the next five minutes only." If you watch much television you also know that this is a pure lie, because the same ad runs pretty much continuously. But the marketing trick is a useful one: It tells us that we had better act quickly, before we think about it, or the opportunity will be gone. Many dens, clubs, and bars have on their walls stuffed fish who succumbed to much the same impulse; fish who would still swim the lakes, streams, and oceans if they had looked a little closer before they bit. The goal of modern marketing is to make you bite before you look.

This is not to say that all advertising is dishonest (and, per the admonition of Chapter 1, you might want to subject to extra scrutiny any sentence that proposes "all" anything), but that all advertising seeks to influence you into taking an action or not taking an action. You have heard of, and, perhaps, experienced "buyer's remorse," that phenomenon which comes about when a frenzied purchase soon proves to be less than the promised miracle. If ever you feel overly cheerful and want to put yourself into a bad mood (I can't imagine why you would, so consider this a rhetorical exercise), think back over all the purchases you have made over your life that you wish you hadn't and that a moment's sober reflection would have prevented you from making; consider how that money, if put in a modest investment, would have grown, and how much better off you would be today as a result.

From all directions we are encouraged to give into whim. Marketing is not limited to goods and services. It applies, too, to political candidates and even to opinions. The battle over your feelings is as powerful as, and in some ways more powerful than, the battle for your money. It is like the old cartoons, in which a devil figure appears on one shoulder and an angel figure appears on the other, and they argue with each other over the action you should take. The problem is, today you must provide your own angel, in the form of your conscience—which manifests itself in self-respect—while practically everyone else is there to provide the devil. This illustration may be a little too harsh: People who have good products and good ideas market those, too. But you will like living with yourself a lot more if you listen to that angel figure and take actions only when they pass muster with it.

It is difficult. Damn near impossible. From our first days of life we learn to put great stock in the opinions of others. One of the first disillusionments of life comes when we discover that we cannot trust everything we are told. Some of us refuse ever to believe that fact. Some of us refuse ever to trust anyone on any subject ever again. That kind of overgeneralization is usually lazy and counterproductive, leading in the first case to disappointment after disappointment and in the second case to cynicism and a world of lost opportunities. The difficult but more rewarding path is to measure every assertion, every claim, every sales pitch, by our own real needs and by our own reasoning. It is said that if a deal seems too good to be true, it probably is; that's true, but it doesn't mean that there is no such thing as a bargain. Your own reasoning is how you separate one from the other. You won't always be right, but if you apply some thought to what you bring into or exclude from your life, you'll improve the odds.

The odds of what?

The odds that late on a dark, sleepless, fitful night you won't be haunted by some decision you made.

Today, whim rules all. Instant gratification is the demand. The clinics are filled with people who thought that a night of intimacy with a stranger was worth the risk (or else gave no thought to the risk at all), and who now have some disease as a trophy. Others employ "protection," as the advertisements that encourage us to engage in such activity euphemistically put it, without thought at the time about what it means to engage in the most intimate of all activities with someone you mistrust to the extent that a physical barrier must be placed between you. Even entertaining such thoughts is now deemed prudish and not with the program. Yet I suspect that the number of people who regret a string of one-night stands and the effect they have had on real intimacy with a loved partner later is greater than the number of men and women who point to the notches in their belts with pride. You may fall into either group, and I am not here to tell you whether you are right or wrong. I am here to tell you that your decision is one you will live with in the hours when your only company is your self-respect.

Sexual promiscuity is merely an example. There are others, far too many to list. Societal mores having to do with abortion, divorce, the importance of meaningful work, the importance of self-reliance, even the idea that there are such things as good and evil, have been cast aside in favor of whatever feels good right now. Persons who claim to mean well (and no doubt some of them do, but some of them also seek only to gain power over you and it is impossible to tell the difference) have sought to remove the consequences from casting aside those societal conventions, many of which were arrived at after millennia of human experience. Those persons can remove some of the consequences, for a while, but they cannot remove how your approach to those issues affects your view of yourself.

We're constantly at battle with our tendency to go along with the crowd. But we also recognize the dangers of the mob. The crowd isn't always right. It isn't even often right. Consider the difference between style and fashion. Style is comfort in one's appearance and social behavior. Fashion is an attempt to impress others. The latter is expensive and rarely satisfying; it is often embarrassing. (Don't think so? Are you old enough to have any pictures of yourself in the fashions of yesteryear, maybe with a necktie wide enough to serve as a bib?) Fashion extends beyond attire. It includes the attitudes and actions we take in an effort to be part of the crowd. If you think the old pictures are embarrassing, consider what a tape recording of your conversations way back when would sound like.

We can feel guilty for actions we have taken against our own better judgment in order to fit in. But we can also feel guilty, perhaps more so, for the times that we have been part of the problem, when we have led someone else astray from his or her own judgment.

Judgment has been given an unfair reputation in recent years and has come to be thought a negative attribute. Doubt me? Hold any hard-line position contrary to another person, and see how long it takes for someone to chide you for being "too judgmental." This is nonsense. Judgment is essential to our existence. It is what tells us whether it would be better to hit the nail or our thumb. It is what enables us to arrive at decisions we can live with on those nights alone. The denunciation of judgment comes primarily from those who believe that their purposes would be better served if we were compliant and easily herded.

Judgment is an essential skill. What is not essential is imposing your judgment on others. While much of our conversation is in the nature of argument in its purest sense—a discussion of the various factors affecting a particular decision—if you persuade someone to go along with something that he or she believes is wrong, even if you believe it is right, you bear the responsibility of the outcome both for yourself and to some extent for the other person as well. This is not to say that the person who is convinced has this to offer as an excuse. It is to say that if you have any regard for yourself, you will bear your full responsibility if you have swayed someone to your way of thinking. There is a term for this. It is "the courage of your convictions," and it is a rare commodity.

The fundamental point, over all, is this: If you are uncomfortable with your actions, whether anybody or everybody else is comfortable with their identical actions, and you take those actions anyway, you will probably feel guilty about it. And you should. Conversely, there are times when others seek to make you feel guilty when your own inner voice tells you there is nothing of which you should be ashamed. (It is possible, of course, to do terrible things and not feel guilty about it. People who are like this are, at their worst, called sociopaths. If you are one of those, your problems are beyond the scope of this book or, for that matter, any other book.)

The bottom-line lesson remains much the same: In most circumstances, you are the best judge of whether you ought to feel good or guilty about your actions. As discussed in the preceding pages, the pressures for you to go along with ideas that you believe are wrong is great. There is also a pressure we put on ourselves to create a kind of moral relativism, looking at those who get away with doing, as in the old confessional prayer, what they ought not to have done, and leaving undone those things which they ought to have done, and divining that if they get away with it, we ought to be able to get away with the same thing. Maybe so, but ultimately your self-respect will suffer if you follow that path.

The pressure to succumb to the manipulations of others does not end with your decision to follow the dictates of your own conscience. At that point, you may well be condemned for your decision; afterward, you may be led to feel guilty for it. Again, you have to live with your conscience—no one else does.

There is one area, though, where people often fall victim to external guilt, and it is one where they can least afford to. It is in the raising of children.

Today, more and more parents subscribe to the idea that they are their children's buddies or pals. That is not and cannot be true, pretty much by definition: You cannot be pals if one of you has supreme control over the other. To relinquish that control in order to be your child's friend is to relinquish your responsibility as a parent.

During the course of raising children, you are going to have to tell your child many things that that child does not want to hear. Given the general trend in society, in which feelings trump demonstrable realities, you may end up being the only person who cares enough about your child to tell him or her those things.

Your child, obviously, will not be pleased—not at the time, anyway, though you might receive thanks in one of those moments dramatized in greeting card advertisements, years later—and will probably strike back at you. Few are the parents whose children have never said the cruelest and most terrible things to them.

It is easy at such moments to feel a failure, to feel guilty for having spoiled childish hopes. Sometimes, what you know to be true—that it is not okay to skateboard off the roof because it looked like fun in the cartoon—is so obvious that you can explain it to your own satisfaction if not that of your child. Sometimes it is not. Sometimes, "No—because I said so" is the best you can do. It is a lonely task, being a responsible parent in today's society, and it feels even lonelier when your own child thinks you are making a botch of it. Rest assured that no matter your decision on any aspect of raising your children, there will be people who will disagree with it and pronounce you a terrible parent. If you do

not let the little scamp drive the skateboard off the roof there is someone out there who will say that you are depriving him of his creativity;
of course, if you do let it happen you can expect a visit from the authorities while you are at the emergency room. Meddling with the way
people bring up baby is a growing industry in society—as if society
could point with any pride at all to its own efforts in that direction such
as public schools, where half the kids are drugged to the gills just to
keep them from going berserk with boredom.

Guilt is peddled in many forms, and it often takes a brave heart to
pass it by. Something called the "United Fund," which has since
become the "United Way," is a consortium of charities that has its hooks
deep in our communities and many businesses, and the pressure on
employees to contribute can be great. But the list of causes to which
United Way contributions are distributed is long, and it is entirely possible for people of goodwill to decide that supporting some of them
runs contrary to one's values. You might well decide to give to the individual charities that you support yourself, without the intervention of
anyone else. Such a decision, no matter how well-reasoned, is likely to
get you branded a heartless creep.

We must all sometimes do things that we do not like to do. The
example above, saying "no," then "NO!" to a child, is one of them.
There are many others. It might be that someone you care about wants
to go to the ballet and wants you to go along, and it might be that you
would rather visit the dentist than go to the ballet. Sometimes it is best
to go along cheerfully. Your right to your own decisions does not necessarily extend to selfishness in your dealings with others. Common
consideration, which should grow as our closeness to those we care
about grows, makes some demands on us which, when properly
approached, can require extraordinary strength.

Let us consider that dreaded ballet performance. If you go, but do so only kicking and screaming, announcing that you are doing it "just to keep the peace" and letting it be known that it is an enormous imposition on you, you cannot be surprised if the effect is as if you had been a graceless jerk—because that is exactly what you have been. It is no gift if you leave the price tag attached. When it comes to those we love, suffering in their behalf must be done in silence, because otherwise it is not suffering in their behalf but instead interpreting one kind of suffering into another kind of suffering, which is then passed along. It is becoming a guilt peddler yourself.

It can be difficult to smile through it all. Yet doing just that is an essential skill.

We best retain our self-respect when we follow our own sense of right and wrong. But as John Donne reminded us, no man is an island. We do not live in isolation. Where two or more people combine for some common goal—a business, a project, a marriage—sooner or later there will be disagreement. Sometimes, rarely, it ends with the parties agreeing to disagree. Sometimes, too rarely, discussion illustrates the wisdom of one choice over the other, shows that the differences between the choices are not worth arguing over, or results in a compromise. Sometimes, all too frequently, it ends with a decision or *de facto* decision, with one of the parties going along with it only grudgingly, ready to spring forward with "Aha! I told you so!" at the first opportunity and far too slow to offer, "Well, it looks as if you were right," if that is the outcome. For some reason, we think that something of us is lost if we admit that someone else is right. For the same reason, we think that if we obnoxiously trumpet it when we are right, we will gain the respect of others. If we learn to swallow those impulses and embrace the triumphs of others while remaining modest about our own accomplishments, we will gain not just the respect of others but the respect of ourselves, too. And our relationships will be smoother, happier, and only then offer the opportunity of achieving real depth, whether those relationships are friendships or romantic love.

This is not selling out. It is recognition that we are ourselves imperfect, in a world populated by other imperfect people.

It all comes down to your ability to look at your life, to own up to your mistakes, and to embrace your personal triumphs—which are not the things you succeed at that are aimed at impressing others, but the things you succeed at that make you think of yourself as a good and decent person. It all comes down to the thoughts that visit you in times of loneliness, times of sadness, whether the guilt comes roaring in or whether you can look at your life and realize that whatever life's travails, you have done your best and taken possession of your own life.

22

REFUSING TO SELL YOUR SOUL

I know of someone who reads the obituaries each day, after which he is profoundly sad. Asked why, he says that it is a listing of people he now will not have the opportunity to know. But surely he has no desire to know everyone—after all, look at the number of people he meets each day whom he makes not the slightest effort to engage in conversation. Yes, he says, but it is not until the obituary appears that one for the first time sees why a person might have been worth knowing.

He has, I suppose, a point. Certainly there is no obituary that carries the headline, "Anonymous W. Smith Is Dead; Always Followed, Never Led."

Leaders tend to be lionized in the obituary columns, but it may well be that leadership is an overrated quality, or at least leadership of the kind that so often draws praise. Leadership is a tool, and a useful one, but like any useful tool it can be put to good use or ill. Possessing the power of persuasion over others is fine, when it is used well, but there is a characteristic that matters even more.

Our heroes, generally, have one thing in common: courage of

some kind. That valuable attribute takes many forms, and most of the time we never hear of those who possess it. But even when we do hear about it, it does not always involve the person who led the charge, who waved the flag, who most harmed the enemy.

Sometimes heroism comprises doing what one believes is right even at the risk of great cost to oneself. The belief cannot be lightly arrived at—then it's not "heroism" but "stubbornness"—and the risk to oneself need not be realized. The person willing to stick to his guns who is never called to do so is heroic, too.

This kind of courage is especially difficult because its only reward usually comes from within. The hero who fought off the enemy is immediately praised by those around him. But today, the enemy is more and more the pressure on you to conform to the conventional wisdom—which is rarely wise—without inspecting or questioning it. Those around you are not likely to raise you up on their shoulders with a hearty three cheers for your refusal to do what they are doing, your decision not to think as they think.

It was an act of heroism on the part of Dr. Peter Duesberg to refuse to remain silent in the face of evidence that AIDS is not as it is conventionally said to be. He has paid a high price for his disagreement, but he can hold his head just as high. It was an act of heroism for Dr. Michael Zasloff to go to work nights and weekends to find the solution to a puzzle, and that heroism is in no way diminished by a bureaucracy that for all the wrong reasons denigrated the value of his discovery.

It is an act of heroism every time a lawyer becomes a voice in the wilderness, seeking to establish some relation between justice and the courts, even as it is an act of heroism when someone resists the temptation to sue solely because a lawsuit is possible.

It was, in its way, an act of heroism for Bill Wilson, on his deathbed, to ask for those three shots of whiskey, just as it is an act of heroism anytime someone recognizes that he or she has been drinking too much and cuts back without pronouncing himself or herself "diseased" as an excuse.

It is heroic to insist on the wages of your work and other actions, and to refuse things you have not earned. It is heroic to stick with your marriage and to keep other commitments you have made, even when it might be easier to abandon those commitments and no one in the society around you would criticize you for doing so.

It is an act of heroism, too, to avoid the impulse to force your notions on others.

Have you ever watched fish being fed in an aquarium? The little flakes of food are dragged in one direction by this fish, then in another direction by that one, then some other way by a third, and so on. It is difficult today not to think of one's life as being like one of those flakes of fish food, so many and so disparate are the forces tugging and dragging at us. A great many people feel that "to get along" it is best if they exert no more control over their lives than that flake of dehydrated insect has over its path through the water, and many conduct their lives with just about as much thought. That is their right, as much as others might wish that they devoted more thought to living the only life they have been given.

A friend of mine was once news editor at a big broadcasting network in New York. The work was unsatisfying, because the network largely rewrote whatever was packaged by the wire services, then broadcast it, but it was not at all difficult and, due to powerful unions, paid a hefty salary. He would spend his workday in a windowless newsroom—and if that is not an appropriate metaphor for today's coverage, I do not know what would be—and then go home. He was respected by others because of his seemingly lofty position, but something bothered him. He could not quite put his finger on it for several years.

One summer he took a cross-country automobile trip. It carried him to the southwestern United States, stopping along the way to see sights that interested him. As timing would have it, he arrived one evening at a place called Monument Valley. You would recognize Monument Valley if you have ever seen old westerns or new automobile commercials. Majestic red monoliths and mesas rise from the red sand desert. It is a beautiful place at any time of day, but this evening it was especially so. It was near sunset, the sun a reddening orb in the west. A nearly full moon was rising in the east. There wasn't much breeze, and around him was silence—"blessed silence," he later called it.

Suddenly that nagging discomfiture, which he had never quite been able to identify, sprang to life. He looked at his watch, which he had kept on New York time. It was dark there, and he could see, even hear and smell, what was going on in the newsroom just then. People were scurrying around doing things they pretended were important but that were not important, in their heart of hearts, even to them. They reported on the world around them but at the same time were oblivious to it. Receiving those big paychecks, they were likely to remain there until it was time to retire.

He imagined himself at retirement age—he was then in his mid-thirties—looking back on a life largely spent in that room, doing those things. He looked around him, there at Monument Valley, and it was inconceivable to him that anyone in that newsroom was even peripherally aware of places such as this, of silence, of how small people are but how big are the things life provides to delight us.

The sun now gone, he got in his car and rushed beneath the moon-lit sky to a place called Tuba City, where he pulled into a place called the Tuba City Truck Stop and grabbed the pay phone. He called New York and quit.

He did not know what he was going to do, but for a little while he basked in the rush of relief that came of knowing what he was *not* going to do. He was fortunate, having no wife or children depending on him; if he had had dependents, his response to the Monument Valley epiphany would no doubt have been different, more considered, yet by recognizing what was bothering him he would have felt a great weight lifted anyway. It took the silence and isolation and pure raw beauty of that majestic place on that night to let him hear his own internal voice. He had been too busy listening to other people in the newsroom, for whom quitting was unthinkable, because they were powerful and important, and to those around him outside the newsroom, in hope of believing them when they told him that he was powerful and important. "An epiphany," he wrote to a friend later, "is the point at which the obvious becomes visible."

His life was not all peaches and cream after that. He did and does writing jobs, magazine articles and the occasional book. He has managed to keep himself fed and, by the standards others would impose on him and for a long time did impose on him, is not ragingly successful. He certainly enjoys nothing approaching the financial affluence that would have been his had he remained at the network; in fact, it has sometimes been a real financial struggle for him.

Does he regret that decision, made nearly two decades ago in a place far away? Not for a second. Not now and not any time since then. Because it was that night that he learned from himself what was valuable to him. It is a nice story, and a sad one—sad because it took a trip of two thousand miles and just the right moment in just the right place for him to hear that which he had kept down, had deliberately refused

291

to listen to in the name of getting along for most of thirty-five years: the voice of his own heart.

The world does all it can to keep us from hearing our own hearts. It tries its best to pull a bait-and-switch on us, to tell us that this thing or that thing is what we *really* want; that we *really* want to believe this thing or that; that *real* happiness comes only from making no waves, even in our own lives.

Who knows what would have happened if he had not visited that place on that night? He doesn't. He doesn't know if he would have continued at the network, possibly even convincing himself that he was happy there, or if he would have ultimately gotten the message that he had been trying so desperately to send to himself.

The world, for its own convenience, would shape us as it wishes. If we wish to be more than a flake of fish food in our own lives, we need to shape our lives to suit ourselves.

23

THE ONLY EXPERT ON YOU IS YOU

Entering the Oracle of Delphi, a visitor would read certain inscriptions. According to the ancient historian Plutarch, one of those is the admonition "Know thyself." Socrates put it even better: "The unexamined life is not worth living." Those were useful notions thousands of years ago, but today they are essential for anyone who hopes to respect himself or herself.

Today, it is impossible to escape others who believe that they know more about you than you do. They believe that it is important that they tell you how to live your life, and they believe that it is essential that you follow their advice. Some do it to increase their wealth, others to increase their power. As we have seen, it is questionable whether they know more about *anything* than you do. Certainly, they do not know more about *you* than you do.

Were we to rely on statistics, no one would engage in the sport of skydiving. It is dangerous, and we should, we are told, avoid danger. Nor would anyone ride a motorcycle, because you are statistically more likely to be killed or crippled if you ride a motorcycle than you would be if you didn't.

Many people die, and others are injured, in automobile accidents; still others die when people start their cars with the garage door down, then return to the attached house for some reason, leaving the garage and then the house to fill with deadly carbon monoxide.

Horseback riding is out—look at the sad case of Christopher Reeve, paralyzed from the neck down, ultimately dying.

I have a friend who cut off a toe in a lawn mower accident, so we should let the grass grow long. Of course, there are also those who die as a result of allergic reaction to the pollen when grass grows long—if you're among them, you must move to a locale where there is no grass.

Eating a steak is out, because of its effect on the coronary arteries, and if ever you drank too much you are forbidden to enjoy an aperitif before you don't eat that steak, for alcoholism is an incurable illness.

Never have fondness for anything. If you care overmuch about the affection you receive from others, you're "codependent." If you enjoy intimate relations, you may well be a "sex addict." If you fail to be up on the current television shows, you're "out of touch." If you are up on all the current television shows, you're a "couch potato."

Smoking? Don't even think of it.

On and on it goes. And that is before we ponder the contradictory claims of what is good for you. Both cannot be right, and if you are devoted to ceding control of your life to others you are left hanging. (Of course, if you were devoted to ceding your life to others, you would not be reading this book.)

Were we to follow all the advice we're given, we would hunker in our homes—after having them checked for radon, which, we are told by people who cannot possibly know, kills thousands annually—cowering in fear. We would run back and forth for an hour each day. We would eat scientifically approved gruel containing the exact amount of nutrition we need. We would avoid cancer-causing sunlight. By so doing, we would live in the best available notion of safety.

And we would receive notice from lawyers seeking to represent us in our class action lawsuits against whoever the lawyers had concluded had money, the charge being that they led to our insanity as a result of our being virtually imprisoned. The lawsuit would be large, but the lawyers would keep most of the money if they won, which they probably would were they able to lure a dozen others from their own cells to serve as a jury.

Pretty bleak, isn't it?

Yet that is the condition, like rabbits in a hutch, in which those who wish to do you the favor of exercising their power over you wish you to be.

So let me clue you in on a little something. No, not clue you in but instead confirm what you already know: Try as you might, your life will end in death. You may well believe that afterward you go to a better place or a worse one, or perhaps that you reappear as a different person or even a different creature—your beliefs are up to you to decide.

What is not up to you to decide, because it is a fact, is that life is a dangerous condition which ends in death. It is also a fact that most of us do not look forward to death and are willing to take action to postpone it.

Let us suppose that we now have the choices before us: following the advice of the "experts" and cowering in fear, or paying no attention to our own safety and flinging ourselves off the rim of the Grand Canyon because impulse piques our curiosity as to what it would look like as we flew past. Let us further suppose, for now, that the "experts" are all absolutely right, so if prolonging our lives is the sole goal we will follow their lead to the letter.

Prison or sudden, violent death. What's your choice?

Probably your choice is "neither."

Life is entirely made up of calculations of risk versus reward. A perfect example is that of Janie P. Morris, a young woman in Florida who was a fine airplane pilot and brilliant airplane mechanic who had, with her husband, come to love skydiving. She knew of its dangers, but learned all that she could, prepared as best she could, to intelligently handle those dangers. One unremarkable day she jumped from the Pilatus Porter airplane high over the south edge of Lake Okeechobee when the unexpected happened. She pulled the ripcord and, instead of a parachute canopy, she saw what she described as "this big wad of laundry" at the end of the shroud lines.

Her parachute had failed to open.

When she had jumped from the airplane, she had two parachutes, a "main" and a "reserve." Now she had to cut away one of them, which had failed. This would leave her with only one, and in that it was not deployed she would have to place her confidence in something she knew nothing about. She cut away the failed canopy—contrary to what is a common cause of death among parachutists, an attempt to "fix" a failed parachute during the fall to Earth—and, when it was clear of her and could not become entangled with the reserve, pulled the other ripcord. The parachute opened, and she floated safely to the ground, to the applause of the others at the airport that day.

She had decided to participate in a dangerous form of recreation. She had done her best to learn all she could to minimize the risk. When that knowledge became essential, she employed it and survived.

What is more, she continued to skydive, not becoming complacent but instead carefully critiquing her actions with the failed parachute, trying to learn if there is anything she could have done better. She stopped skydiving only when she learned that she was pregnant and was now responsible for two lives and would continue to be.

Later, at age forty, she decided that she wanted to become a physician. The experts will tell you that it is foolish to decide to start medical school at age forty. And she did lack some of the prerequisite coursework needed even to be considered for medical school. With no guarantee at all that it would pay off in admission to a course of study that is highly competitive and which sends most applicants away disappointed, she studied for and passed the examinations necessary to meet the requirements, then applied to medical school.

Since this is not a biography of a woman of remarkable accomplishment, let's merely note that she is today a highly successful physician who each day makes instant decisions involving life and death.

We cannot know, but it is not ridiculous to think, that the good sense involved in her approach to skydiving, her belief that she could learn enough to overcome any contingencies, was the same thing that gave her enough self-respect to believe that after having done the coursework required as a prerequisite she would be admitted to medical school. Nor is it unreasonable to think that her cool approach to a situation that threatened her own life, combined with her decision to abandon a sport she loved when another life was at stake, makes her better at making the decisions she must make daily when it involves the lives of others.

Perhaps, even, her knowledge that she could act coolly in a crisis gives her confidence to make the tough choices that save lives in the operating room, rather than hide behind some defensible statistic and let the patient die. But had she been interested in the statistics and only concerned for her own safety, she would never have jumped out of an airplane to begin with.

A remarkable example, admittedly, and one chosen for precisely that reason.

The satisfaction of life comes from a weighing of risks versus rewards. Not all the risks involve sudden, violent death, as is the case with a skydiver. (And what motorcyclist or driver has not experienced moments of sheer terror? Or, for that matter, what pedestrian?) If the experts are all entirely correct, each time we light a cigarette, or eat a luxurious meal, or, really, do anything, we run the risk of shortening our lives. Or, more accurately, increase the risk of shortening our lives.

The experts are wrong, for three reasons. The first, as we have seen, is that they are often motivated by things other than a search for truth, a very difficult commodity to obtain in the best of circumstances. Their studies are variously too broad, too narrow, or too statistical. They look good on paper but, as with the one which tells us that we should devote one-twenty-fourth of our lives to walking five miles per day, too removed from a sensible prescription for all of humankind—some of whom may have spent the day loading and unloading heavy objects and who, therefore, are scarcely in need of the exercise, while others simply do not need it because of the nature of their physiological makeup. The second reason derives from the first. Any study of large numbers of people can at best produce an average. The problem is that there is no truly average person. Each of us is unique. The effects of any of a multitude of activities upon you might well be entirely different from those effects on me, and they are certain to be different to some extent.

The third reason, and perhaps the most important one, is something that no study can quantify: satisfaction. That is simply a different way of expressing the risk-reward ratio. The idea of risk versus reward is important in the investment world, with the market telling us that the greater the risk, the greater the potential reward. (Though it is not exactly the same thing, this extends to odds on horse races and sports gambling. The greater the perceived risk of loss, the higher the return if the bet pays off.) But with the vast number of disparate experts telling you what to do, weighing these factors, determining the risk, and appraising the reward is actually more difficult. The experts have an agenda different from yours. They are seeking to promote their view, to gain power by influencing people's lives. You are seeking to live the richest life possible—to achieve satisfaction, to obtain self-respect.

"The really big mistake comes when you treat people as authority figures when they are not expert but simply well known," says the philosopher Jamie Whyte in an interview in *New Scientist*. "There is a terrible tendency to treat people as reliable sources of fact when in fact they are simply 'important' people or people who happen to be in the news. It is doubly perverse when you consider who gets counted as 'important.' For example, the victims of train accidents appear on television as authorities on rail policy and celebrities endorse presidential campaigns as though they are expert on politics. It's sheer insanity."

Self-respect can come only from having control over your own life and from respecting the right of others to have control over their lives. If you are lost and ask directions, you understand, as does the person helping you, that you are not obligated to follow the advice you're given. And if someone asks directions of you, you surely understand that you are not dictating the directions that the person who asked must now take. It is as simple as that, but in that simplicity lies much of the problem in the modern world.

Yet when we give directions, we tend to think that it somehow elevates us, that it is an insult if our directions are not followed. We set ourselves up as experts, whether we claim that title rightly or not. Whyte notes that in a very complicated world there is no way that we can be experts on everything, so it is a sensible division of labor for people to specialize and to make their learning available to others. But even acknowledged experts tend to overreach. Says Whyte:

> Scientists are vulnerable to this kind of celebrity issue. Some scientists have a certain amount of star quality that gives their opinions more weight than they ought to have. Worse, scientists have a terrible tendency to pronounce on issues where they don't recognise that they are not expert.
>
> Take the British Medical Association, which is always making policy recommendations. A recent example was that the government should tax the fat content of food. Why does the BMA think it knows anything about how we should live? It may know that if I live a particular way I'll become unhealthy, but why does it think that it can tell me that I should value my health more than my chosen way of life? What makes its members think that they are in any privileged position to answer questions like that?
>
> Also, how do they know what the effects of a tax on fatty food would be? They're not specialists in the way that prices affect consumption and the way the economy will be affected by redistribution of spending from one part to another. They can't even anticipate the health effects of these things. They should shut up.

The British Medical Association is unlikely to shut up, of course, nor is the American Medical Association or the American Bar Association or any of the other groups, scientific establishments, or others who believe—sometimes with the best of intentions—that they should leverage a finite amount of knowledge into sweeping plans for the way you should live. Of course, these groups often send conflicting messages. Perhaps these can cancel each other out, but they also create a lot of noise in the process.

Among the conflicting signals, you need to learn to listen to and count on yourself—and be responsible for the outcome. Have you ever been ill and noticed that for a period of time you are not hungry, but then you are ravenous? It might well be that by listening to your body, by rejecting food even when those who are well-intentioned want to force it on you, then seeking such food as you crave, you hasten your recovery. The human body—in all its variations, which total the number of humans on the planet—is a remarkable thing. Listening to it is a skill worth cultivating.

But beyond that, there is value, value beyond the scope of any scientific study, in following your passion, so long as that passion does not require the involuntary participation of others or, in some cases, break the law. (If heroin is your thing, it is not something that good sense would recommend, precisely because it is against the law, though the responsibilities inherent in self-respect suggest that any desire for it be closely examined to find out if it is a mask for some underlying issue that needs attention beyond the heroin palliative. I do not suggest that heroin is permissible, because it is not, but instead to illustrate the far end of risk-reward and to note that there are risks that outweigh the rewards in all imaginable circumstances.)

It is said that each cigarette reduces one's life by eleven minutes. That may be true, though there is no reason to suppose that it is, but let's accept it as fact. If the satisfaction of the after-dinner cigarette is worth the expenditure of eleven minutes of your life to you, there is no reason to deny yourself that pleasure. (The eleven minute question is, again, why "expert studies" are of limited practical value.) If you are a trencherman and your life is enriched by eating richly, that is your right. You might want to seek out, among their diminishing number, a physician who looks at individual patients rather than some chart based on generalized studies, and if you have children it is your responsibility to do so. But even if there is no question that your eating habits are detrimental to your health, it is up to you to decide whether the satisfaction of eating as you like is worth the risk of shortened life.

While we still have any power at all over our lives, the most annoying thing about those who use phony science to gain control over us is that it robs us of our ability to exercise that power. While the medical profession requires among its ethics that we make informed decisions, the information is all lost in a haze generated by academicians in search of grants, government studies aimed at broad-swath reduction of government expenditures (as if the government is not of the people but over the people), and once-trusted advisors who now fear the marauding herd of lawyers. Claiming to "help" us, all of the sources of information now merely mislead us, all for their own purposes.

What to do? Now more than ever, we must rely on ourselves and make our own choices based on our expert knowledge of ourselves. As with the skydiver who learned enough to save herself, we need to become as skillful as we can. We need to make our choices, weigh the risks, count on ourselves to limit those risks where we can, and decide for ourselves whether that choice is a life recklessly shortened, a life made meaningless by the effort to prolong it, or something in between.

What most of us would not choose is to live a life dictated by others, governed by fear of death, which is in any case inevitable. Such a life, though, is your choice, too, though by making that choice, by ceding power over your existence to someone else, by never having experienced life on your own terms, you must not be surprised if, in its final moments, you wonder why you bothered to live at all.

You are the architect of your own life. Everyone else is just a spectator in your life, as you are in theirs. They have no right to tell you how you must live, nor do you have the right to dictate to them how they shall live.

Only you know whether you find it worthwhile to spend time in the gym in hope of gaining an extra year or two of life. Only you are capable of balancing your choice of life's dangers—and everything in life does have dangers—to achieve the admixture of safety you want and the actions without which you would not find life rewarding.

Unfortunately, wherever you look today there is someone seeking to take away that right and responsibility from you. Gaining and keeping control over your own life is more difficult than ever before. Just remember: No matter what the advice is that you are receiving, no matter what the warnings or claims, you are the one who will live with the consequences. The decision is yours. Surrounded by warnings, you and only you can make the choice: Will you, in an effort to prolong your life, give up living it?

In the summer of 2004 the *New York Times* reported on a study of "bullying bosses," conducted by Dr. Harvey A. Hornstein, a retired professor at Columbia University. Supervisors are unpleasant to subordinates for a variety of reasons, Hornstein determined. "But most often, Dr. Hornstein found, managers bullied subordinates for the sheer pleasure of exercising power," the *Times* reported.

Not a big surprise, is it?

ACKNOWLEDGMENTS

As I wrote in my last book, *The Tyranny of Experts,* "A wag once said that stealing the ideas and words of one person is plagiarism; stealing from many people is research." I must be one of the world's greatest researchers! I'm not sure I've ever had an original idea or thought or phrase. What I can do occasionally is put disparate ideas, notions, and phrases into a new perspective. I hope I've done that here. But since so much I read and hear sticks in my head in such strange ways, I cannot give specific attribution and acknowledgment to all of the many writers and other people whose ideas and words I have incorporated in my thinking and writing.

But there are some specific acknowledgments that are essential. First, I have never, to the best of my recollections, used an agent. My colleague, friend, and publisher of Jewish Lights, Stuart Matlins, put me in touch with Dystel & Goderich Literary Management, who offered me an agent in nonfiction work, Jessica Papin. Jessica, with beauty and enthusiasm in her voice, recognized quickly that I was overwhelmed with the complex, multifaceted aspects of a book I was hungry to share with the

ACKNOWLEDGMENTS

public. Even though I am tempted to foolishly label or categorize myself as a misanthrope, in truth, my life, experience, and behavior do not fit my self-imposed label. The proof of that lies in the person Jessica suggested could help my disorganized mind communicate with people: Dennis E. Powell.

If ever a marriage of ideas and expression to help people respect themselves came about, it was Dennis Powell. He had done much excellent writing before and is still producing more. He was taken with my wife, who devotes herself supremely well to computers and teaching older people how to learn from and about them, and because Dennis is involved in Linux and other computer activities, they hit it off, which allowed our relationship to grow and expand successfully.

A third person who deserves mention is Mark LaRochelle, a writer and organizer for the *National Journal* who started collecting, organizing, and writing some material for the book. In the course of his work, he married for the first time, and the demands of his nuptial relations led to his need to no longer go on working with me.

As the manuscript was being completed, Jessica Papin married, and, as if that were not in this day and age adventure enough, she and her new husband took a sabbatical to Egypt. I was worried that without the ultra-competent Jessica it might be far more difficult to shepherd the manuscript to publication. That worry was unfounded; the task was more than ably undertaken by Michael Bourret, who provided advice, friendship, and more than a little handholding—writers tend to fret.

To the extent that the ideas herein succeeded in making the journey from my mind to pages that readers can understand, credit must go to my editor, Joel Miller, whose comments and changes were without a single exception friendly and pertinent. The editor's job is to make books better, and I cannot imagine anyone more competent to carry out that daunting task.

My assistant of longstanding, Lila Campos, also tolerated the demands, mood swings, and other changes of temperament that go with a creation of pride, and she deserves thanks also.

My wife, Marion, who is responsible directly or indirectly for the unbelievable life and experiences I have enjoyed, must be noted beyond the usual acknowledgment authors toss to their mates.

With all these many rightful acknowledgments, the faults and criticisms are mine and should be directed to me.

—Morris E. Chafetz, M.D.
Washington, D.C.
March 17, 2005

NOTES

While I've cited most of the sources for quoted material in the text itself, in some cases the reader may find useful citations of material that contributed to general conclusions or pointers to additional material. Hence these notes. In some cases, the URLs of sites on the Web are given; by the nature of the Web, these sites may change over time.

Chapter 1 — The Danger of Generalization

Dr. Abraham Maslow's work is available in his book, *Personality and Motivation*, 2nd ed. (New York: Harper & Row, 1970).

Chapter 2 — It's All Point of View

To get a sense of just how carefully marketers approach their work, the reader is encouraged to read the publications of the Marketing Science Institute of Cambridge, MA, available on the Web at http://www.msi.org.

Dr. A. Bernard Ackerman's views on the questionable value of sunscreen products were the subject of an article in the July 20, 2004, *New York Times* and are discussed in numerous places on the Web, notably at the "Cancer Decisions" Web site, http://www.cancerdecisions.com/082204_page.html, and at "DermQuest," http://www.dermquest.com/articleIndex.do?aid=education.ackerman.ackerman Home.

Chapter 3 — I'm Okay, and If You Were Like Me, You'd Be Okay, Too

Nathaniel Branden's books and other material pertaining to his views on self-esteem are available in most large bookstores and on the Web at http://www.nathanielbranden.net/.

NOTES

Chapter 4 — Playing God as an Institutional Right

The British House of Commons "Health Third Report," which discussed the allegedly morbidly obese three-year-old, can be found on the Web at http://www.publications.parliament.uk/pa/cm200304/cmselect/cmhealth /23/2302.htm. The reference that gained so much attention in Great Britain is the second paragraph of the Introduction, which reads, in full: "Dr Sheila McKenzie, a consultant at the Royal London Hospital which recently opened an obesity service for children, offered a powerful insight into the crisis posed to the nation's health. Despite only being in existence for three years, her service had an eleven-month waiting list. Over the last two years, she had witnessed a child of three dying from heart failure where extreme obesity was a contributory factor. Four of the children in the care of her unit were being managed at home with non-invasive ventilatory assistance for sleep apnea: as she put it, 'in other words, they are choking on their own fat.'"

Chapter 5 — The New Gods Don't Know Either

The story of how HTLV-III, later HIV, came to be blamed for AIDS is excruciatingly detailed in the 1994 "INVESTIGATION OF THE INSTITUTIONAL RESPONSE TO THE HIV BLOOD TEST PATENT DISPUTE AND RELATED MATTERS," Staff Report, Subcommittee on Oversight and Investigations Committee on Energy and Commerce, U.S. House of Representatives, also known as the "Dingell Committee." Most readers will find the executive summary, which itself runs many pages, sufficiently detailed to answer any questions they may have. The report, related documents, and the executive summary are online at a Canadian AIDS site, http://www.healtoronto.com/gallodocs.html.

Dr. Peter H. Duesberg describes his arguments against the HIV-AIDS connection in *Inventing the AIDS Virus* (Washington D.C.: Regnery, 1996). A detailed account of the academic price of Duesberg's dissention is found in *Oncogenes, Anueploidy, and AIDS: A Scientific Life and Times of Peter H. Duesberg,* by Harvey Bialy (Berkeley, CA: North Atlantic Books, 2004).

The dispute over whether psychotherapy should be backed by scientific studies rather than individual efficacy is covered in "For Psychotherapy's Claims, Skeptics Demand Proof," in the August 10, 2004, *New York Times.*

Chapter 6 — The Environmental Mess

The disappearance in America of the vast herds of bison and the extinction of the passenger pigeon are both generally attributed to over-hunting. The story of the dodo, a huge, flightless relative of the pigeon, is different, even though the turkey-sized, flightless bird was hunted for food. Native to the Indian Ocean island of Mauritius, the dodo had few natural enemies until the arrival of Dutch sailors in the early 1500s. When the Dutch established a penal colony on the island, they brought pigs, some of which escaped, as did monkeys and rats. These creatures devoured the eggs in the dodos' ground nests, and by 1681 the last dodo had died.

A serious consideration of the errors in Rachel Carson's *Silent Spring* and the devastating effects of her conclusions being made public policy is "Silent Spring at 40" in the June 2002 *Reason*.

Paul Ehrlich is still at it. On April Fool's Day 2004, *One with Nineveh: Politics, Consumption, and the Human Future* (Washington D.C.: Island Press), cowritten with his wife, Anne, was published; it continues to thump the Malthusian tub of overpopulation resulting in disaster. A review by Ronald Bailey, entitled "We're Doomed Again. Paul Ehrlich has never been right. Why does anyone still listen to him?" was published in the *Wall Street Journal*, May 20, 2004, and is online at http://www.opinionjournal. com/la/?id=110005103.

As this book was going to press, Congress was close to approving oil exploration in the Arctic National Wildlife Refuge. Commentary at the time suggested that with the price of oil nearing sixty dollars per barrel, opposition to use of a small portion of ANWR for oil production was not politically survivable by politicians from any but the most leftist locales.

According to Congressional testimony, February 12, 2002, by James F. Jarboe, domestic terrorism section chief, Counterterrorism Division, Federal Bureau of Investigation, the Earth Liberation Front, and an associated organization, the Animal Liberation Front, have "emerged as a serious terrorist threat." The testimony was given before the House Resources Committee, Subcommittee on Forests and Forest Health.

Chapter 7 — Global Warming: More Heat than Light

The reader interested in following the vagaries and outright silliness of the global warming and environmental cataclysm movements will find satisfaction in the current work of Dr. Michael Crichton. His novel, *State of Fear* (New York: Harper Collins, 2004), is based on the global warming hysteria, and he has written several essays and speeches on the subject, among them being "Aliens Cause Global Warming," which is online at http://www.crichton-official.com/speeches/speeches_quote04.html.

Chapter 9 — Alcohol and Alcoholism

My views on alcohol consumption have received some notice over the years, and it seems only appropriate that I point to some of it. Not everyone in the field agreed with my book, *Drink Moderately and Live Longer: Understanding the Good of Alcohol* (Lanham: Madison Books, 1995), with the most criticism coming from my belief that people who had abused alcohol could learn to drink moderately. A broader consideration of the topic can be found in *Encyclopedia of Understanding Alcohol & Other Drugs* (Facts on File, 1999) of which I was a coauthor.

Information on the early use of alcohol beverages in hope of fighting infectious disease can be found in Gerard Koeppel's *Water for Gotham: A History* (Princeton, NJ: Princeton University Press, 2001).

The study that indicated that alcohol consumption reduced tissue damage in heart attacks was published in the Fall 2004 edition of the journal *Microcirculation.*

Chapter 10 — Mushrooms and the Misuse of the Public Health Model

An interesting history of the U.S. Public Health Service can be found online at http://www.usphs.gov/html/history.html.

The full transcript of the FDA advisory panel hearing on Locilex can be found online at http://www.fda.gov/ohrms/dockets/ac/99/transcpt/3500t1.pdf. The Adobe Acrobat Reader program is required.

The National Institutes of Health are now employing the question used in the Yale study, "Is your health excellent, good, fair, or poor?" in its literature for estimating life expectancy. The material on this method is online at http://symptomresearch.nih.gov/chapter_14/Part_3/sec4/chspt3s4pg1.htm.

Chapter 13 — Bad Science and Tobacco

There has been so much written on all sides of the tobacco debate that it is difficult to provide a mere few pointers to readers who would like to look more closely at the issue. One good discussion was conducted by the Cato Institute. Entitled "The Science and Politics of Tobacco," it can be found online at http://www.cato.org/pubs/policy_report/smoke-pr.html.

The Congressional Budget Office summarizes studies involving the medical costs of tobacco users in "Life-Cycle Estimates of the Cost of Smoking," online at http://www.cbo.gov/showdoc.cfm?index=407&sequence=7. This summary notes that factors other than smoking may have skewed study results.

"The taxes of sin. Do smokers and drinkers pay their way?" A study by W. G. Manning, E. B. Keeler, J. P. Newhouse, E. M. Sloss, and J. Wasserman of the Department of Health Services Management and Policy, University of Michigan, published in the March 17, 1989, issue of the *Journal of the American Medical Association,* concluded that smokers do in fact themselves bear the burden of any medical expenses associated with smoking.

The famous "tobacco settlement" between tobacco companies and numerous states can be read (if not necessarily understood) online here: http://www.lawpublish.com/settle.html.

The National Cancer Institute's tirade against "secondhand" smoke, "I Mind Very Much If You Smoke," is online at http://dccps.nci.nih.gov/TCRB/I_mind_if_you_smoke/mindsmo.html.

The Cato Institute's consideration of claims that secondhand smoke contributes to breast cancer is available at http://www.cato.org/special/junkscience/case-study.html.

Chapter 14 — Addiction

An English-language account of the French study of rats and cocaine can be found here: http://www.news-medical.net/?id=4067.

The National Academy of Sciences Institute of Medicine report, "Marijuana and Medicine: Assessing the Science Base," is on the Web at http://www.nap.edu/html/marimed/.

Chapter 15 — Obesity

The alleged connection between smoking cessation and obesity is described in "The Economics of Obesity," by Inas Rashad and Michael Grossman, in the Summer 2004 issue of *The Public Interest*. The article is online at http://www.thepublicinterest.com/archives/2004summer/article3.html.

The CDC study, "The spread of the obesity epidemic in the United States, 1991–1998," was published in the *Journal of the American Medical Association*, October 27, 1999, and is not, as far as I can tell, available online except through subscription services aimed at physicians.

Chapter 16 — Revolt Against the Machines

Ralph Nader's attack on the Chevrolet Corvair was published as the first chapter in his book, *Unsafe at Any Speed* (Grossman, 1965).

The effects of tort litigation run amok, along with many links describing its effect on numerous industries, including general aviation, are found in "Tort Reform Facts," published by the American Tort Reform Foundation and available online at http://www.atrafoundation.org/tort_facts.html.

In considering the new power of bloggers and their ability to call the press and others to account, one need look only at the events surrounding the September 2004 broadcast on CBS that employed apparently phony documents in support of a claim that President Bush had shirked his duties in the Texas Air National Guard. Within minutes of the broadcast, there were reports on sites such as FreeRepublic.com and PowerLineBlog.com saying that the documents could not, based on their appearance, be as CBS represented them to be. A heated national debate ensued; ultimately, CBS fired several employees and *Evening News* anchor Dan Rather stepped down a year earlier than planned. This new medium is at first blush a force to be reckoned with. The incident is described in some detail in Chapter Nineteen.

Chapter 17 — The Attack on Business

The issue of vaccines allegedly causing autism was considered in an editorial in the *Wall Street Journal* of February 16, 2004, "Autism and Vaccines: Activists wage a nasty campaign to silence scientists." The editorial can be read online at http://www.opinionjournal.com/editorial/feature.html?id=110004700.

The "Trial Lawyers, Inc. Annual Report" is available online at http://www.triallawyersinc.com/.

Chapter 18 — Terrorism and Other Worries

Mortality statistics are published by the National Center for Health Statistics at the Centers for Disease Control. They may be viewed online at http://www.cdc.gov/nchs/about/major/dvs/mortdata.htm.

Readers interested in the proliferation of lawyers in the United States will find a great deal of information on the Web site http://www.overlawyered.com/.

The disbarment of lawyer Delany is described in some detail online at http://www.law.cornell.edu/nyctap/comments/i96_0012.htm.

The history of "no-fault" divorce is covered in great detail by Judy Parejko in her book, *Stolen Vows* (InstantPublisher, 2002).

INDEX

—A—

Ackerman, Dr. A. Bernard, 21
Acquired Immune Deficiency Syndrome (see AIDS)
Adams, John, 257
Administrative Office of United States Courts, 226
Aedes aegypti mosquito, 62
Afghanistan, 231
   Afghan war, 232
Africa, 48–49, 62, 162, 238
Ager, Susan, 179–180
AIDS, 42–49, 63, 113, 119, 288
Air Force One, 231
Alar, 115
Alaska, 68
Albuquerque (New Mexico), 216
Alcoholics Anonymous (AA), 85–86, 94–95, 98
Alcolac Inc., 219
al Qaeda, 231
Alschuler, Albert, 203
amanitin, 105
Amazon.com, 211–212
American Bar Association, 248–249, 251, 253, 257, 300
   House of Delegates, 253
American College of Sports Medicine, 192
American Diabetes Association, 123

INDEX

INDEX

Index

English sparrow, 54
Enron, 264
Environmental Defense Fund, 57
Environmental Protection Agency (EPA), 57–59, 115, 128
epilepsy, 217
Eritrea, 60
Eton, 165
Eucharist, 97
Europe, 55, 66, 165

—F—

Federal Aviation Administration (FAA), 187, 231
Family Research Library, 205–206
fatigue, 165
FBI, 208
fetal cocaine syndrome, 164
Fixx, Jim, 240–241
   Complete Book of Running, The, 240
Flega, Katherine, 191
Florida, 54, 231, 256, 296
   State University, 208
flu, 237–238, 240
fluoroquinolones, 123–124
Ford, Gerald, 257
Ford, Harrison, 185
Fortune, 75
Foster, Jodie, 84
France, 248
   French, 44–45
Franklin, Benjamin, 239
Freud, Sigmund, 165
   über Coca, 165
Frist, Bill, 178
Frito-Lay, xiv

—G—

Gallo, Dr. Robert, 44–46
Gallup, 208
Genealogical Society of Utah (GSU), 205
General Motors, 222

INDEX

Georgia, 206, 256
   House Judiciary Committee, 256
Giamatti, Bart, 170
global warming, 71–76, 78, 173
Gogek, Jim, 92–93
Goldstein, Susan, 205
Gore, Al, 67, 73
   Earth in the Balance: Ecology and the Human Spirit, 67
Gramm, Phil, 180
Grand Canyon, 295
Gray, Hanna H., 207
Great Britain (see England)
Greece, 55
Greeks, the, 161
Green Party, 66
Greenpeace, 61
Gross Domestic Product (GDP), 217, 220
Guardian, Manchester, 37
Gwadz, Robert, 64

—H—

Haggart, Elinor, 82
Halliburton, 257
Hart, Peter, 208
Harvard College, 96
Harvard University, 149, 207
   Medical School, 219
   School of Public Health, 182
Hasleton, Elaine, 206
Hatch, Orrin, 258
Hawaii, 239
headaches, 165, 219
Health and Fitness Initiative, 177
Health and Safety Hall of Fame, 89
heart disease, 131, 147, 219, 237–238, 240
Heckler, Margaret, 44
hepatitis, 97, 131
Heritage Foundation, 72
heroin, 163, 166
Heston, Charlton, 230
Hinkley Jr., John W., 84–85

322

Index

Human Immunodeficiency Virus (HIV), 45–49, 63, 113, 119
Holroyd, Kenneth, 125
Homo sapiens, 65
Hoover, Bob, 271
Hornstein, Harvey A., 303
House of Commons, 37
Huber, Peter, 217–220
    Galileo's Revenge: Junk Science in the Courtroom, 217
Human T-cell Leukemia virus type-III (HTLV-III), 44–45, 113

—I—

impetigo, 123
Improved Nutrition and Physical Activity Act (IMPACT), 178
Independent, London, 38
Independent Institute, 212
India, ix, 55, 60–62
Indian Ocean, 239
Institute of Medicine, 218
International Pesticide Action Network, 61
Iowa, 255
   State Bar Association, 255
Ireland, ix
IRS, 178
Islamic, 229–234
Is Our Food Safe, 128
Italy, 55

—J—

Jacobson, Michael, 179
Japan, 44, 248
Jefferson, Thomas, 156
Jefferson City (Missouri), 255
Jesus, 96–97, 161, 200
Johannesburg, 64
Jordan, Michael, 185
Journal of Agriculture and Food Chemistry, 56
Journal of American History, 203
Journal of the American Medical Association (JAMA), 184, 189–190, 217–218
Judeo-Christian, 161
Judge, Mark Gauvreau, 86

INDEX

—M—

MIT, 73
Monkkonen, Eric, 203
Montagnier, Luc, 45
Monument Valley, 290–291
Morgan, Edmund, 202–203
morning sickness, 218–219
Morris, Janie P., 296
Mozambique, 60
Mugabe, Robert, 61
Müller, Paul, 55
Murrah Federal Building, 237

—N—

Nader, Ralph, 67, 199
NAFTA, 61
National Academy of Sciences, 46, 92–93, 166, 191
   Immunization Safety Review Committee, 218
   Institute of Medicine, 166, 192
National Archives, 206
National Audubon Society, 56
National Cancer Institute, 153
National Center for Education Statistics, 225
National Center for Health Statistics, 191
National Center for State Courts, 225
National Center on Addiction and Substance Abuse, 170
National Conference of Commissioners of Uniform State Laws, 253
National Endowment for the Humanities (NEH), 202, 207
National Enquirer, 218
National Highway Traffic Safety Administration, 222
National Institute for the Humanities, 212
National Institute on Alcohol Abuse and Alcoholism, 89
National Institutes of Child Health and Human Development, 120
National Institutes of Health (NIH), 44–46, 61, 64, 120, 122, 127, 178, 181–182, 185
National Review, 207
National Review Online, 264
Natural Resources Defense Council, 115
Nature Biotechnology, 47
Nebraska, 231
Nelson, James S., 254
nerve damage, 219

INDEX

Index

Stallone, Sylvester, 185
Stanford University, 126
Stanley Works, 261
stare decisis, 3
State University of New York, 47
Steinburg, Joel, 262–263
Stoutt Jr., Glenn R., 187
substance abuse, 13
Sudden Infant Death Syndrome, 153–154
Sullum, Jacob, 128–129, 246
Surgeon General, 111–113, 148–149, 156, 177, 192
    Advisory Committee on Smoking and Health, 147
Sutro Library, 205
Sutton, Willie, 261
Sweeney, Edmund, 58–59

—T—

Taiwan, 56
Temperance movement, 96–97
Texas, 68
Thanksgiving, 96
Thomas, Dylan, 102
Thompson, Tommy, 178
Three Mile Island, 66–67
Thurber, James, 173
    Fables for Our Time, 173
Tickell, Chrispin, 76
Tillinghast-Towers Perrin, 217
Time, 175, 179
Topeka (Kansas), 239
Torah, 161
Tour de France, 240
Trial Lawyers, Inc., 222–224
trichinosis, 107
Truth.org, 150
Tuba City, 290
    Tuba City Truck Stop, 291
Twain, Mark, 1, 105
typhoid fever, 97
typhus, 55, 63

INDEX

INDEX

World Bank, 60, 222
World Health Organization (WHO), 56, 62, 182
World Trade Center, 230–231, 235, 237, 241
World War II, 20, 55
World Wildlife Fund, 64
Wyeth Laboratories, 217

—X/Y/Z—

Yale University, 45, 132, 170, 179, 208
    Law School, 208
    Medical School, 132
yellow fever, 63

Zambia, 56
Zamora, Ronnie, 82–83
Zanzibar, 56, 61
Zasloff, Michael, 120–122, 125–127, 288
Zero Population Growth, 65
Zimbabwe, 61